European Community Economics

European Community Economics
A Modern Introduction

T. Hitiris
Senior Lecturer in Economics
University of York

HARVESTER • WHEATSHEAF
NEW YORK LONDON TORONTO SYDNEY TOKYO

First published 1988 by
Harvester ● Wheatsheaf
66 Wood Lane End, Hemel Hempstead
Hertfordshire, HP2 4RG
A division of
Simon & Schuster International Group

Printed and bound in Great Britain by
Billing & Sons Ltd, Worcester

British Library Cataloguing in Publication Data

Hitiris, T. 1938–
European Community economics : a modern
introduction
1. European Economic Community. Economic
policies
I. Title
337. 1′42
ISBN 0–7450–0366–4

1 2 3 4 5   92 91 90 89 88

For Niki and Nana

Contents

List of Tables

List of Figures

Preface

This book is concerned with the objectives, successes and failures of economic policy in the European Community. It is designed for students and other persons interested in European integration, who wish to acquire a reasonably comprehensive introduction to the major economic policy issues of the European Community. They are assumed to have no prior knowledge of economics beyond an introductory course on economic principles. In an attempt to evoke and maintain the readers' interest and make the book intelligible and self-contained, a conscious effort has been made to explain specialised terms and concepts within the text, and to use only the necessary minimum of numerical data. For the same reasons, footnotes are not used and the number of references is kept very low.

Chapter 1 presents an introductory exposition of the objectives, policies and effects of Regional Economic Associations. Chapter 2 surveys the institutional background of policy-making in the European Community. Chapters 3–11 deal with contemporary economic policies of the European Community. Clearly the coverage is selective, but it is hoped that it includes most areas of major economic activity in the Community.

A feature of the book is its emphasis on economic analysis of public policy rather than detailed description of European Community institutions. The chapters are integrated closely and conform to the following standard format: 1. Presentation of the problem; 2. Set of possible solutions; 3. The solution chosen by the EC; 4. Effects of the EC choice; 5. Evaluation and conclusions.

The book started to take shape a few years ago when I was asked to teach a one-term undergraduate course on the economics of the European Community at the University of York. In preparation for this course I had the opportunity to read a number of good books, collections of essays and articles dealing with European Integration and related issues. In contrast to their treatment of the subject, the approach followed here aims at a differentiated product, which attempts to explain the origin of EC policies and their effects. In this, account is taken of the limits of power which the treaties conferred on the Community, and of the constraints on the choice and exercise of Community economic policy that the governments of the member states have imposed. Novel features of the book are that: a) It is concerned with positive economics, explaining what the EC policies are and why, rather than speculating on what they ought to be or dispensing unsolicited advice to policy makers; b) It aims at a balance between theory, policy and facts, and follows an integrated and consistent treatment of the whole subject of policy-making in the context of European integration; c) It includes the latest developments, and up-to-date information and policy decisions, such as statistics from all the 12 member countries of the Community, the January 1987 realignment of exchange rates in the EMS, and the changes in the Treaty of Rome introduced by the Luxembourg Summit of December 1985.

It should become clear from the following that this book is concerned primarily with economic policy-making in the European Community. But the reader should not forget the dictum of the first President of the European Commission: 'Make no mistake about it. We are not in business; we are in politics' (Walter Hallstein in *Time Magazine*, 6th October 1961).

T. Hitiris
York, October 1987

Abbreviations

ACP	African, Carribean and Pacific countries: signatories of Lomé Convention
CAP	Common Agricultural Policy
CCP	Common Commercial Policy
CCT	Common Customs Tariff, also CET
CET	Common External Tariff, also CCT
CFP	Common Fisheries Policy
CMEA	Council of Mutual Economic Assistance, also referred to as COMECON
COREPER	Committee of Permanent Representatives
EAEC	European Atomic Energy Community, also referred to as Euratom
EAGGF	European Agricultural Guidance and Guarantee Fund, also referred to as FEOGA
EC	European Community, comprising the EAEC, ECSC and EEC
EC-6	The first six members of the EEC: Belgium (B), Germany FR (D), France (F), Italy (I), Luxembourg (L), Netherlands (NL) (from 1958)
EC-9	The first six members of the EEC plus: Denmark (DK), Ireland (IRL) and United Kingdom (UK) (from 1973)
EC-10	The first nine members of the EEC plus Greece (GR) (from 1981)
EC-12	The 12 members of the EEC (from 1986)
ECJ	European Court of Justice
ECOFIN	Council of Economic and Finance Ministers
ECSC	European Coal and Steel Community

ECU	European Currency Unit (also ecu)
EDF	European Development Fund
EEC	European Economic Community: the members are 12: Belgium (B), Denmark (DK), Germany FR (D), Spain (E), France (F), Greece (GR), Ireland (IRL), Italy (I), Luxembourg (L), Netherlands (NL), Portugal (P), and United Kingdom (UK)
EFTA	European Free Trade Area
EIB	European Investment Bank
EMCF	European Monetary Cooperation Fund
EMF	European Monetary Fund
EMS	European Monetary System
EMU (a)	European Monetary Union
EMU (b)	Economic and Monetary Union
EP	European Parliament
ERDF	European Regional Development Fund
ESC	Economic and Social Committee
ESPRIT	European Strategic Programme for Research and Development in Information Technology
EUA	European Unit of Account (also eua and ua)
GATT	General Agreement on Tariffs and Trade
GDP	Gross Domestic Product
GNP	Gross National Product
GSP	Generalised System of Preferences
LDC	Less Developed Country/ies
MCA	Monetary Compensatory Amounts
MFA	Multi-Fibre Arrangement
MFN	Most-Favoured-Nation
NCI	New Community Instrument
NIC	Newly Industrialising Countries
REA	Regional Economic Association
SAP	Social Action Programme
UNCTAD	United Nations Conference on Trade and Development
VER	Voluntary Export Restraint
VAT	Value Added Tax

1 Regional Economic Associations: Objectives, Policies and Effects

1.1 FORMS OF ECONOMIC ASSOCIATIONS

The term Regional Economic Associations, or REAs, defines collectively the various forms of economic integration among independent states. The relevant literature distinguishes five forms of REAs as presented in Table 1. This classification is taxonomic, and does not represent the different stages of integration of actual REAs which usually combine characteristics from two or more forms.

It is important to note that economic integration has an internal dynamic. The only stable levels of regional economic association are minimal (that is the Free Trade Area) or maximal (that is Complete Integration), with of course no definite time setting for the completion of either of these processes. Thus, a Customs Union would inexorably lead to higher forms of economic integration—provided, of course, that the members agreed to it. The dynamics of integration arise from increasing openness and political and economic interdependence among the participating countries, both of which reduce their ability to follow an independent course or to diverge significantly from the performance of the group as a whole. Progressive interdependence generates policy conflict among the members of the economic association. In an attempt to resolve this conflict the members of the economic association either adopt policies which lead them further into economic integration or, alternatively, they decide to retrace their steps back to a looser, and stabler, form of international interdependence, the Free Trade Area. In the latter case the need for 'policy compatibility' or 'harmonisation', additional to that already required of countries engaged in international trade, is minimal and can be handled by existing intergovernmental channels of negotiation and consultation.

Table 1.1 Forms of Regional Economic Associations (REAs)

Forms	Free Trade among the Members	Common External Tariff	Free Mobility of Factors of Production	Harmonisation of Economic Policy	Unification of Economic Policy
1 Free Trade Area, FTA	*				
2 Customs Union CU	*	*			
3 Common Market CM	*	*	*		
4 Economic Union EU	*	*	*	*	
5 Complete Economic Integration EI	*	*	*	*	*

In REA forms more advanced than the Free Trade Area there is a need for policy compatibility. This involves the imposition of constraints on policy objectives, and the adoption of rules which require new elaborate international agreements and ultimately the establishment of special supranational institutions for their administration (Johnson, 1968). The taxonomy in Table 1.1 shows distinctly that as openness increases and the degree of economic interdependence rises, intervention in the market in the form of international coordination or 'harmonisation', becomes more intensive. For example, beginning with Customs Unions, the abolition of restrictions on intra-market trade and the unification of national tariff schedules disturbs the motive of national tariff policy, that is the economic and social reasons on which each member country based trade intervention prior to the establishment of the REA. Thus, not only are tariffs eliminated from the instruments of national policy, but also the targets of tariff policy are exposed by participation in the Customs Union. If these targets are incompatible with the aims of the REA, they will be completely abandoned or appropriately modified. In the latter case, new instruments have to be found for the continuation of the policy. Similarly, following the formation of a Common Market, free mobility of factors of production will alter the endowment of production resources available to a member country (and their prices), and thereby the pattern, the pace and the limits of that country's economic growth.

Consequently, harmonisation within REAs actually is a set of intervention policies, the need of which arises from market liberalisation and from the emerging divergence between the objectives pursued, in common by the economic union, and individually by each member state as a sovereign national economic unit. For example, if all the members of a Customs Union want a surplus in the balance of trade with their partners, not all of them can possibly succeed. Harmonisation in this case is an interventionist policy which attempts to make the conflicting targets of the participants compatible.

In general, if the main economic objective of countries participating in a Customs Union is to increase their own national welfare, it seems more likely that this would now have to be pursued within a framework of additional constraints imposed by the harmonisation of both targets and policies. Therefore, not all the participants in the union will succeed in realising fully their private objectives Similarly, free trade in commodities and factors of production within an Economic Union cannot be mutually beneficial for all the participants without some policy of harmonisation. In this case, harmonisation will aim at some sort of equality in the distribution of the costs and benefits arising to the members from operating a freer market in commodities and factors of production. But then, harmonisation is another form of intervention which includes among its results the increase in the degree of interdependence among the participating states.

Consequently, our contention is that there are only two truly stable forms of REAs: (a) Free Trade Areas; and (b) Complete Economic Integration. All other forms of REAs simply constitute intermediate and temporary stages in the process of the voluntary integration of national states by piecemeal methods. These transitional forms of REAs for economic, political, and other reasons are inherently unstable. These arguments do not imply that countries embarking upon some form of REA will necessarily end up integrated into some sort of federal or unitary state. In fact, examples of voluntary subjugation of independent states in a multi-state federation, i.e. an advanced form of integration, are rare. According to history, most of the existing federations or unifications of states have been formed after wars, not by peaceful negotiations (e.g. USA, Italy, etc.).

The progress towards integration depends on the willingness of national authorities to confer real powers to the supra-national authorities of the REA. In fact, integration is a process during which the power of the national authorities of the member countries to exercise independent national economic policy is progressively diminished, while at the same time the power of the central authority of the REA to design and implement common policies is rising. The 'surrender' of power and the 'loss of sovereignty' of the national authorities is very often strongly resisted. Hence, in practice and during a long period of transition, an Economic Union may appear to be rolling from crisis to crisis (as, e.g., the EEC), though willingness among the members to accept compromise and to reach consensus usually leads to the survival of the association, but at a higher level of interdependence and integration. Alternatively, if the participating countries either are unwilling to accept further curbs in their economic and political independence, or if by their intransigence they fail to resolve their differences and conflicts, the complete dissolution of the REA must not be discounted. This is not a remote theoretical possibility, but a fact which is confirmed by the large number of failed attempts for economic integration.

An issue of critical importance for the success or failure of the REA is the nature of its objective, that is the purpose for which hitherto free and independent states might willingly sacrifice a considerable part of their national sovereignty for the sake of integration with other countries of similar inclination. Associations between states aim in general at the realisation of a benefit. It is important to emphasise that this benefit may not be primarily of an economic nature even if it is described by the term *economic* association. For example, some of the participants in the economic association, or all of them, may have strictly political, nationalistic, defence or other objectives. However, all economic associations invariably have positive and/or negative economic implications, and these economic implications should be subject to examination. Inevitably, this means that countries may proceed with the formation of a Regional Economic Association although the economic effects they expect to derive from it are positive but negligible, or even negative overall. On the other hand, even if the potential economic benefit for a country from participation in an economic union might be large, its membership in the union is not necessarily a foregone conclusion. Many countries value their independence and national identity more than the prospect that within an economic union they might become more prosperous.

In general the causes and the objectives of REAs between developed countries are different from those between developing countries:

a) REAs Between Developed Countries
The essential requirements for a successful economic association between developed/industrial countries are: first, that the participating countries are more or less of comparable levels of economic development; and, second, that they are actually very similar, but potentially very complementary, in the structure of both their production and demand.

The formation of an economic association between developed economies aims at the realisation of this potential complementarity. The abolition of trade restrictions between the members bring about immediate general benefits to the participants, the so called static economic effects of the association. In the longer run, the resulting intensification of competition is expected to accelerate development, and to increase welfare by the dynamic effects of economic integration which consist of:

- improvement in the allocation and utilisation of resources,
- specialisation according to comparative advantage,
- enlargement of the market and realisation of scale economies in both production and demand.

The full extent of these benefits cannot be accomplished easily, if at all, by the efforts of one country on its own, especially if it happens to be economically 'small'.

b) REAs Between Developing Countries

Developing countries on the whole are both actually and potentially similar. Therefore, economic associations between developing countries cannot aim at the maximisation of static welfare. On the contrary, developing countries form REAs in an attempt to foster growth and to bring about fundamental changes in the structure of their production and trade. By these means they attempt to fashion a regional trade mechanism which will help to orient their economies in the direction of regional specialisation. These aims are usually pursued by: (1) The pooling of scarce resources essential for economic growth, such as capital, skilled labour, foreign exchange, entrepreneurship, etc.; (2) The avoidance of unnecessary and uneconomic duplication in capital investment, research expenditures, and the application of modern technology; (3) The enlargement of the market for the purpose of realising economies of scale.

The nature of these goals implies that developing countries are not attempting to (and in fact cannot) make short-run gains; they have instead a longer-run perspective for forming economic associations. Hence, the rationale of integration among developing countries is not based on the expectation of static benefits accruing from changes in the existing pattern of trade, which necessarily reflects the existing pattern of their production. On the contrary, it is based on the dynamic effects, the expectation that integration will develop regional markets which in turn will shape a new developed structure of production capable of generating a greater volume and range of trade. Therefore, the success of a REA among developing countries must be judged in the longer run, after the development of a productive sector capable of responding to increases in inter-regional demand. An additional justification for the formation of economic associations among developing countries might be that regional cooperation may increase the group's bargaining power in its economic and sometimes political external relations.

However, with the prospect of deriving benefits after a long time interval, the economic associations among developing countries contain in a sense elements of self-destruction. They consist of a number of countries each one of which individually aims at the same objective—acceleration of its own development which it cannot easily achieve with its own resources. They try therefore to raise their individual shares out of the resources available for collective development. This process leads to conflicts among the members of the economic association which are difficult to resolve and result in long periods of strife and inactivity. In these circumstances, the economic associations among developing countries very rarely survive long enough to reap actual economic benefits. Recent experience has shown that most of them disintegrate prematurely in an atmosphere of hostility and recrimination, or otherwise they become inactive and continue to exist, but only on paper (e.g. East African Economic Community, Central American Common Market, Latin American Free Trade Area, and many others).

1.2 TRADE PROTECTION

As we have seen, each of the forms of REAs entails the abolition of trade restrictions on intra-regional trade between the members. Therefore it is reasonable to start with the study of the effects of instituting trade restrictions, and to follow with the effects of abolishing trade restrictions within a REA.

In this section we examine: a) The instruments of commercial policy; b) The effects of tariffs; and c) The differences between tariffs, quotas and subsidies.

a) Policy Instruments

Theory shows not only that every country can benefit by engaging in international trade but also that free trade is the best, welfare maximising policy. However, for a number of economic and non-economic reasons, most countries intervene in the market to protect their economy from foreign competition. The aim of the present section is to show the effects of protective policies.

The commonest form of protection involves the levying of a tariff on imports. The tariff is a tax levied usually *ad valorem*, that is on the price of imports, but it may take the alternative form of a specific duty per unit of imports. In general, tariff policy discriminates in favour of domestic production, and against foreign production of competitive commodities. Among the many instruments of similar policies we distinguish the following:

Tax discrimination (1) in favour of the domestic producers. If the instrument is indirect taxes on commodities, this policy has effects equivalent to those of tariffs.

Quotas (2) which are quantitative restrictions, limiting the total volume (or sometimes the total value) of imports allowed into a country per time period.

Subsidies (3) which reduce production costs and provide the domestic producers with advantages in competition with foreign producers. In contrast to the policy of levying discriminatory taxes or tariffs which penalise the foreign suppliers (negative discrimination), subsidies reward the domestic suppliers (positive discrimination).

State trading (4) The state, which is a relatively large economic unit, does not necessarily obey the rules of the free market. On the contrary, the market outcome can be affected by government demand or supply: state purchases can affect market prices or may favour domestic suppliers, while state sales of inputs may be provided to domestic producers at favourable low prices.

Exchange controls (5) is a policy of administrative restrictions on transactions involving foreign exchange. Restricting the amount of foreign exchange available for imports in general, or imports of certain commodities, affects prices and provides the domestic producers of competing commodities with unfair advantages.

Import prohibition (6) of certain commodities is sometimes used by government in an attempt to eliminate completely foreign competition from the domestic market.

Other non-tariff barriers (7) to trade include mostly administrative red tape and similar bureaucratic devices (such as the discriminatory enactment of sanitary and safety standards, quality controls, buy-at-home campaigns, etc.), which discriminate against imports.

b) Effects of Tariffs

For the partial equilibrium analysis of the effects of tariffs we consider the market for a commodity in a small price-taking country operating under conditions of perfect competition. We assume that the commodity is homogeneous, but while domestic production and imports supply the market with perfect substitutes, i.e. identical units of the commodity, the domestic supply is given priority over imports. Hence imports, M, are always equal to the *excess demand*, that is the difference between the domestic demand, D, and the domestic supply, S:

$$M = D - S \qquad (1)$$

This case is illustrated in Figure 1.1, 1A, where D is the domestic demand curve for the commodity, S is the domestic supply curve, and W is the perfectly elastic world/foreign supply curve. Under free international trade, equilibrium in the domestic market will be established at price Po, which is the domestic as well as the world price of the commodity. Domestic demand will be Q4, domestic supply Q1, and imports Q1Q4. Consequently, consumers' expenditure on this commodity is the rectangular area Po×Q4, which is composed by Po×Q1 consumers' expenditure on domestic production— hence, domestic producers' revenue—and by Po×(Q1Q4)

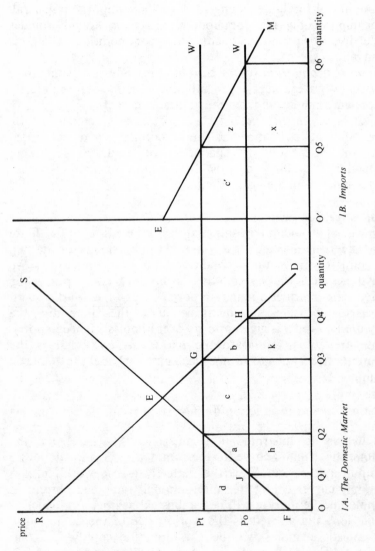

Figure 1.1: Effects of Tariffs

consumers' expenditure on imports. Next, the government decides to levy a tariff on imports, e.g. because it wishes to increase the share of the domestic supply in the market, to save foreign exchange spent on imports, to raise tariff revenue, etc. The *ad valorem* tariff at t per cent shifts the foreign supply curve upwards from W to W' with the following effects:

Price effect: (1) Under the specified assumptions, domestic prices rise by the full per cent of the tariff. Thus, for world price remaining at Po, the domestic price, Pt, becomes

$$Pt = Po\,(1 + t) \qquad\qquad (2)$$

The policy of levying the tariff has created a distortion between domestic prices and free trade/international prices.

Demand effect: (2) The increase in the price induces consumers to reduce their demand from Q4 to Q3. The utility value of this reduction is represented by the area (*b* + *k*). The rectangular area *k* represents the social value of the reduction in demand, while the triangular area *b* represents the social waste stemming from consumption distortion after the levying of tariffs.

Production effect: (3) Higher market prices attract more domestic resources in the production of the commodity and thus domestic supply increases to Q2. The area under the supply curve represents the opportunity cost of the factors that are employed in the production of the commodity. Increases in the price raise production by attracting factors which (under the full employment assumption) were before employed elsewhere in the economy. This process increases the area under the supply curve by (*h* + *a*). However, the overall effect of the increase in production must be considered as welfare reducing. The rectangular area *h* is equal to the world cost of producing the quantity Q1Q2, while the triangular area *a* represents the excess domestic cost of producing this quantity at home instead of importing it. Therefore *a* should be counted as a waste caused by the distortive effect of the tariff on relative prices.

Import effect: (4) Decrease in domestic demand and increase in domestic production imply that the residual between demand-supply, the excess demand which is identical to imports, will be reduced by precisely the sum of demand and production effects. Thus, the reduction in the quantity of imports is (Q1Q2 + Q3Q4), the tariff policy leaving only the quantity Q2Q3 to imports from foreign sources.

Foreign exchange saving effect: (5) Reduction in the volume of imports under the constant import price Po implies that expenditure on imports is also reduced. In Figure 1.1 this reduction at domestic currency valuation is equal to the area *(h + k)*. [As imports are paid for in foreign currency, the foreign exchange saving due to the tariff is *(h + k)/r*, where *r* is the foreign exchange rate defined as the cost of one unit of foreign currency in terms of domestic currency].

Tariff revenue effect: (6) The levying of a non-prohibitive tariff yields revenue to the government equal to the tariff per unit of imports times the volume of imports, area *c* in Figure 1.1. Under our assumptions, the tariff is a tax on the domestic consumers of the imported commodity. Hence, the tariff revenue constitutes an income *transfer* from these consumers to the government of the country.

Distribution effect: (7) The levying of the tariff has changed the total consumers' expenditure on the commodity from (Po × Q4) to (Pt × Q3). This amount of expenditure exceeds what consumers would have paid for the same quantity of purchase under conditions of free trade by the area sum *(d + a + c)*. The latter area in fact is the increase in the price per unit of the commodity (i.e. the tariff per unit) *times* the total consumption of the commodity, that is Po × t × Q3. As we have seen, area *c*, the tariff revenue, is a transfer from the consumers to the government, while area *a* is a waste of domestic resources. The remaining area *d* is an increase in the total revenue over total cost which accrues to the domestic producers as profit. Therefore, area *d* is also an income transfer, but this time from the consumers to the producers. Therefore, as a result of the tariff policy and the consequent reallocation of expenditure between imports and domestic production and the re-distribution of income, the consumers end up worse off, while the two other economic groups in the country, the producers and the government, benefit from the effect of trade restrictions.

Welfare effects: (8) Taking into consideration the costs incurred and the revenues received consequent upon the levying of the tariff, we end up with two items which cannot be accounted for and therefore they constitute a clear waste, that is a net loss for the whole economy. These are the triangular areas *a* and *b*, respectively the resource waste, and the social waste of the distortive effects of the tariff. Hence, the sum (*a* + *b*) is the total welfare cost of the tariff.

c) Tariffs, Quotas and Subsidies
Under the assumptions of perfect competition in the production, supply and demand of the commodity, quantitative restrictions have effects on prices and quantities identical to those of tariffs. Hence, in this case the quota and the tariff are *equivalent* because both produce the same import level and therefore an equal discrepancy between foreign and domestic prices. In Figure 1A, a quota of Q2Q3 volume of imports is equivalent to the tariff of t per cent which produced the same level of imports. However, only if the government auctions import licences, is the equivalence between tariffs and quotas complete, with area *c* collected by the government as revenue from the sale of import licences under quotas, or tax revenue under tariffs.

With tariffs and quotas having many effects, it is not always easy to pinpoint the exact reasons for their use in government policy. However, owing to their relatively large negative welfare effects, we can state that in general what tariffs or quotas can do, other policy instruments can do much better. Assuming, for example, that the specific objective of the policy is to raise the share of domestic production in the market, the subsidy is a better policy instrument than the tariff. In Figure 1.1, the tariff of t per cent raised domestic production from Q1 to Q2. The same increase in production can be achieved by subsidising the domestic production at rate *s* per unit of output, where *s* is equal to the tariff charged per unit of imports, $s = (Po \times t)$. The following results obtain under the subsidy policy:

(1) Domestic prices remain unchanged at the level of world prices, Po.

(2) Demand remains at the free trade level, Q4.
(3) Imports are reduced by the quantity Q1Q2 with saving of import expenditure equal to area h in domestic currency terms.
(4) There is no tariff revenue for the government which instead incurs additional budgetary expenditure equal to the area sum $(d + a)$ for the financing of the subsidy.
(5) There is no direct transfer from the consumers to the government and the producers. Of course, the budgetary cost of the subsidy is ultimately contributed by the taxpayers (who are not exclusively the consumers of this commodity).
(6) The welfare effect of this policy is still negative but restricted to the loss of only the triangular area a, which is the waste caused by the distortive effect of government intervention in the production side of the market.

Therefore, other things being equal, protection by tariffs or quotas is an inferior policy for promoting domestic production. However, the comparison between tariffs, quotas and subsidies has also to be extended over the administrative costs of operating each policy. The sums allocated to subsidies have first to be collected by taxation and then distributed to producers according to some exact plan of intervention. In contrast, import duties are relatively inexpensive to collect, they perform the tasks assigned to subsidies equally well and provide the government with the added bonus of a revenue.

The tariff is both a tax on consumers and a subsidy to producers, without having to be actually collected and distributed. However, the tariff as an instrument of policy is considered to be inflexible because, every time a change in tariffs is contemplated, the government has to ask the legislature for changes in the tariff law. Quotas are in general more adaptable, administratively more flexible (their modification usually involving simple procedural requirements), and more efficient for preventing the volume of imports to exceed pre-specified levels. Hence, despite the valid theoretical objections against tariffs and quotas and the economists' preference for subsidies, both tariffs and quotas are still widely used instruments of government commercial policies.

1.3 TRADE LIBERALISATION

We have stated that, from the welfare point of view, free trade is the best policy. A customs union and other more advanced forms of REAs entail the abolition of barriers to trade among the members and the adoption of a common external tariff on trade with non-member countries. Therefore, these forms of economic association combine a move towards free trade among the members with the retention or increase of impediments to trade against non-members. This is a case of discriminating trade liberalisation by abolition of protection only on trade with the union partners. Elimination of one distortion in the presence of others does not necessarily improve welfare. This is an example of the theory of *second best* according to which, if one of the conditions for optimality cannot be made to hold, there is no presumption that attainment of all the others will produce the best solution, i.e. maximum welfare. Consequently, formation of a regional economic association has both positive and negative trade and welfare repercussions upon: (1) The members of the association; (2) The non-member countries; (3) The world as a whole. Whether the overall effect of the formation of the REA is negative or positive cannot be accurately predicted. In the following we illustrate this problem with a study of the short-run trade and welfare effects of tariff changes following the formation of a Customs Union between two price-taking countries.

In figure 1.2, 2A and 2B illustrate the markets for a commodity in countries A and B respectively. The demand-supply curves are DA, SA in country A and DB, SB in country B. We assume that both countries face increasing production costs, but country B, for reasons relating to her demand and supply conditions, is able to reach self-sufficiency, SB = DB, at a lower price than country A. For convenience we, in fact, assume that country B's market reaches equilibrium at the world supply price, Pw, so that B does not need protection from foreign competition. However, counry A, facing world supply SW protects her domestic industry by an *ad valorem* tariff of t per cent. Hence, in A the world supply curve shifts to SWt and the domestic price of the commodity is Pt. Therefore, the following situation exists in the markets of the two countries, before the formation of the customs union:

		Country A	Country B
1	Price	Pt	Pw
2	Demand	Q2	Q3
3	Supply	Q1	Q3
4	Imports	Q1Q2	nil

All other effects of tariffs occur in A as previously described.

Next, we assume that country A forms a customs union with country B, retaining the tariff of t per cent as the common external tariff. Hence, while the world supply SW is subject to the tariff, the partners' supplies are not. Therefore, B's producers are provided with a higher selling price and an expanded market where, up to a certain point, the only competition they face comes from the less efficient producers of country A. Consequently, B's producers increase production to meet A's demand. But, at rising production costs and therefore prices, B's excess supply for exports originates, first, from increase in production and, second, from decrease in domestic demand. In Figure 1.2, this process will continue until equilibrium in the market of the customs union is reached, that is until the supply from A and B equals the demand of A and B. Equilibrium in the combined market implies that the exports from B equal the imports of A. Consequently, after the formation of the customs union, the following situation is observed:

		Country A		Country B	
		level	change	level	change
1	Price	Pu	–(Pt – Pu)	Pu	+ (Pu – Pw)
2	Demand	Q5	+ Q2Q5	Q6	– (Q6Q3)
3	Supply	Q4	– Q4Q1	Q7	+ (Q3Q7)
4	Imports	Q4Q5	+ (Q4Q1 + Q2Q5)	nil	nil
5	Exports	nil	nil	Q6Q7	+ (Q6Q7)

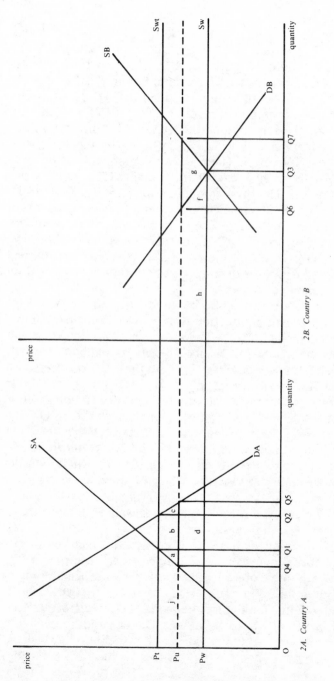

Figure 1.2: Customs Union

2A. Country A

2B. Country B

Disaggregation of A's imports, Q4Q5, is of particular importance. The total of A's imports comes from its partner in the customs union, country B, and is due to three effects: (1) The substitution of imports from country B for imports from the world: the import quantity Q1Q2. (2) The substitution of imports from country B for domestic production: the import quantity Q4Q1. (3) The increase in domestic demand following the lowering of the price: the import quantity Q2Q5. The first two components of imports are the *inter-country substitution* effect of the formation of the customs union. The third component of imports results from the reallocation of consumers' expenditure towards purchases of the commodity whose (relative) price has fallen by the abolition of the tariff. This import component constitutes the *inter-commodity substitution* effect of the customs union. Therefore, the imports of country A have undergone a change of origin and an expansion.

The expansion was caused by a reduction in the supply of high-cost domestic production, Q4Q1, and an increase in the domestic demand, Q2Q5. Therefore, the import expansion associated with these two events is beneficial and has a positive welfare effect, the area $(a + c)$ which in the context of customs union theory is termed *trade creation*.

The change in the origin of imports involved the replacement of low cost imports from the world, Q1Q2, by higher cost imports from country B. Therefore, this re-location of the supply of imports is detrimental for country A and causes a negative welfare effect, the area d, which is here termed *trade diversion*. Area b, which before the formation of the customs union was part of the government's tariff revenue, and area j which was a transfer from consumers to producers, remain now with the consumers.

The elimination of tariffs within a customs union affects each member's imports as well as exports. In fact, one of the principal economic objectives of a country's participation in a customs union is to increase its exports. Import effects can be achieved by unilateral tariff reductions, but export effects require tariff reductions by others. Under conditions of full employment, the additional demand for exports, which is created by the abolition of tariffs, is met by diverting productive resources from other activities to the export producing sector, where they will enjoy higher rewards. Hence, the gain for the export side should be measured by the excess reward which these resources obtain over and above the remunerations they received in their previous occupation. Figure 2B presents the effects of the formation of the customs union for the exporting country B. The increase in prices from Pw to Pu enables B's producers to hire more factors of production and expand their supply to Q7. However, when the price of the commodity rises, the consumers in B cut down their consumption to Q6. As a result of these changes, B's producers gain the area sum $(h + f + g)$, while B's consumers lose the area sum $(h + f)$. Under the assumptions employed in the construction of Figure 2B, while area h is a transfer within country B from consumers to producers, area f is an outright loss for the consumers. However, B's producers gain the area f and g from the consumers of country A as profit from exports. Therefore, B's net benefit from the customs union with country A is the export expansion Q6Q7 which is associated with a positive welfare effect for the economy equal to area g. This net welfare benefit can be considered as the *trade creation* effect of the exporting country. Consequently, the welfare effects of the customs union, arising from trade liberalisation of the commodity under discussion, equal the area sum $(a + c + g - d)$ and are distributed among the participating countries as follows:

	Country A	*Country B*
1 Trade creation	$(a + c)$	g
2 Trade diversion	$-d$	nil
3 Net welfare effect	$(a + c - d)$	g

These effects emerge in the comparison of 'before' vs. 'after' situations from the abolition of the tariff on the intra-union trade of a single commodity. With many commodities being traded, each one of the partners will realise trade and welfare effects as importer of certain commodities and as exporter of other. The net outcome of these effects can be negative for certain countries and positive for others, with net welfare effect for the customs union as a whole negative or positive. This clearly is a case of the theory of second best.

The import and export effects as presented above and illustrated in Figure 1.2 depend on a number of simplifying and restrictive assumptions. First, that supply curves are either upward-sloping or horizontal, thus excluding the case of scale economies; different assumptions about costs will provide different results. Second, that the elimination of trade barriers, enlargement of the market, and intensification of competition improve efficiency, but only through trade, not through the import-competing and non-trade goods sectors. Third, that the main issue concerning the customs union is the short-term reallocation of a given endowment of resources, and not the long-run growth and optimal allocation of productive factors. These assumptions have to be relaxed when one considers the long-term and the dynamic effects of the formation of REAs. However, the dynamic effects can neither be accurately estimated nor easily predicted.

The static effects arise from inter-country and inter-commodity substitution which give rise to trade creation and trade diversion. The extent of these effects depends on the economic structure of the countries participating in the customs union. Thus, a high level of tariffs in trade between the prospective partners, combined with high elasticities of demand and supply of the commodities traded between them (before and after the formation of the customs union), may raise welfare through substantial trade creation. Also, a low level of tariffs in trade with the outside world and low elasticities of demand for imports from non-participating countries may lead to relatively low trade diversion.

It is important to repeat at this stage that the analysis of the static effects of discriminatory tariff alterations applies to the market for a *single* commodity. However, despite the aggregation problems and the probable violation of certain crucial assumptions, such as that factor prices remain constant while commodity prices change, or that factor supply elasticities are always infinite, this same procedure has been employed in the estimation of the total static effect of actual or potential customs unions (see Appendix for methodology). The results are invariably unimpressive. Low estimates of import demand elasticities, low tariff rates, and relatively low average propensities to import, mean that the measures of the static trade and welfare effects of tariff changes are necessarily very small. But even if they were larger, they should not be considered crucial for deciding whether a customs union ought to be formed. The reason is that these effects are just static, and static efficiency is not a good predictor of, nor a necessary precondition for, dynamic efficiency. As we have emphasised, the dynamic effects which derive from the intensification of competition within the area of the regional economic association are the important ones.

1.4 APPENDIX: MEASUREMENT OF THE TRADE AND WELFARE EFFECTS OF TARIFFS

Figure 1.1, 1B, illustrates the import side of the domestic market as described by equation (1). Since imports are allocated a residual share in the market, with domestic demand equal to domestic supply, as at point E, imports are nil. Free trade imports Q1Q4 are exactly equal to imports $0'Q6$, and imports Q2Q3 under tariff protection exactly match imports $0'Q5$ in Figure 1.1, 1A and 1B respectively. Similarly, the area under the demand and supply curves in Figure 1A exactly match the areas under the import demand curve in Figure 1B. Namely: $c = c'$, $z = a + b$, and $x = h + k$.

We have seen that the effects of tariffs are caused by their distortive increase in prices. The increase in the market price leads to two reactions of particular importance: (1) A decrease of the quantity demanded by the consumers; and (2) An increase of the quantity supplied by the domestic producers. The size of these effects obviously depends on the sensitivity of demand and supply to price changes, that is on the demand and supply price elasticities. Thus, from the definition of the price elasticity of demand

$$e_d = (dD/dP)(P/D) \qquad (A1)$$

where D = quantity demanded, P = price, and d denotes a change, the effect of the change in price on the volume of demand is

$$dD = e_d \, (dP/P)D. \qquad (A2)$$

With reference to Figure 1.1, $dP = Pt - Po$ and since the price change is entirely due to the imposition of the tariff, $Pt = Po(1 + t)$. Therefore: $(dP/P) = (Pt - Po/Po) = (t/1 + t)$, and equation (A2) can now be written as

$$dD = e_d \, (t/1 + t)D \qquad (A3)$$

where, of course, $e_d < 0$.

Similarly, from the definition of the price elasticity of supply

$$e_s = (dS/dP) \, (S/P) \qquad (A4)$$

where S denotes the quantity of supply. After substitution we obtain that the supply effect of levying the tariff is

$$dS = e_s \, (t/1 + t)S \qquad (A5)$$

where $e_s > 0$.

As we have seen, the import effect of the tariff is equal to the sum of the reduction in demand and the increase in domestic supply, that is the demand and the supply effects. Hence:

$$dM = dD + dS = (e_d D + e_s S) \, (t/1 + t) \qquad (A6)$$

where M denotes the quantity/volume of imports. However, from the definition of the price elasticity of the demand for imports

$$e_m = (dM/dP) \, (P/M) \qquad (A7)$$

we obtain

$$dM = e_m \, (t/1 + t)M. \qquad (A8)$$

Hence, under the specific assumptions we employed in the construction of Figure 1.1, from equations (A6) and (A8) we obtain the following relationship between the three price elasticities:

$$e_m M = e_d D + e_m S \qquad (A9)$$

and

$$e_m = e_d (D/M) + e_m (S/M). \qquad (A10)$$

Since it is relatively easier to obtain estimates of price elasticities of demand and imports rather than of supply, in empirical measurements of the effects of tariff policies equation (A8) is used more frequently than equations (A3) and (A5).

Welfare cost of the tariff is the sum of the area *a* and *b* in Figure 1A , or the equivalent area *z* in Figure 1B. The measure of the latter area is

$$z = 1/2[dM \, Po \, t] \qquad (A11)$$

or, substituting for dM from equation (A8),

$$z = 1/2[e_m (t^2/1+ t)MPo]. \qquad (A12)$$

The product MPo is in fact the initial, or base-year, value of imports, Vm. Hence, the measure of the waste caused by the tariff is

$$z = 1/2[e_m (t^2/1 + t)Vm]. \qquad (A13)$$

The import contraction and the welfare loss which follow the imposition of the tariff are, of course, reversed to import expansion and welfare gain when the tariff is abolished. Taking into consideration Figure 1.1 and the relevant equations for the estimation of demand, supply and import effects, we observe that in general the effects of the abolition of a tariff are greater:

(1) the larger the price elasticity of domestic demand, domestic supply and imports;
(2) the higher the level of tariffs;
and (3) the larger the initial value of imports.

REFERENCES

Balassa, B. (1962), *The Theory of Economic Integration*, Allen and Unwin, London.

Cooper, C. A. and Massell, B. F. (1965), 'Towards a General Theory of Customs Unions for Developing Countries', *Journal of Political Economy*, 73, 461–76.

Hitiris, T. (1982), 'Progressive Interdependence and Economic Integration: a General Case', in Dosser, D. *et al.* (eds), *The Collaboration of Nations*, Martin Robertson, Oxford.

Johnson, H. G. (1968), 'The Implications of Free or Freer Trade for the Harmonization of Other Policies', in English, H.E. (ed.), *World Trade and Trade Policies*, University of Toronto, Toronto.

Krauss, M. B., (ed.) (1973), *The Economics of Integration*, Allen and Unwin, London.

Lipsey, R. G. (1970), *The Theory of Customs Unions: A General Equilibrium Analysis*, Weidenfeld and Nicolson, London.

Meade, J. E. (1955), *The Theory of Customs Unions*, North-Holland Amsterdam.

Robson, P. (1980), *The Economics of International Integration*, Allen and Unwin, London.

Winter, A. L. (1987), 'Britain in Europe: A Survey of Quantitative Trade Studies, *Journal of Common Market Studies*, 25, pp. 315–35.

2 Structure of the EC: Objectives, Policies and Constraints

2.1 THE EUROPEAN COMMUNITY

The European Community (EC) comprises three Communities: The European Coal and Steel Community (ECSC) established by the Treaty of Paris on the 18th April 1951 but not fully implemented until February 1958; the European Atomic Energy Community (EAEC or Euratom), and the European Economic Community (EEC). The last two were established respectively by the Euratom Treaty and the Treaty of Rome, both signed in Rome on the 25th March 1957. After ratification by the member states' national parliaments, they entered into force on the 1st January 1958. The signatories of these Treaties agreed, by a Convention annexed to the Treaty of Rome, to establish common institutions (Assembly, Court of Justice and Economic and Social Committee) for all three Communities. By the 'Merger Treaty', signed in Brussels on the 8th April 1965, the three Communities agreed to create a single 'Council of the European Communities', a 'Commission of the European Communities' and an 'Audit Board'. This agreement came into force on the 1st July 1967 and the established institutions, in the form that they are known today, began to operate from that date. The three Communities were designated 'the European Community' by the Resolution of the European Parliament of the 16th February 1978. Signatories of these Treaties were the original EC members, the Six: Belgium (B), FR of Germany (D), France (F), Italy (I), Luxembourg (L) and the Netherlands (NL). Under Article 237 of the Treaty of Rome 'any European State may apply to become a member of the Community'. In the same spirit, the signatories also called 'upon the other peoples of Europe who share their ideal to join in their efforts' (Preamble). The prequisites for considering applications for entry are: (1) The applicant state must be European. (2) It must be democratic (summit declaration October 1972, confirmed by the European Council 1978). (3) It must accept the political and economic objectives of the European Community (Articles 2 and 3). The United Kingdom (UK), Irish Republic (IRL) and Denmark (DK) signed treaties of accession and joined the EC on the 1st January 1973 (first enlargement, EC-9). Greece (GR) became an associate member of the EEC in 1962. When the political requirements for entry were met, and after lengthy negotiations, Greece joined the EC on 1st January 1981 (second enlargement, EC-10), and Portugal (P) and Spain (E) on 1st January 1986 (third enlargement, EC-12).

2.2   COMMUNITY INSTITUTIONS

Under Article 4 of the Treaty of Rome and the 'Merger Treaty', the operation of the EEC is entrusted to four principal bodies: (1) The Council, (2) The Commission, (3) The Court of Justice, and (4) The Assembly or European Parliament. Among the auxiliary institutions are included: a) The Court of Auditors, b) The Economic and Social Committee, c) The European Investment Bank.

The Council of Ministers (1) is the principal decision-making body of the EC, and it is the only body which explicitly represents the Governments of the member states. The Council takes the final decisions in response to proposals from the Commission, and after consulting the European Parliament and the Economic and Social Committee. Each member country has one representative in the Council of Ministers. For major decisions the Council consists of the Foreign Ministers of the member countries but, depending on the subject under discussion, meetings of other Ministers are held and are known by subject, e.g., the Agricultural Council, the Transport Council, etc. The office of the President of the

Council is held for a term of six months by each member state in turn, in alphabetical order. A new six year alphabetical cycle began on 1st January 1987. After the first cycle, that is in 1993, each pair of countries will be inverted, in order to ensure that the presidency falls to every member state in the important first half of the year (when decisions about farm prices, etc. are taken).

Under the Treaties the Council may take decisions by unanimity, simple majority, or qualified majority. The vote is weighted (10 each for Germany, France, Italy, and the UK; 8 for Spain; 5 each for Belgium, Netherlands, Greece and Portugal; 3 each for Ireland and Denmark; and 2 for Luxembourg), giving a total of 76, of which 54 votes are required for a qualified majority. On matters regarded as of particular importance for the member states, it has been the Council's normal practice to proceed only on the basis of unanimity. However, protracted disagreements on a number of issues finally led to the 'Luxembourg compromise' of the 29th January 1966, whereby it was tacitly agreed that, despite the majority voting provisions of the Treaty of Rome, a member state can insist on a unanimous decision in the Council when its vital national interests are involved. In this way the right of national veto was introduced, which has been used by some countries in a number of cases.

Amendments to the Treaty of Rome were introduced by the Luxembourg agreement of December 1985. Accordingly, qualified majority replaced the requirement of unanimity for a number of issues associated with the objective of creating a single internal market, transport, and research, such as: (i) changes in customs duties (Article 28), (ii) liberalisation in the trade of services (Article 59), (iii) liberalisation of movements of capital (Article 70.1), (iv) the opening up of markets in the field of transport (Article 84). The Council meets about 5 times a month. A large part of the preparation for these meetings is carried out in COREPER which is the Committee of Permanent Representatives of the Member States, that is ambassadors accredited to the EC.

The Treaty of Rome does not stipulate that the Heads of Government of the EC member states constitute a decision-making institution. However, during the 1960s occasional summit meetings became necessary. The first two summits, at

Paris and Bonn, were held in 1961, when leaders of the Six agreed to meet 'at regular intervals to exchange views, to concert their policies and to arrive at common positions in order to facilitate the political union of Europe'. The next summit meeting took place after an interval of six years on the occasion of the 10th anniversary of the Rome Treaty. Since the Paris summit of December 1974, the Community Heads of Government decided to meet on a regular basis three times a year 'and whenever necessary', with a view to solving outstanding problems and making more rapid progress on Community policy. Heads of State (France) or Government (all other members) and their foreign ministers and the president and one vice-president of the Commisssion meet as the *European Council*, which deals with major Community matters arising out of the treaties and with general economic and political cooperation. The presidency of the European Council rotates every six months in conformity with that of the Council of Ministers. The European Council, whose meetings usually last two days, does not normally take formal decisions. This function is instead delegated to a separate meeting of foreign ministers convened immediately after the summit. Since 1986, the European Council meetings are restricted to two yearly.

The Commission (2) has five main roles:

(i) It acts as Community guardian and ensures that the provisions of the Treaties and Community decisions are applied by the member states, with recourse, if necessary, to the Court of Justice.

(ii) It initiates policy, drafts the detailed measures needed for its implementation, and steers legislative proposals through the European Parliament.

(iii) It acts as a mediator at meetings of the Council, frequently amending its own proposals in order to reach a compromise acceptable to all the member states.

(iv) It negotiates on behalf of the Community, for example in matters relating to international trade.

(v) It has certain powers in administering Community rules, and limited power to legislate, mainly in the detailed implementation of the Common Agricultural Policy.

The Commission, which is based in Brussels, consists of 17 members—two each from Germany, France, Italy, UK and Spain, and one from each of the other 7 member countries. They are nominated by the national governments of the member states for a renewable four-year term of office. The Commission is headed by the President and six Vice-Presidents who hold office for a two-year renewable term. Decisions are made by majority vote. The Commission, which is strictly independent of the national governments, heads an administration of approximately 12,000 international civil servants (of which $\frac{1}{4}$ are in the nuclear research establishment), organised in 20 directorates-general, each responsible to one of the Commissioners.

The Court of Justice (ECJ) (3) deals with the interpretation, application and development of Community Law. It comprises 13 judges, drawn one from each member country plus one from the larger states on a rota basis, and six advocates-general, appointed for six-year renewable terms by agreement between the member governments. The role of the Court is to ensure that the Law is observed in the interpretation and application of the Treaties and of the legislation deriving therefrom (Articles 164–88). The Court has jurisdiction in disputes between member states on Community matters, between member states and Community institutions, and in actions brought by individuals against the Community. It also has the right to review the legality of Directives or Regulations issued by the Council or the Commission. In general, Community law in the fields covered by the Treaties forms a special, *autonomous legal system*, independent of the legal systems of the member states. Community law is not incorporated into any national law but has direct applicability to the member states where it takes precedence over national law. Consequently, any provision of national law which conflicts with Community law is invalid. In general, the nationals of each member state are governed by two legal systems, national law and Community law, and therefore they are citizens of two interdependent entities, the member state of their origin and the European Community.

At the request of national courts, the Court of Justice gives 'preliminary rulings' on questions of interpretation of Community Treaties and Community Law. Under the Treaty (Article 189), the Community makes use of five legal instruments: (1) *Regulations*, which are laws directly and uniformly applicable, in all member states, to those who are parties to legal relationships under Community law (e.g., member states, citizens, firms, etc.); (2) *Directives*, which are addressed to member states and are binding as to the end, but the means of implementation are discretionary; (3) *Decisions*, which deal with specific problems and are binding in every respect on those to whom they are addressed; (4) *Recommendations* and (5) *Opinions*, both of which have no binding force.

The European Parliament (EP) (4) or European Parliamentary Assembly—as it was initially called—'which consists of representatives of the peoples of the states brought together in the Community, shall exercise the advisory and supervisory powers which are conferred upon this Treaty' (Article 137). Consequently, while the Council of Ministers represents the states, the European Parliament represents the people. Relatively to the national parliaments of the member states, the European Parliament has rather limited powers. It mostly

Table 2.1: Members of European Parliament

Country		Members
B	Belgium	24
DK	Denmark	16
D	Germany, FR	81
E	Spain	60
F	France	81
GR	Greece	24
IRL	Ireland	15
I	Italy	81
L	Luxembourg	6
NL	Netherlands	25
P	Portugal	24
UK	United Kingdom	81*
Total		518

Note: *Scotland 10, Wales 5, N.Ireland 3, England 63.

acts as a *consultative* body on Community affairs, but has no general right to be involved in the decision-making process. However, it can amend the 'non-obligatory' expenditures of the Community Budget and, under very specific conditions and by two thirds majority, it may also enforce the resignation of the Commission. But this has never happened as yet. The direction of the Parliament is in the hands of the President and twelve Vice-presidents, elected every $2\frac{1}{2}$ years. Much of the Parliament's work is done by specialist committees. The Parliament's administrative seat is Luxembourg, but plenary sessions are now held in Strasbourg. The Parliamentary committees normally meet in Brussels. Since 1979, the Members of Parliament are elected by direct elections for a fixed term of five years. The member country representation in the European Parliament is presented in Table 2.1

In addition to these four constitutional authorities there are a number of auxiliary institutions. The most important of these are:

The Court of Auditors (1) has twelve members, one from each member state. It was set up by amendment treaty in 1975, on the initiative of the Parliament, to exercise control over the Community's expenditure and revenue.

The Economic and Social Committee (ESC) (2) is made up of 189 members, representing employers, trade unions, farmers, the professions and 'representatives of the general interest'. They are appointed by the Council according to quotas allocated to each member state and from lists supplied by them. The members of the ESC serve in their personal capacity and are not bound by any mandatory instructions. The Committee is convened, at the request of the Council or the Commission, to be consulted with matters relating to the Euratom and the EEC treaties, but it also has the power to embark upon enquiries of its own. The Consultative Committee carries out similar tasks for ECSC affairs.

The European Investment Bank (EIB) (3) was set up as one of the institutions of the EEC Treaty (Article 129–30) to promote economic and social integration. It operates independently as a

Table 2.2: *Basic statistics of the community*

Member Country	Area 1000 sq. km	Population 1000s 1984	Employment per cent, 1985 Agr.	Ind.	Serv.	GDP per head (1985)* PPP value	% on EC average	% on EC highest	Annual Growth rate of GDP per head, 1979–84	Gross Value Added by branch, 1984 Agr.	Ind.	Serv.	Foreign Trade percent on GDP, 1984 Imports	Exports
B	30.5	9855.3	3.0	29.9	67.1	12701	104	79	1.9	2.5	34.4	63.0	77.5	79.2
DK	43.1	5111.6	7.1	26.8	66.0	14633	120	91	1.2	6.3	27.7	66.0	35.8	36.9
D	248.7	61175.1	5.6	41.0	53.4	14426	119	89	1.5	1.9	40.9	57.2	28.1	30.6
E	504.8	38386.8	16.9	28.9	55.1	9055	74	56	4.1	16.7	50.0	33.3	20.4	23.3
F	544.0	54947.1	7.6	32.0	60.4	13740	113	85	1.5	4.1	35.8	60.2	25.2	25.4
GR	132.0	9895.8	28.9	27.4	43.7	7005	58	43	-0.3	18.5	28.5	53.0	29.3	21.0
IRL	68.9	3535.0	16.0	28.9	55.1	8433	69	52	2.8	16.7	50.0	33.3	60.1	59.8
I	301.3	57004.9	11.2	33.6	55.2	11225	92	69	0.8	5.2	39.1	55.7	27.2	26.8
L	2.6	365.9	4.2	33.4	62.3	16163	133	100	1.5	3.2	35.4	61.4	†	
NL	41.2	14424.2	4.9	28.1	67.0	13450	110	83	1.5	4.6	34.8	60.6	58.0	63.1
P	92.1	10089.3	23.9	33.9	42.2	6649	55	41	0.2	8.2	37.7	54.1	46.0	38.8
UK	244.1	56487.8	2.6	32.4	65.0	12949	106	80	1.7	1.7	40.8	57.5	29.0	29.1
EC-10	1656.4	272802.0	7.2	34.0	58.9	—	—	—	—	3.4	38.4	58.1	31.5	32.4
EC-12	2253.3	321278.8	8.6	33.8	57.6	12168	100	75	1.6	—	—	—	30.8	31.8

Notes: *Current prices in ECUs.
†Luxembourg's trade figures included in Belgium's

Source: Eurostat (1987), *Basic Statistics of the Community*, 24th ed., Luxembourg.

public non-profit-making organisation. The Bank's task is to contribute to the balanced and stable development of the Community by making or guaranteeing loans for investment projects, principally in industry, energy and infrastructure. The EIB facilitates the financing of: (i) investment that contributes to the economic development of the less-developed regions of the Community; (ii) projects which contribute to the economic integration of the Community or serve other Community objectives; (iii) investment projects for modernising or converting undertakings or for developing new activities, particularly in energy saving, import diversification, transport and telecommunications.

The Bank does not normally contribute more than 40 per cent of the cost of any project. The Bank's resources consist of reserves, capital subscribed by member states, and funds raised (i.e., borrowings) on capital markets inside and outside the Community. The EIB has received a mandate to administer New Community Instrument (NCI) loans for the account and at the risk of the Community. The NCI (or the Ortoli facility) was established in 1978 and has as its objective the financing of investment projects which contribute to greater convergence and integration of the member states' economic policies and, through the dissemination of new technology and innovation, reinforce the competitiveness of the Community economy. The EIB is also participating in the Integrated Mediterranean Programmes (IMP) and is responsible for Euratom project appraisals and loan management. By permission of the Board of Governors, the Bank may grant investment finance for projects in a country or group of countries under association or cooperation agreements with the Community. Most of the finance is in the form of loans at subsidised interest rates. This facility has been used by a number of countries (by 64 countries in 1985).

2.3 OBJECTIVES OF THE EC

Table 2.2 presents economic statistics for each of the 12 member states of the EC. These statistics reveal substantial differences between the countries comprising the European Community, with reference to:

Physical Size (area, population). The smallest member in both area and population is Luxembourg, the largest in area is France and the largest in population is Germany. The EC 12 make up a market of more than 321 million people, nearly ⅓ more than the population of the USA which is 4 times larger in area than the EC.

Structure of Employment. In every member the services sector predominates, while agriculture is the least significant sector of the economy. However, important differences in the structure of employment still exist, e.g., employment in agriculture is 28.9 per cent in Greece and only 2.6 per cent in the UK.

Economic Size. With GDP per head taken as a measure of the level of economic welfare and development, the least developed member (Portugal) reaches only 41 per cent of the level of the most developed member (Luxembourg). In general, seven countries occupy places above, and the remaining five below, the EC 12 average level of GDP per head.

Composition of Value Added. As with the structure of employment, the services sector predominates. But agriculture is still important for Greece (18.5 per cent), Ireland (16.7 per cent) and Spain (16.7 per cent), while for four countries (Belgium, Germany, Luxembourg, UK) the value-added contributed by this sector is below the EC 10 average (3.4 per cent).

Openness to Trade. Here, the smaller, more developed countries are also the more open to trade. Belgium and Spain are respectively the most and the least open economies of the Community.

These statistics confirm that, in general, the 12 members of the EC do not constitute a homogeneous group. Consequently, diversity in their physical characteristics and in their economic structures, both of which may determine a diversity in interests and growth potential, mean that the search for common objectives and common policies within the Common Market is not an easy process.

The EC does not fit easily into any of the forms of Regional Economic Associations which we discussed in the previous chapter. It is clearly something more than a Customs Union because it has certain sovereign rights conferred to it by the member states, and a government separate from national governments, the EC Commission. On the other hand, the EC is not a federal state because its sovereign rights are limited to specific areas and it lacks the right to create new powers. The Community is instead an organisation of independent national states which have renounced part of their sovereignty in favour of an association of states aspiring to economic integration.

The Commission is in effect the executive body of the Community. However, its executive powers are limited to clearly defined areas: the 'primary' powers conferred to it by the Treaties and the 'derived' powers devolved on it by the Council. In principle, it is the member states themselves that have to ensure that Community rules are applied in individual cases.

The Community has been given by the member states its own budgetary resources. Therefore it is unlike other international organisations, which are financed by subscriptions from their member states. But the Community Budget, unlike the budgets of the constituent states, is relatively small and heavily concentrated on one particular sector, agriculture. With the exception of the latter sector, integration of economic policy within the EC is still minimal. There is a common commercial policy and only the beginning of a common monetary system and fixed exchange rates. Tariffs have gone on intra-EC trade, but impediments to free trade are still many. The freedom of factors of production to move from one member country to another is still limited.

The Treaty of Rome specifically states that an objective of the EC is to 'promote throughout the Community a harmonious development of economic activities, a continuous and balanced expansion, an increase in stability, an accelerated raising of the standard of living and closer relations between the States belonging to it' (Article 2). These objectives will be achieved by the creation of a single internal market free of restrictions on the movement of goods; the abolition of obstacles to the free movement of persons, services and capital; the institution of a system ensuring that competition in the common market is not distorted; the approximation of laws as required for the proper functioning of the common market; and the approximation of indirect taxation in the interest of the common market. All these objectives will be realised by the application of two sets of policies, those taken in common at the level of the EC and those taken individually by the member states but in coordination with each other. With the establishment of the Common Market, common policies will be specifically inaugurated in commerce, agriculture and transport.

Article 3 of the Treaty states that the customs duties and quantitative restrictions on intra-EC trade of commodities and services are to be abolished, and common commercial policy to be established with a common customs tariff on imports from third countries. The six original members of the Community removed all internal quantitative restrictions and tariffs by July 1968. The three members of the first enlargement (DK, IRL, UK) did the same in July 1977. Greece followed in December 1985. The two new members, Portugal and Spain, are required to remove immediately on entry all import quotas and to phase out all customs duties on trade with their Community partners by 1st January 1993. By this time, they will also have adopted the Common External Tariff, which is already in force in the other 10 members.

The free Community market will be completed by the elimination of technical obstacles to trade which result from disparities between the laws, regulations and administrative provisions of member countries. Within the Community, impediments to the free movement of factors of production, persons and capital, will also be lifted. In this way the economic frontiers between the member states will be removed and enlargement of the market for commodities, services and factors of production will ensue, leading to improvement in the allocation of production and exchange. With the Common External Tariff this enlarged market is also transformed into a large trading power acting externally as a single unit. The Treaty provides that, in addition to commerce, two other sectors, agriculture and transport (which at the national level of the member countries are riddled with regulations and distortions) will come under common policies exercised at the level of the Community.

Realisation of market efficiency will lead to the ultimate objective of the economic union, which is to increase economic welfare and the rate of growth of Community GDP for the benefit of its peoples. These aims are to be pursued within a system of external and internal stability (Articles 3 and 104), which should be taken to mean: a) full employment of productive resources and stable prices in the short run, and b) an accelerated growth rate along a stable growth path in the longer run. These objectives will be pursued, if possible, within an environment of free markets and perfect competition.

Competition can be interpreted in a number of ways: a broad definition would be that competition means freedom: for firms to produce what and where they wish; for consumers to have a wider range of material choice and cultural enjoyment; for people to live and work where they desire. A more legalistic interpretation with reference to the EEC would be that competition is the means to an end, and this end is explicitly specified. The Treaty of Rome declares that the contracting parties decided to create the EEC 'determined to lay the foundations of an ever closer union among the peoples of Europe, resolved to ensure the economic and social progress of their countries by common action to eliminate the barriers which divide Europe, affirming as the essential objective of their efforts the constant improvement of the living and working conditions of their people.' (Preamble).

It can also be argued that ultimate objective of the EC is the economic and political unification of Europe and the establishment of a federation, the United States of Europe. But, if this is the aim of the EC, it is nowhere in the treaties spelled out in so many words. However, the Articles of the Treaty of Rome and of subsequent agreements and declarations of Heads of States, and the course the EC has hitherto followed, show clearly that aim of the 'high contracting parties' is the realisation of 'an ever closer union among the European peoples' and therefore economic integration is a prime parallel route towards the 'desirable objective' of establishing a European Union.

The Treaty provides that the Common Market shall be established within 12 years in three stages of four years each (Article 8). However, this objective was not achieved. A new date was set by the Single European Act at the Luxembourg

Summit (December 1985) for the end of 1992. The Act, which after ratification by the member states came into force on 1st July 1987, entails the simultaneous implementation of six policies: (1) The establishment of a large market without internal frontiers; (2) Economic and social cohesion leading to greater convergence; (3) A common policy for scientific and technological development; (4) The strengthening of the European Monetary System; (5) The emergence of a European social dimension; and (6) Coordinated action relating to the environment. The objective of the Single European Act is the foundation of a European Union (EC, 1987).

2.4   POLICIES AND CONSTRAINTS

The economic interdependence among the members of the EC, which will be increased by the integration of the markets for goods services and factors of production, leads to progressively increasing needs for consultation, coordination and finally integration of national economic policies. Membership in an economic union entails for each participating country a weakening of autonomy in the design and exercise of national economic policies. It influences each member country's macroeconomic policy by both rendering each economy more sensitive to developments in the economies of the partner countries, and lessening the access to and the efficacy of various economic instruments. Economic interdependence gives rise to policy externalities and, through them, to policy conflict.

Policy conflict can stem from inconsistency in the national economic objectives of the partners in the EC. Harmonisation of objectives, or in the Community's terminology 'medium-term coordination of economic policies', means adjustment of the members' policy objectives so that they become compatible with one another. In the course of pursuing national economic policy, externalities may occur from the application of instruments. The effects of these externalities on the economies of partner countries can be positive or negative. Obviously, positive externalities provide benefits and are welcome, while negative externalities have to be stopped by inter-country cooperation.

Harmonisation applies to both the instruments and the targets of policy. In general, the objectives of economic policy will be reached faster, and the possibility of negative externalities on fellow member countries will be reduced, when national instruments are adjusted to reach national and partner/Community targets. The greater the degree of interdependence among the partners, the greater the required degree of coordination of both objectives and instruments of policies. Effects of the coordination and harmonisation of policies will be that adjustments are speeded up, and that the likelihood of cyclical approaches to equilibrium or over-shooting of the targets will be reduced. With closer cooperation among the partners of the economic union there will be considerable economies from efficient assignment of policy instruments. Hence the Community gains not only from the reduction/elimination of the negative externalities of economic policies, but also from the saving and efficient allocation in the use of instruments. Coordination of policies leaves national frontiers intact. Integration transforms the policies from national to common, applicable throughout the Community.

Establishment of the European Community can create four types of effects on the powers of the national authorities: (1) It leaves them unchanged; (2) It modifies them—hence, the need for consultation and coordination among members; (3) It limits them, by binding constraints; and (4) It abolishes them, by the introduction of common policies.

The constraints on the exercise of national economic policy, which are imposed by increasing interdependence, are well recognised by the Treaty of Rome which provides general principles for the regulation and coordination of national economic policies. Its aims are to enhance the effectiveness of measures taken at the national level, to emphasise the need for concerted action aiming at speedier progress towards integration, and to diminish the possibility of incompatibility between the objectives of policies. Thus, the Treaty specifies that in pursuing their common aims the EC partners will consider their national economic policies 'as a matter of common interest. They shall consult with each other and with the Commission, on measures to be taken in response to current circumstances' (Article 103). Furthermore, it is stated that in their domestic policy 'each member state shall pursue the economic policy necessary to ensure the equilibrium of its overall balance of payments, and to maintain confidence in its currency, while ensuring a high degree of employment and the stability of the level of prices' (Article 104).

Maintenance of balance of payments equilibrium requires coordinated application of economic policies and consistent patterns of economic development among the partners, particularly in regard to trends in productivity, nominal incomes and prices. The policy instruments which each member may employ to achieve balanced trade with its partners include: fiscal, monetary and exchange rate policy, provided that 'each Member State shall treat its policy with regard to exchange rates as a matter of common interest' (Article 107); trade controls *vis-à-vis* non-member countries; mutual assistance 'recommended by the Community'; and, in the last resort and subject to Community approval, temporary 'protective measures' against other members, provided that 'such measures shall cause the least possible disturbance in the functioning of the Common Market' (Article 109).

The exchange rate is not included among the recommended instruments of policy. This is taken to mean that the Treaty assumes implicitly a commitment on the part of the members to maintain fixed exchange rates, that is the *de facto* establishment of an 'exchange rate union'. This implicit requirement is in accordance with the international system of exchange rates in operation at the time of signing the Treaty of Rome, which was that of fixed exchange rates.

The Treaty does not deal only with macroeconomic policy co-ordination among the members. It also provides an outline for the free movement of factors of production, at a later stage of the integration process, for the purpose of achieving optimisation in resource allocation within the wider area of the Common Market: 'The free movement of workers shall be ensured within the Community' (Article 43); 'Member States shall ... progressively abolish as between themselves restrictions on the movement of capital' (Article 67). The free movement of factors of production may indirectly contribute towards the economic and political unification of the member states. Indeed, many reports and Summit declarations have set explicitly as a long-run objective of the Community the establishment of a European Union.

During the early stages of integration the member states of an economic association are functioning as independent economic units, but within an environment of added restrictions imposed by the need for intra-union policy coordination and harmonisation. The liberalisation of factor movements may entail the gravitation of productive factors from slow-growth areas to fast-growth areas, and this may cause economic imbalances and inequality unacceptable to some member states. Hence, after an initial push towards achieving a common market with free trade in commodities, the process of integration slackens. Reallocation of resources aiming at optimisation might become possible in the longer run, when aggregate concepts, such as Community welfare as opposed to national (or even private) welfare, become politically acceptable and a central authority can have control over both growth policy and income distribution in the common market. But, when this stage of integration is reached, the central authority of the common market is invested with powers beyond those conferred by the member states to an appointed Commission. It is an authority which should have a mandate to govern; in other words, it should be an elected government. Therefore, after a certain threshold, economic integration cannot be advanced further without a parallel move towards political unification.

In the meanwhile, during the intermediate stages of integration, instead of an optimal, the economic association may pursue a balanced allocation of resources as a means for balanced economic development. During this phase of the process of integration the members tend to pursue 'convergence' in the form of equalisation of economic performance. Convergence is an objective which conflicts with the optimal allocation of resources within the area of the common market by imposing constraints on the growth rate of income of individual member countries, and thus on aggregate Community income. Therefore, convergence is an inferior policy which can be justified as a temporary political objective aiming at cohesion among the members until the conditions allow a faster move towards economic unification: 'In order to promote its harmonious development overall, the Community shall develop and pursue its actions leading to strengthening its economic and social cohesion' (Single European Act, *Bulletin EC* 11–1985).

In the EC both political and economic convergence have been advocated as prior requirements for faster progress towards integration and the long-run objective of establishing the European Union. The enlargement of the Community from the homogeneous group of EC-6 countries to the less homogeneous EC-9 countries made the realisation of the ultimate goal more remote. Notwithstanding the problems involved, the Heads of State of the Community countries reaffirmed at the Paris summit of December 1974 that the original objective of European Union has not changed. Following this summit, the Tindemans Report (1976) stressed the need for a new impetus for accelerating the establishment of the European Union which would be based on the following principles:

(1) A united front to the outside world.
(2) The interdependence of the economic prosperity of the Member States and a common economic and monetary policy.
(3) The solidarity of the peoples of the Community and action through social and regional policies to lessen inequalities.
(4) Action to help protect people's rights and improve the quality of life.
(5) The existence of institutions with the necessary powers to determine a common and all-inclusive political view 'with the efficiency needed for action and the legitimacy needed for democratic control'.
(6) A gradual, step-by-step approach, with priority given to objectives likely to succeed.

According to the Tindemans Report these principles were to be given practical application in the form of a 'two-tier'

Community in which a core of the strongest members would press ahead with faster policy integration, while the other members would follow at a slower pace. But the Heads of States, while endorsing most of the Report's recommendations, did not make any specific decisions upon its content. The enlargement of the Community from nine to twelve member states has diluted further the homogeneity of the EEC, and thus it has postponed till another day the realisation of the ultimate goal, establishment of the European Union. With the same objective and two more enlargements which added more members unable to follow the pace of the stronger countries, revival of the Tindemans Report in the future is not excluded.

We will understand better the EC policies if we consider that they are not related solely to an economic objective defined in terms of private consumption oriented concepts of welfare economics, but to a political one, that of establishing a single internal market. This entails costs in terms of traditional concepts of economics, but it may bring about benefits which in the longer run may be proved to be much more important for the peoples of Europe. Subject to this caveat we can state that, in relation to the policy developments which we will examine in the following chapters, the main objectives of the European Community are *enlargement of the market, and changes in production structures leading to improvement in efficiency through specialisation and economies of scale.* The aim of Community policy is to generate the conditions which will improve the competitive structure of the market so that, with few but notable exceptions such as the Common Agricultural Policy, the market mechanism will provide solutions to economic problems. This is the leitmotive of the economic policies of the European Community.

REFERENCES

Bulmer, S. (1985), 'The European Council's First Decade: Between Interdependence and Domestic Politics', *Journal of Common Market Studies*, 24, Dec.
Cooper, R. (1969), 'Macroeconomic Policy Adjustment in

Interdependent Economies', *Quarterly Journal of Economics*, 83, pp. 1–26.

EC Commission (1976), *European Union* (Tindemans Report), *Bull. EC.*, Supplement.

EC (1981), *The European Community's Legal System*: European Documentation, Luxembourg.

EC (1985), 'Texts from the European Council', (Single European Act), *Bull. EC* 11, pp. 9–20.

EC Commission (1987), 'The Single Act: A New Frontier', *Bull. EC.*, Supplement 1

Louis, J. V. (1980), *The Community Legal Order*, EC, Commission, Luxembourg.

Noël, E. (1979), *The European Community: How it Works*, Commission of the European Communities, Brussels.

3   The Community Budget

3.1   INTRODUCTION

As we have seen, the EC objective is integration and enlargement of the market, with predominantly market–determined solutions to economic problems. The emphasis on the market mechanism does not mean that the EC completely abstains from application of economic policies. On the contrary, integration requires the active participation of the central authority in policy making, particularly when an objective of the common policy is a community target, and the process of integration involves costs or brings benefit which must be shared among the participating countries. One of the most important instruments of national economic policy is the budget. The budget is also a major instrument of economic policy in regional economic associations and in the EC. In the following we examine the structure and the objectives of the Community Budget.

Government budget is the account of Revenues received and Expenditures incurred by the government in a period of a financial year. Analysis of the structure of the budget is the study of: a) The origin of government financial resources; b) The destination of those resources; and c) The effects of the composition of revenues and expenditures, and of the overall position of the budget, i.e. the budget surplus or deficit.

In general, the budget mirrors the political, economic and social aims of the government in power. For the economists, the budget is the policy instrument which is used by the government to pursue fiscal policy objectives or expenditure objectives relating to: 1) the allocation of resources; 2) the distribution of income: 3) stabilisation, and 4) economic growth. Ultimately, these objectives constitute part of the more general target of the economic policy of the government, the improvement in social welfare.

The relative importance of the budget as an instrument of policy is to be found in:

(1) The size of the budget: whether it is large or small in relation to a certain base reference, such as the national income.
(2) The structure of the budget: the composition of its credit and debit sides.
(3) The net position of the budget: whether the budget shows an overall surplus or a deficit.

3.2   THE EC BUDGET: GENERAL CHARACTERISTICS

a) Background
One of the basic aims of the Treaty of Rome is 'to establish the foundations for an even closer union among the European peoples', that is an economic and political union rather than another international organisation. To reach this objective the member states must gradually confer to the Community certain of their functions and activities and the powers to operate them. These will be the common targets which will be pursued by common policies at costs shared by all the participants. The Treaty of Paris (1951) had provided the ECSC with its own budget, financed by a levy on coal and steel production and by borrowing. Euratom also started with its own budget, financed by national contributions. In accordance with the terms of the Treaty of Rome, the EEC Commission was given an operational budget and the task of administering two funds, the Social Fund and the Agricultural Fund. In 1967, following the 'Merger Treaty', the budget of the three communities were brought together in a single general budget, the Community Budget.

Initially, the Budget consisted of financial resources made available, and expenditures allocated in accordance with decisions taken in common by the contracting parties. The Budget was *specific*, the revenues consisted of fixed financial contributions made by the member states on an agreed scale, and the expenditures were directed to clearly specified activities (Article 199–209). The Treaty also required the Budget to be (annually and overall) 'in balance as to revenues and expenditures' (Article 199). Hence, this Budget was not substantially different from the budgets of other international organisations, which usually have more moderate aims than those of the European Community.

In order to pursue successfully the objective of economic integration by common policies, the government of the economic union must be provided with the power to choose what revenues to collect and how to spend them, that is with its own budget. As in the case of a federation of states, community financing means the transfer of resources from the national to a common supra–national level. In the EC, the target of this process is the provision of resources which would be used in operational activities geared to the integration of peoples and countries. Hence, the EC, although it is not a federation of states, has specific objectives in many ways similar to those of a federation, and they can be realised only if an adequate budget becomes available. But little has been done towards this direction:

(1) In 1970, in accordance with the provisions of the Treaty (Article 201), the Council decided gradually to replace the financial contributions of member states to the Community Budget by revenues from appropriately allocated 'own resources' directly paid to the Community as of right. An advantage of this new system of financing the Community Budget is that the Commission gained a certain degree of power by loosening its financial dependence on the member states.

(2) At the current phase of European integration, the Community Budget is based on narrow foundations and continues to remain relatively insignificant in size. To a large extent, the EC Budget is still functioning as 'public expenditure estimates', an account of revenues from specific resources and expenditures for specific purposes, in *ex-post* equilibrium as required by the Treaty.

(3) But, if the ultimate policy objective of the contracting parties is to establish a European political and economic union, the present small Community Budget cannot function as an effective policy instrument. That role can be played only by a larger and more independent Community Budget, which could progressively absorb many of the functions currently coming under the jurisdiction of the national budgets.

The Community Budget thus perfectly reflects the present stage of economic integration in Europe. There is as yet no question about using this Budget as an instrument for pursuing Community policies at large, other than those explicitly specified in the Treaty of Rome. Unemployment, inflation, low rate of growth and other macroeconomic problems at the level of the Community have not as yet come to be regarded as common, and are not subject to consideration by Community Budgetary policy. They are still considered as the prerogative and responsibility of the national governments of the member states and are still pursued at the strictly national level. There is still very little cooperation in the area of macroeconomic policy within the EC, and not enough attention has been paid to whether the integration of policies would make them more effective and bring gains to the Community.

b) Budgetary procedure

The Community Budget, which is denominated in ECUs, is drawned annually for a calendar year. Supplementary budgets are added during the year, whenever necessary. Since 1975, the Parliament and the Council are the 'Budgetary Authority', with the Commission responsible for executing the Budget. Both the annual Budget and the supplementary budgets are subject to the same procedures.

Three of the Community's decision-making institutions are involved in the preparation and adoption of the budget.

- On the basis of estimates submitted to the Commission by five Community institutions (the Council, the Commission, the Parliament, the Court of Justice, and the Economic and Social Committee), the Commission prepares the *preliminary* draft budget which it submits to the Council by 1 September.

- The Council, acting by a qualified majority, prepares the *draft budget* which it forwards to the Parliament by 5 October.
- The Parliament approves, amends or rejects the draft budget, which in the latter two cases is referred back to the Council for modifications.

The Parliament can however reject the draft budget *in toto* and ask for a new draft to be submitted. Final adoption of the budget is the prerogative of the President of the European Parliament.

This is a simplified version of a procedure which is rather complex, and it frequently leads to delays in the approval of the budget beyond the required date for completion (usually December). The complications arise mostly from the Treaties, because the texts laying down rules and regulations are not very clear. Most frequently problems emerge from the classification of expenditure as *compulsory* or *non-compulsory*. Compulsory is 'expenditure necessarily resulting from the Treaty or from acts adopted in accordance therewith' (Article 203). Currently, about 85 per cent of the total expenditure is compulsory, such as the expenditure for the CAP. The Parliament has the power to determine only the non-compulsory/discretionary expenditure, and only within pre-specified limits.

The latest dispute between the Council and the Parliament, concerning the classification of expenditures, was resolved in July 1986. The point at issue was that in December 1985 the Parliament had added 1.9 per cent expenditure on the 1986 Budget without previous consultation with the Council, which objected to the increase and appealed to the European Court of Justice. The Court ruled that the Parliament was technically in the wrong and had exceeded its legitimate powers. Namely, the Parliament can disapprove of the entire budget; but it cannot, without Council approval, change the compulsory parts of the budget item by item. Nor can the Parliament raise the discretionary part of the budget above a ceiling set by the Council. The Court also confirmed that drafting the budget was a task in which the Council and Parliament were jointly, though not equally, involved.

After the end of the budgetary year, a fourth Community institution, the Court of Auditors, scrutinises all Community revenue and expenditure, and decides whether financial management has been sound and regular. Finally, after the Parliament has examined the accounts, deliberated on the report of the Court of Auditors and considered the recommendations of the Council, it grants *Parliamentary Discharge*, confirming that the Commission's management of Community funds during the preceding year has been approved.

3.3   THE EC BUDGET DURING THE PERIOD 1980-6

In 1985 the Community budget was approximately 28,430 million ECUs (or nearly £15,800 million). It looks like a very large sum, but actually it is less than 1 per cent of the EC countries' gross domestic product of the same year (which was 3230.7 billion ECU). In contrast, the national budgets of the member states currently take up a large (and in some cases increasing) share of national GDP. For instance, this share currently is in France 32 per cent, in Germany 33 per cent, in the UK 42 per cent, in Italy 43 per cent, in Denmark 56 per cent. The Community Budget is equal to only 2.5 per cent of the sum of budgets of the EC-10 countries. But this makes it approximately equal to the budget of Denmark or to the sum of Greece's and Ireland's national budgets.

The composition of the Community Budget of the period 1980-86 was as in Table 3.1. The analysis of its structure is as follows:

a) Revenues
(1) Customs revenue from the application of the Common Customs Tariff (CCT) on goods imported from third countries. The customs duties are collected at the point of entry in the Community, which can be in a country other than the country of final destination or consumption of the imported commodity. It is therefore revenue from operating a Community policy, and it rightly goes to the Community purse.

(2) Variable import levies on imports of agricultural products from third countries arising under the Common Agricultural Policy. Reasons similar to (1) above apply for directing this revenue to the Community rather than the treasury of the country collecting it. Agricultural levies are designed to offset the differences between the (usually much higher) Community price and the price of imports. The sugar levy, which is a charge on the production and storage of sugar and isoglucose of member states, is also included here.

(3) The revenues collected from (1) and (2) above are inadequate relative to the functions allocated to the Community Budget (approximately 35 per cent and 12 per cent in 1980) and fluctuate widely from year to year. In the longer run their relative shares in the Budget may further diminish as international trade is liberalised and more special agreement for free or freer trade are concluded between the EC and third countries. Consequently, the Community (in accordance with Article 201 of the EEC Treaty) decided to create an additional and more secure source of budgetary revenue by allocating to the Community as 'own resource' a proportion of the imputed yield of each member state's Value Added Tax (VAT).

The VAT yield has been chosen in preference to other tax yield, because: a) Under the Sixth Directive of the 17th May 1977, VAT is a tax paid by all the Community citizens; and b) As an indirect tax charged at the consumption stage, the VAT is supposed to reflect each member state's spending capacity, that is their ability to pay. The latter reason is, however, incorrect, since at the current stage of European integration, sales tax harmonisation means only that VAT is the common sales tax and that it is assessed on a common basis, but VAT rates are not equal in the different member states (see chapter 4: Tax Harmonisation).

The 1970 agreement to assign to the Community 'own resources' set a ceiling for members' contribution to 1 per cent of VAT revenue as imputed according to a common definition. But, delays in the introduction of VAT in some EC countries meant that the replacement of all member states' financial contributions by VAT payments was not completed before 1980. In the meanwhile, budgetary expenditures kept rising and, after two years of operating the new system, the ceiling of 1 per cent was reached, with the implication that the Community had exhausted its finances before fulfilling its legal obligations. A new ceiling of 1.4 per cent was set in June 1984 at the Fontainebleau summit of EC Heads of State, and came into force on 1st January 1986. The new agreement provides that, under certain conditions, by a new unanimous decision of the Council and after ratification by the member states in accordance with national procedures, the ceiling could be raised to 1.6 per cent from the 1st January 1988.

b) Expenditures

Expenditures from the Community budget are in the form of direct payments to recipients in individual member states or to countries outside the EC, such as: agricultural intervention boards, government departments of member states, research establishments, private firms, or foreign governments as aid, etc. Items (1) to (4) in Table 3.1 have become known as the *allocated* budget expenditures. They account for more than 80 per cent of total expenditure. The rest of Community expenditure, the *unallocated*, goes either to recipients outside the Community or to administrative outlays at the headquarters. Another distinction of expenditures is drawn between *payment appropriations* (amounts which can be paid out in the year) and *commitment appropriations* (amounts which can be legally committed for payment over a number of years ahead).

The relative shares in total expenditure of the various economic sectors to a large extent reflect relative growth of Community intervention, that is the areas of active Community (as contrasted to national) policy. Thus the highest proportion of the Community budget is spent on agriculture. Expenditures under the Regional, Social, and other Funds aim at improvement of the economic conditions either in disadvantaged regions or for disadvantaged categories of people. It is assumed that expenditure from these funds constitutes a supplement to, and not a substitute for, similar expenditures incurred by the national governments of the member states. The expenditure on energy, industry, transport, research, and development aid has remained low.

Table 3.1: EC Budget Allocation, 1980–86

	1980	1981	1982	1983	1984	1985	1986
Revenues %							
1. Customs Duties, Agricultural Levies, Sugar Levy	51	45	42	40	46	38	36
2. VAT	49	55	58	60	54	62	64
Expenditures %							
1. Agriculture & Fisheries Guarantee	69.6	61.9	60.9	65.1	64.1	71.1	62.8
Guidance	3.7	3.2	3.2	3.1	3.1	2.2	3.1
2. Social Policy	4.7	4.7	5.2	4.2	5.3	4.9	7.2
3. Regional Policy	6.8	12.6	14.7	9.9	5.6	5.7	6.7
4. Research, Energy, etc.	1.9	2.1	2.1	5.4	4.2	2.6	2.2
5. Development Aid	3.1	4.8	3.8	3.3	3.5	3.7	3.3
6. Administration	5.0	5.3	5.0	4.6	3.1	4.7	4.5
7. Reimbursements to Members	5.2	5.4	5.1	4.4	7.2	3.8	9.5
8. Contingency Reserves	–	–	–	–	3.9	1.3	0.7

Sources: Eurostat 1984.
Bull. EC 9–1985 and 6–1986.

The new members of the EC (Greece 1981, Spain and Portugal 1986) are covered by transitional arrangements for the first five years of their membership. During this period they contribute to the budget as full members, but in return they receive a refund equal to a progressively diminishing share of their contributions.

3.4 PROBLEMS WITH THE BUDGETARY IMPACT AMONG THE PARTNERS

Table 3.2 presents the distribution of the burden of the EC budget among the partners for the period 1980–2. The data show that two of the members, Germany and the UK, have consistently been net contributors to the Budget, while all other countries are net recipients from the Budget. The UK's

Table 3.2: Net contributors (–) to, and Recipients (+) from EC allocated budget, 1980, 1981, 1982

Member State	1980 Total*	1980 Per head†	1980 GDP‡	1981 Total*	1981 Per head†	1981 GDP‡	1982 Total*	1982 Per head†	1982 GDP‡
B-L	+439	+43	115	+515	+50	107	+510	+50	98
DK	+327	+64	125	+279	+55	126	+294	+57	127
D	–1,526	–25	126	–1,684	–27	123	–2,085	–34	124
F	+431	+8	118	+576	+11	117	+14	+0.3	115
IRL	+650	+191	51	+582	+169	54	+721	+207	59
I	+737	+13	67	+788	+14	68	+1,586	+28	70
NL	+454	+32	115	+239	+17	109	+302	+21	112
UK	–1,512	–27	90	–1,419	–25	98	–2,040	–36	97
GR			40		+18	42		+71	44

Notes: *million ECUs.
†ECUs.
‡Per head as a percentage of EC average, current prices, market exchange rate.

Source: 1. *Official Journal of the European Communities*, 1985.
2. *Eurostat Review*, various issues.

contribution to the Community Budget has been regarded as particularly disproportionate to her position in the per capita income scale within the EC. The reasons for differential inequality in the impact of the Budget are to be found in the narrowness of its structure, which affects both the receipts from it and the contributions to it by member states. In particular:

a) Receipts

The budgetary impact of the CAP(1) A member state's production of agricultural output may exceed its own consumption. The surplus output is disposed of by: (i) Exports to other member countries at current Community prices; (ii) Sale to Community agencies at support prices; (iii) Exports at prices subsidised by the Community. Over the last decade the Agricultural Fund (EAGGF) has been using more than 70 per cent of the total revenue of the Budget. Hence, a substantial share of Community expenditure is directed towards member states with relatively large agricultural sectors, which are surplus producers and exporters of highly-supported temperate foodstuffs, such as wheat, dairy products and beef. On the other hand, member states with relatively small agricultural sectors, which are importers of agricultural products covered by the CAP tend to be net contributors to the budget. Table 2.2 in chapter 2 shows that Germany and the UK belong to the latter category of member countries, with share of agriculture in Gross Value Added equal to 1.9 per cent and 1.7 per cent respectively (1984). Changing the budgetary impact means reforming the CAP itself, which is a difficult proposition.

Other budgetary expenditure (2) The sums remaining after subtracting the CAP expenditures are relatively small and, therefore, unable to counterbalance the impact of the CAP on the member countries. In other words, the CAP takes up too much money, creates imbalances, and leaves too little to the other sectors.

b) Contributions

The revenues from customs duties and agricultural levies (1) depend on the level of imports from non-EC countries.

The Netherlands and Belgium, which have large ports through which imports destined for other members of the EC arrive, appear to be contributing high duty payments to the Community Budget. But some of the burden of the customs revenue collected by the Netherlands and Belgium will in fact be borne by consumers elsewhere in the Community. The level of agricultural levies is not necessarily related to the level of GDP. Thus countries with a relatively small agricultural sector who are net importers of food from outside the Community, both contribute more to the budget and receive less out of it than members with relatively large agricultural sectors. The problem with the UK's contribution to the Community Budget arises from the fact that the UK is both a relatively small producer, and a major importer (for historical reasons, mostly from outside the EC) of agricultural products. Since accession in 1973, the pattern of UK's trade is changing direction with the proportion of imports from non-EC countries declining rather rapidly. Nevertheless, the UK continues to have a large share of its trade with non-member countries (see Table 8.1 in chapter 8).

VAT contribution (2) This reflects levels of expenditure on goods and services and the rate of VAT charged in each member, so that the overall VAT contribution to the Community Budget is only indirectly related to the level of GDP and the ability to pay.

The basic problems of the impact of the Community Budget were predicted and debated even before the UK acceded to the Community. After accession, the UK argued that its contribution to the Budget is disproportionate since (unlike Germany), it is not one of the richest members of the Community (sixth from the top, see Tables 2.2 and 3.2). When repeated complaints failed to solve this problem, the UK finally claimed that a case of 'unacceptable situations' had arisen and that 'the very survival of the Community would demand that the institutions find an equitable solution' (in accordance with supporting documents of the Treaty of Accession).

In an attempt to reduce expenditure on the CAP, the Commission proposed that production targets be set for every agricultural sector. Once these were reached producers would be required to contribute to the expenses or the intervention guarantee could be reduced. Although this device, which is known as the 'coresponsibility levy', was selectively applied (notably on sugar and milk), the problems of budgetary finances and impacts on the members were not solved. After repeated negotiations, the principle for compensating the UK for excess payments was accepted in 1980, when it was agreed that the UK would get for 1980 and 1981 a fixed refund, approximately equal to $\frac{2}{3}$ of its own contribution. These refunds were paid out of the Community Budget the year following that to which they applied. Since the contributions of the members were governed by the 'own resources' provisions of the Treaty and were 'mandatory', the refunds to the UK were granted on a temporary *ad hoc* basis, partly by direct payments to the British Treasury and partly in the form of 'extra EC spending on approved projects'. This agreement was extended to 1982 and 1983.

A new and more permanent solution agreed at the Fontainebleau summit in June 1984 set the UK refund at 1000 million ECU for 1984, and for subsequent years at 66 per cent of the difference between what it pays in VAT and what it receives from the Community Budget. Hence, in the future the UK refund will be in the form of a reduction in contribution and not as additional budgetary expenditure on specific projects. In exchange for this settlement of the problem, the UK conceded the VAT ceiling to be raised to 1.4 per cent. In case this ceiling needs to be raised by a new unanimous decision of the Council, the UK refund provisions will have to be renegotiated. The agreement states that not only the UK but 'any Member State sustaining a budgetary burden which is excessive in relation to its relative prosperity may benefit from a correction at the appropriate time'. This means that problems as those which for a long time affected the EC–UK relations should not arise in the future. Portugal is expected to be eligible for a refund of her contributions after she becomes a full member of the Community.

In an attempt to solve the Budget's financial crisis the Fontainebleau agreement introduced 'budgetary discipline', a check procedure on the growth of budget expenditure.

Accordingly, the Council early in the year establishes in collaboration with the Commission a 'reference framework' setting the maximum level of expenditure which it considers it must adopt to finance Community policies during the following financial year. An additional constraint is also imposed, that the net expenditure relating to agriculture, calculated on a three-yearly basis, should increase less than the rate of growth of the own resources base. The Commission is required to observe these limits when making its initial (draft) budget proposals. If ministers agree to any measures which threaten to result in the budgetary limit being exceeded, the Commission has the power to suspend it. However, this mechanism for reducing the growth of expenditure has not taken into consideration events which are outside the Community's control and can have effects on the budget.

In the first half of 1986 the dollar fell by approximately 11 per cent and thus the ECU appreciated making the EC output more expensive. This in turn increased the cost of EC export subsidies. As a consequence, the sums allocated to the CAP were rapidly depleted, exports ceased and the Community was forced to hang on to its food mountains. But, with financial resources tied up in unsold agricultural commodities, a substantial drop in customs revenues due to the fall in the price of oil, and shrinkage in budget receipts arising from a general decline in economic activity in the member states and thus the VAT 'take', the Community faced another budgetary crisis. The Commission requested and received more emergency funds from the member states and thus the final outcome was a budget much larger than the draft budget which the Council had rejected a few months earlier as being excessive.

The Commission came up with a temporary solution involving the introduction of 'creative accounting', that is deferring payments until the next year, when it was hoped that the situation might have improved. But this device did not work as expected and half way through the financial year the Budget came apart with a shortfall of £500 million. In September 1986 the Commission released figures showing that the £22 billion budget, agreed only two months earlier, was unworkable. Without having yet solved the budgetary problem for 1986, the budget ministers prepared the European

Community's 1987 draft budget. In an attempt to safeguard funds for spending on farm support, the draft budget included cuts in development aid, food aid, spending on transport and funds for agricultural improvements. As we have seen, current expenditure on agriculture is such a dominant factor of the EC that the Community Budget is built for the sole purpose of serving it first; all other needs have to wait.

At the beginning of 1987 the Commission came up with the proposal that the Community Budget should rise by 30 per cent from its current level by the end of 1992. To ensure that the farm policy does not swallow up extra funds, the Commission proposed that the size of the Budget should determine the extent of agricultural spending. This would involve the introduction of 'budgetary stabilisers', that is set limits for the guarantee section of expenditure on agriculture, determined by the size of existing stocks of output and current prices in the markets of the Community. The expectation is that the overall farm budget would increase by no more than the natural, annual increase in Community revenue, which is estimated to be about 2 per cent in real terms.

By June 1987 the Community finances had reached a new crisis. The Commission's original plans to effect savings of £500 million through CAP price support curbs and other measures were all but destroyed by the determination of governments to preach austerity, but secure the best deal for their own agricultural sectors. The net result was that the Community once again ran out of money. A proposal to levy a consumption tax on fats and oils, which was scheduled to add £1.4 billion a year to the Community's coffers, was opposed by the UK, Germany and the Netherlands who argued that it could seriously damage trade relations with the United States. With no other alternative in sight, the Commission estimated that either the VAT contribution should be raised from 1.4 to 1.9 per cent, or the Community would be unable to meet its commitments and avoid a new large deficit. At the same time, the Parliament made known that it would no longer be prepared to put up with creative accounting measures designed to delay the Community's day of reckoning. With the Community staggering from one financial crisis to another, it is remarkable that till now the day of reckoning has been postponed eight times in as many years. The repeated crises have helped, inadvertently, to produce a widespread consensus for long-term budgetary reform. If this consensus survives the detailed negotiations to come, it could provide the basis for a saner and fairer budget system, to the benefit of all EC countries and the course of European integration.

3.5 EVALUATION

Where a federal level of government has over the years acquired wide powers of raising taxes and spending, complex patterns of equalisation both of revenues and of expenditures may make sense. However, the Community Budget is at the moment relatively small and questions about its impact seem to be out of proportion: the UK contribution to the Community is about 0.3 per cent of UK public expenditure.

Nevertheless, the Community Budget is structurally unsound. By having a narrow base both of revenue and of expenditure, it gives rise to net positions of the member states that are highly sensitive to yearly changes in economic conditions.

When a member country is a net contributor to the Budget, a transfer of resources takes place from that country's taxpayers to the beneficiaries of Community policies in other member countries which are net recipients of budgetary policies. Net contributions and net receipts provide a measure of budgetary transfers within the Community. However, there are limits to what these figures represent. Budgetary transfers should not be confused with the costs and benefits of membership in the Community. Community policies have many and varied economic effects, and the budgetary accounts provide a partial and highly distorted view of what is actually happening. In general, net budgetary transfers do not, by definition, take account of costs and benefits outside the Budget and therefore they cannot become the basis for measuring the costs and benefits of economic integration. They are effects of a certain activity at the Community level, but there are many other activities which do not involve the Budget. These activities must be considered for an evaluation of total costs and benefits. Some of the missing elements for the completion of the picture are:

(1) Gains and losses for individuals from operating the Common Agricultural Policy regarding the increase in the prices of agricultural commodities within the EC. Consumers pay more for their food than they would in the absence of the CAP, while farmers receive higher prices for their sales than they would receive otherwise. These payments and receipts are not passing through the EC budget and remain unrecorded.

(2) Gains and losses from operating the customs union, that is from intra-community free trade in manufacturing commodities, services and factors of production. These gains or losses accrue to economic agents, firms or individuals, within the Community and arise from the enlargement of the market, the intensification of competition, the realisation of economies of scale, and the protection of the market from foreign competition by the Common External Tariff. Activities like these are not part of the Budget, and therefore they are not counted when the net budgetary impact on the member countries is evaluated.

(3) But even those costs and benefits which accrue through the Budget may misrepresent reality. Gross contributions collected in a member state may not accurately reflect the burden on the taxpayers of that state. The attribution of customs duties and levies to a country whose ports act as entrepôts for onward movement of imported commodities to other member countries inside the Community is clearly incorrect (the 'Rotterdam-Antwerp effect'). Similarly, gross receipts paid to residents of a member country, such as MCAs, may not accurately reflect the benefits to citizens of that state, if cross-border exchange has taken place.

(4) It is important to recognise that for most policies undertaken in common there is a substitution effect between Community and national expenditure: Community spending is frequently complementary to national spending: what is spend by the Community often represents saving for the national budgets. Therefore it is important to estimate whether the benefit from spending in common outweighs that from spending individually at the national level. There is no doubt that for the largest part of the budgetary expenditure (e.g. for

agriculture or research) this indeed is the case. However, this should not be of crucial importance since a common general budget which is oriented towards policies and not individual issues entails allocational inequalities in both costs and benefits.

These considerations do not exclude the possibility that certain member countries are net losers from the overall operation of the Community. However, the concept of net contributors to, and net beneficiaries from the Budget during the process of integration should be considered as of little consequence—except if they give rise to 'unacceptable situations' which may threaten the existence of the Community. Progress towards integration and equality of contributions and benefits are incompatible. The problem is related to the links between revenue and expenditure. There are two general principles: one is that a *specific tax source* should be made available for a specific form of expenditure. This principle is usually associated with the notion of equality between costs and benefits, the *fair return* argument.

The other principle is that of a *common pool of funds* from which community expenditure is financed. This principle is usually associated with the 'ability to pay'. Clearly, neither of these principles is applied to the Community Budget. However, the notion that each member should receive from the Budget an amount equal to that it contributed, so that the net position of every participant is balanced at nought, undermines the concept and aims of integration. Even in single national states each region and each individual do not receive from the budget an amount equal to their contribution. If this was the case, then the distributional aims of the budget would disappear. However, problems with the Community Budget exist, because at this stage of integration it is small, it is not an instrument for income redistribution and, with one notable exception, it has very little impact on the macroeconomic policy of the member states. The Community's target of 'harmonious development of economic activity' suggests that the Community Budget has an important role to play in the process of integration. Harmonious development does not, of course, mean equality of performance. However, *convergence at a higher level of performance* might be a requirement for harmonious development. This is a very important target for the EC, which should become the objective of a larger and more ambitious Community Budget.

REFERENCES

Denton, G. (1984), 'Re-Structuring the EC Budget: Implications of the Fontainebleau Agreement', *Journal of Common Market Studies*, 22, pp. 118–40.

EC (1984), 'The Budget', *Bull. EC*–6.

EC (1986), *The European Community's Budget*, 4th edition, European Documentation, Luxembourg.

H.M. Treasury (1982), *The European Community Budget: net Contributions and Receipts*, Economic Progress Report Supplement, October.

Prest, A. R. (1983), 'Fiscal Policy', in Peter Coffey (ed.), *Main Economic Policy Areas of the EEC*, Martinus Nijhoff, The Hague.

Strasser, D. (1980), *The Finances of Europe*, EC, Brussels.

Wallace, Helen (1980), *Budgetary Politics: The Finances of the European Communities*, Allen and Unwin, London.

4 Tax Harmonisation

4.1 THE PROBLEM

Abolition of trade barriers among the members of the customs union does not necessarily imply that a common perfectly competitive market has been completed. Impediments to the smooth functioning of the competitive markets for commodities, services and factors of production are still many. Differences among the tax systems of the members of the customs union are one of the most important of these impediments.

Tax systems may differ between countries in a number of ways associated with a) What is taxed: the tax base. b) By how much it is taxed: the tax rate. c) By what particular kind of tax is taxed: tax type.

Tax harmonisation attempts to make different tax systems compatible with one another and with the objectives of the economic union. The aim of tax harmonisation is 'to encourage the interplay of competition in such a way that integration and economic growth ... may be achieved simultaneously and gradually' (The Neumark Report, *Report of Fiscal and Financial Committee*, 1963, p. 188). The scale of compatibility ranges from nil to perfect and exactly what degree of compatibility/tax harmonisation is ideal for a particular economic union will depend on the degree of integration the members are aiming at. In a Free Trade Area, where only tariffs among the members are abolished, the required tax harmonisation is minimal. But even fully independent states may choose to coordinate their tax systems, e.g. for reasons relating to tax avoidance, double taxation etc. In a Regional Economic Association aiming at complete economic and political integration, complete tax harmonisation may become inevitable, and this means that the members will have to adopt a unified tax system.

In general only two approaches to tax harmonisation in economic unions have received much attention: a) The equalisation approach, and b) The differentials approach.

(1) The equalisation approach

advocates 'standardisation', that is uniformity of tax base and equalisation of tax rates among the members of the union. Standardisation can be reached with or without actual unification of the tax system under a single fiscal policy authority. The equalisation approach is supported primarily for two reasons: 1) It accords with the aims of the economic union designated simply as 'enhancing competition on equal terms'. 2) It is the favourite of those who consider tax harmonisation as one of the means of moving forward with economic and later political integration, where equalisation of rates and uniformity of taxes are regarded as necessary.

The problem of tax harmonisation under the equalisation approach consists of selecting the set of taxes and tax rates which will direct the economic union towards achieving its objective. This objective is economic integration and maximisation of welfare for the economic union as a whole.

(2) The differentials approach

is based on the principle that the tax system of each country functions as an instrument of policy for attaining major economic objectives. Therefore, it is argued that the same principle should apply at the scale of the economic union, with the proviso that the externalities of each country's tax systems on other countries should be minimised by close coordination among the members. Under the assumption that the sum of the members' welfare adds up to the welfare of the economic union, the problem of the differentials approach is to select for each participant the set of taxes and tax rates which optimises its own welfare. This principle is based on the presumption that private (member's) benefit and social (economic union's) benefit coincide.

It should be obvious from the above discussion that tax harmonisation encompasses in general both the equalisation and the differentials approaches. Tax harmonisation ranges between the one extreme of *zero change* in taxes and tax rates and the other extreme of *unification of taxes and complete equalisation of rates*, with all the variations in between. The differentials approach covers most of the cases, while the equalisation approach occupies only the upper limit of this range.

Taxes are used by governments as instruments of budgetary, social or economic policy. With changes in taxes and tax rates consequent upon tax harmonisation there will be effects on both the instruments and the objectives of economic policies. In general, tax harmonisation is multi-dimensional, affecting all the functions of the tax system. The principal functions of a tax system are: 1) Allocation of resources; 2) Economic stabilisation; 3) Economic growth; 4) Income distribution; 5) Balance of Payments; and 6) Tax revenue. Every government's policies relate to these functions, but different governments have different sets of objectives and therefore different priorities and rankings of these functions. Tax harmonisation affects both the functions of the tax system and the order of their priority.

The equalisation approach gives precedence to the common goals of the economic union, placing them above the goals of the individual members. Unification of tax rates or even agreement for closer alignment of rates will severely restrict the members states' capacity to manipulate these rates for short-term economic policy purposes. Moves towards a uniform tax system, with common tax rates, imply that the members have considered and endorsed the transfer of the necessary power for policy making from themselves to the policy-making authority of the economic union. In other words, the members would adopt tax harmonisation in the form of tax equalis-ation, only if they have already decided that the ultimate objective of the economic union is economic (and political) integration, and that a common tax system is a way towards that goal. Equalisation provides a common tax system, just as in the case of a single national state. If at any time departures from uniformity might be deemed necessary, they would no longer be pursued by a tax policy; they would be taken care of by other policies, such as public expenditure, regional policy, etc.

Under the differentials approach the presumption is that for the time being the economic association will not move towards full integration and, more specifically, that fiscal policy will remain in the domain of each member state. Tax harmonisation in this case is akin to tax coordination and is not free of complications. The members have to decide the degree of economic integration they aim at, before deciding the exact form of tax harmonisation they require. For example, they may have to consider: 1) Whose welfare they attempt to improve by tax harmonisation. Conflicts may arise between individual members and the economic union as a whole with regard to diverse objectives, the ranking of tax functions, the effects of harmonisation, the degree of coordination imposed by the adopted system, the effects on the distribution of income among the partners and so on. 2) Whether the tax system will be used to restrain or to enhance intra-union factor mobility. With factor mobility, the framework of the REA is that of a common market, without it is a customs union. 3) Whether there will be a general harmonisation of the whole tax system or a partial harmonisation of those taxes whose effects impinge on the functions of the economic union. 4) Whether the harmonisation will be introduced gradually or at once. 5) Whether the harmonisation will be constrained by *tax neutrality*, that is whether it will leave the tax revenue undisturbed.

In general, changes in a tax system, implemented either within an economic union through tax harmonisation or individually by a national state through tax reform, change a number of economic variables and have welfare implications. Tax changes and their effects take place within the framework of 'second-best' conditions. Therefore, whether tax changes would lead to an improvement or a deterioration in social welfare, cannot be decided on *a priori* considerations.

In general, tax changes affect relative prices and therefore the terms of trade within the economy and between the economy and other countries, so that the pattern and the volume of trade may also be affected. Changes in the terms of trade imply redistribution of income between: i) the citizens of the country, ii) the country and its partners in the economic union, iii) the economic union and the outside world. The effects are similar with those derived from changes in tariff structures. Consequently, changes in relative domestic/foreign prices originating from tax changes give rise to welfare effects, the trade creation and trade diversion effects of tax harmonisation.

4.2 TAX HARMONISATION IN THE EC

The tax systems of the Six signatories of the Treaty of Rome differed substantially in a number of ways: Sales taxes were in the form of Value Added Tax (VAT), turnover tax and taxes on gross value. Excise taxes differed in the extent to which goods were taxed, rates and mode of evaluation. Different systems of corporation taxation had different implication on capital and investment. In some countries (e.g., Italy) a separate corporation tax did not exist; it was partially integrated with the personal income tax system. The personal income tax system differed among the contracting states in rates, allowances, administrative procedures, compliance and enforcement. Furthermore, the social security obligations and the social benefits to individuals were also different. In general, the tax systems of the Six were greatly diversified, reflecting important differences in the members' economic and social structures and policy objectives.

The Treaty of Rome specifies that 'harmonising the legislation ... concerning turnover taxes, excise duties and other forms of indirect taxation' (Article 99) is a principal objective of the EC, and that laws in general—including tax law—should be approximated (Articles 100–102). Details about what tax harmonisation and approximation of laws would involve are not provided in the Treaty. The missing details are usually specified by specially constituted Study Committees and Working Parties of experts. Their proposals and recommendations are published in Reports. When their proposals are approved, they are issued as Directives and become binding on the member states.

Tax harmonisation in the EC always aimed at two objectives: 1) Competition on equal terms among the EC partners; this implies the abolition of tax frontiers; 2) Acceleration of the process of integration and unification of the market. The following quotation from general guidelines issued by a member of the Commission presents an official view of the objectives of tax harmonisation in the EC very clearly:

> We want to carry tax harmonization as far as is required by the objectives of the Common Market. We must harmonize where this is necessary to eliminate tax frontiers and avoid distortions of competition: we must harmonize in order to facilitate mergers across the internal frontiers of the Community and to help build up a European capital market. We must also harmonize as a part of the work to be done before we can arrive at a common economic policy, and quite simply with a view to achieving the aims of a number of common policies in various sectors of our activity.
> (Vice-President of the Commission Haferkamp, quoted in Schneider, 1973).

In practice tax harmonisation was proved more difficult than envisaged. The complexity of the problem, and the widely held principle that tax sovereignty is one of the fundamental components of national sovereignty, meant that rather little could be achieved, and at a very slow pace. For the same fundamental reasons all the measures adopted or proposed are confined to the harmonisation of tax structures and bases of assessment under strict neutrality. Decisions on tax rates are still regarded as a sensitive issue which must remain with the national authorities of the member states.

Table 4.1 presents the structure of taxation in the EC countries, that is the relative tax burden in the form of the ratio of taxes on GDP, the share of sales taxes on GDP and the contribution of different taxes to total tax revenue. The data show considerable differences among the EC countries in both the burden of taxation and the composition of tax revenues. This is the situation at present, despite many years of economic cooperation and after many attempts at tax harmonisation. These attempts and their results are examined in the following with reference to certain basic taxes:

Table 4.1: Relative Size and Composition of Receipts of General Government

Country	Taxes % on GDP (a) Total	VAT & Excise	Taxes % in total receipts, (b) production and imports	income and wealth	capital	social contributions
B	46.9	10.06	25.7	41.8	0.6	31.8
DK	40.4	15.71	38.0	57.7	0.4	3.9
D	40.7	9.04	31.9	30.0	0.2	37.9
F	43.5	11.41	35.0	20.6	0.9	43.5
IRL	32.7	17.13	48.5	35.6	0.3	15.6
I	38.6	8.32	29.0	36.4	0.2	34.5
L	48.5	10.28	32.2	39.1	0.4	28.3
NL	46.3	9.19	25.0	28.7	0.4	46.0
UK	39.1	9.79	41.2	39.3	0.5	19.0
EC 9	41.2	7.05	33.8	31.7	0.4	34.1

Notes: (a) 1982, (b) 1984, except for L (1982), IRL (1983) and EC-9 (1982)

Sources: Eurostat, (1985), *Basic Statistics of the Community*, 23rd and 24th eds.
EC (1985), *Completing the Internal Market*, Document.

a) Sales taxes

Indirect taxes enter the final prices of goods and services on which they are imposed. Therefore, under similar production cost conditions, different levels and principles of taxation will be reflected in different price levels.

Indirect taxes are levied according to the *origin* or *destination* principles of taxation. Under the origin principle taxes are levied at the production stage and the tax revenue accrues to the country of production. Therefore exports from a low tax country to a high tax country enjoy an artificial comparative advantage. Under the destination principle, which is used in international trade worldwide, taxes are levied at the consumption stage and the tax revenue accrues to the country of consumption. Therefore under the destination principle countries make border tax adjustments, that is they levy taxes on imports and refund taxes on exports. Countries can gain an unfair advantage by taxing imported products at rates higher than those levied on similar domestic products, and by refunding taxes on exports greater than those actually paid. This amounts to imposing disguised customs duties and subsidising exports, hence it is specifically forbidden in common markets (EEC Treaty Articles 95 and 96).

The destination principle of taxation, which (barring unfair practices) treats imported and home-produced goods alike, does not lead to distortions of competition and in general does not upset comparative costs (Musgrave, 1969). The origin principle would have had similar effects only if all trading countries applied a common tax rate, but this condition is never met in practice. Therefore the origin principle of taxation upsets comparative costs, trade flows, and the international allocation of production.

While the first moves for trade liberalisation among the members of the Community had started, the Commission appointed in 1959 a working group to study the effects of differing systems of indirect taxation on trade. The group's report revealed substantial distortions in trade caused by differing national policies regarding tax rebates to exporters and the fiscal treatment of imports. Following this report the Commission appointed a group of experts, the Neumark Committee, to review the fiscal systems of the member states and to recommend methods for harmonising them. The Neumark Committee issued its Report in 1962 recommending the introduction of a common system of sales tax, the Value Added Tax, VAT. This tax was chosen as the common sales tax because it had been shown to have a number of advantages over the traditional forms of sales taxes (turnover, single stage, etc.), for instance, it may provide more neutrality as regards saving, investment and work decisions, particularly if the tax base is wide and there is a single rate of tax. Moreover, VAT facilitates exact refunding of taxes on exports and, therefore, it can lead to abolition of fiscal frontiers within the Community.

The Neumark Committee dealt also with the question of the jurisdictional principle of taxation on internationally traded goods and services. The Report proposed the *restricted origin principle* of taxation, whereby goods crossing borders within the economic union carry the tax of the country of production (the origin principle), whilst goods imported from outside are taxed by the country of consumption (the destination principle). Hence, the restricted origin principle is a composite which includes features from both constituent parts. An advantage of the origin principle of taxation is that it eliminates fiscal frontiers between member countries, thus contributing to the creation of a single market and the elevation of the Regional Economic Association to a more advanced form of integration. This in turn means that, in the longer run and without internal border controls, competition among the members of the economic union will necessarily bring about a tendency towards tax-rate equalisation.

It is important to emphasise that VAT is a method of taxation and not a new kind of tax. By VAT taxes are levied on a piecemeal basis, stage by stage, while avoiding double taxation, so that the tax collected in relation to final product price will be precisely equivalent to that obtained by a single stage tax levied on the same aggregate base with the same *ad valorem* rate. Therefore, VAT is neutral as between production by a vertically integrated enterprise and production by several independent firms. In contrast, a multi-stage cascade tax levies a lesser tax burden on production undertaken within the same enterprise and therefore it encourages the vertical integration of firms. On the other hand, VAT may involve heavy administrative costs for both the tax authorities and the taxpayers.

The calculation of VAT is usually based on the indirect or invoice method: that is the tax is applied to total sales of the firm, but the tax already paid on input purchases is subsequently subtracted. This method, which is known as the 'tax credit' method, introduces into the tax system a self-policing operation which helps tax collection. An advantage of VAT is that at every stage of production the exact amount of the tax paid is known, therefore tax rebating on exports is accurate and cannot be used as a disguise for granting export subsidies.

The Community accepted the Neumark Committee's proposals for introduction of VAT. It decided, however, that, for as long as the process of building up the common market is in progress, it should apply the destination principle of taxation. The preference for the destination principle arose from the need to avoid distortions of competition, and to allocate internal indirect tax revenues to the country levying the tax. As a long-term solution, the Community formally adheres to the introduction of the origin principle (First VAT Directive, 1967), which is the principle usually adopted by federations.

Since 1969, six Directives were issued setting up VAT as the common sales tax of the Six, and of all new members joining the Community at a later date. Tax harmonisation at the ongoing phase of integration in the EC meant only that a common sales tax structure was to be adopted, but no attempt was made to impose on the members a common VAT rate. Acting on the proposition that fundamental changes in the tax field impinge on the prerogative of national parliaments, sales tax harmonisation in the Community was based on the operational principle of structural uniformity first and rate equalisation later. The sixth Directive of 1977, on the uniform basis of assessment for VAT, aimed at closer structural harmonisation, with the introduction of a common list of taxable activities and exemptions, including a common lower limit of exempted transactions, the tax threshold. Uniformity of assessment was also deemed necessary after the decision to allocate a share from the VAT imputed revenue to the Community's 'own [budgetary] resources'.

Table 4.2 presents the 1987 VAT rates of the member countries. It can be seen that considerable differences still exist as regards the number of rates and their levels: there is a single rate in Denmark and four rates in four other countries; 12 per cent standard rate in Luxembourg and 25 per cent in Ireland. Differences also exist with regard to what products are wholly or in part *zero rated* (that is, subject to reduced or zero rate of VAT on output, but receiving credit for tax paid on inputs). Certain broad categories of VAT exemptions are: agricultural and food products (D, B, F, I, IRL, L, NL, UK); pharmaceutical and medical products (D, B, F, I, IRL, L, UK); fabrics, clothing and footwear (IRL, I, UK). Owing to different exemptions, the VAT coverage of private consumption is only 35 per cent in Ireland and 44 per cent in the UK, whereas most of the other member states cover about 90 per cent. Therefore, a uniform base has not as yet been reached. As an illustration of the existing different exemptions

Table 4.2: VAT rates per cent, 1987

Country	Standard	Reduced	Increased	VAT as % of GDP[3]
B	19	6 and 17	25 and 33	7.67
DK[1]	22	–	–	9.84
D	14	7	–	6.34
E	12	6	33	4.50
F	18.6	5.5 and 7	33.3	9.19
GR	18	6	36	5.00
IRL[2]	25	10	–	8.22
I	18	2 and 9	38	5.48
L	12	3 and 6	–	6.04
NL	20	6	–	6.83
P	16	8	30	4.75
UK[2]	15	–	–	5.22

Notes: [1] single rate
[2] zero rate also
[3] estimate for Greece, Spain and Portugal

Sources: EC, (1985), *Completing the Internal Market*, Document, Luxembourg.
The Financial Times 1986, various issues, and *The Independent*, 6 July 1987.
OECD, *Country Report: Spain*, 1986.

and tax rates among the EC partners, Table 4.3 presents the VAT rates on newspapers, magazines and books.

The drive for completion of the single market by 1992 requires that at least the indirect taxes are fully harmonised as a precondition for the abolition of frontier controls. In an attempt to end tax discrepancies and trade distortions, the Commission prepared in July 1987 a plan for 'VAT approximation' by squeezing all VAT rates in the Community within two bands—from 4 to 9 per cent for necessities and from 14 to 19 per cent for other goods and services. The Commission recommended no exemptions, and abolition of zero rates, which are nothing more than disguised exemptions, but it accepted that member governments should be able to apply to the Council of Ministers for special treatment for politically sensitive items. The plan also called for harmonised rates of excise duty for tobacco, wine, spirits, beer and petrol. However, the Council has not reached consensus with regard to the implementation of these reforms. Since changes in

Table 4.3: VAT Comparisons in the European Community

Country	VAT Rates Newspapers	Magazines	Books
B	0	0	0
DK	0	0	22
D	7	7	7
E	6	6	6
F	7	4	7
GR	0	3	3
IRL	10	23	0
I	0	2	2
L	3	6	6
NL	6	6	6
P	0	0	0
UK	0	0	0

Sources: *The Independent*, 6 July 1987.
    OECD, *Country Reports*, various issues.

Community taxation law require unanimous agreement of all the twelve governments, it is anticipated that some modified form of the plan will probably be accepted, but not without a long period of negotiations.

b) Excise taxes

Positive measures to harmonise the structure of excise taxes have still to be approved by the Community. Exception is the excise on cigarettes which has been partly harmonised since 1978.

Excise duties are specific taxes on certain products which are characterised by their relatively large share in consumers' expenditure (up to $1/3$) and small price elasticity of demand. Excises are levied mainly for revenue-raising reasons, but sometimes also in order to decrease consumption, e.g. of tobacco and spirits for health reasons. The yield of these taxes depends on their specific rate and the taxable quantity. Therefore, only an increase of the quantity purchased or the tax rate will increase the tax revenue, which does not automatically keep pace with changes in prices. The tax rate varies from country to country, but in general it is very high. Expressed as a percentage on retail price, the average rate among the EC countries reaches 69 per cent on cigarettes and 52 per cent on petrol. But the deviations from the average rate among countries are wide; for example, in absolute terms the highest basic rate of excise duty on alcohol in Denmark is almost forty times the lowest rate in Italy. High rates mean that excises have a high incidence on prices and, in general, a wide economic impact. Therefore differences among the members with regard to structure, rates and administration of excise taxes have serious effects on competition.

In assessing the proposals for harmonisation of excise taxes, the most important consideration is the revenue effect. In some members of the Community excise taxes contribute more than 25 per cent of the total receipts from taxes and social contributions. Further complications arise from the fact that in some countries some commodities, which are subject to excise duties, are traded by state monopolies (e.g. tobacco in France and Italy) and some others (such as mineral oils, tobacco, alcohol) are inputs to further processes whose output is subject to different systems of taxation.

The harmonisation of excise duties in an economic union aims at the abolition of distortions to competition and the elimination of fiscal frontiers. The first steps for a common policy concern the coverage of excise duties, that is which excise duties are to be retained and harmonised. Traditionally three broad groups of commodities are subject to excise in most countries: hydrocarbon oils, manufactured tobacco, and alcoholic beverages. In the EC countries, as in many other countries, most of the revenue from excise duties is collected from 'the big five': tobacco products, beer, spirits, mineral oils and wine (but wine is not taxed in Greece and Italy, while only sparkling wine is taxed in Germany, and only imported wine in Luxembourg). However, a variety of other commodities are subject to excise in different countries (e.g. sugar in Belgium, spices in France, coffee in Germany, matches in Italy, and even cars in Denmark). Besides the coverage, there is also variation in the rates charged by different countries. Among the EC countries the heaviest taxation is to be found in Denmark, Ireland and the UK.

Over the years the Commission put forward a number of proposals, mostly concerning the harmonisation of tax structures rather than tax rates. However, despite the many attempts, very little has been achieved. The failure is officially attributed to the budgetary impact of excise tax harmonisation which for certain members is estimated to be substantial. But actually the basic reasons for slow progress are those observed in every attempt to introduce common policies, the conflict between national priorities and Community targets. At the moment, only the excise on cigarettes is partly harmonised. After a long period of deliberations, the member states agreed on a compromise system of tax structure for cigarettes, which are now subject to a tax partly specific (a fixed sum per unit) and partly *ad valorem* (a percentage on retail price). Since 1978 the specific duty must not be less than 5 per cent or more than 55 per cent of the total tax burden on cigarettes, the remainder being an *ad valorem* tax. At a later stage of harmonisation, the specific element of the tax is to be narrowed to a band of 10 per cent to 30 per cent. At the moment the actual rates of tax vary significantly, from 0.28 ECU per twenty cigarettes in Greece to 1.96 ECU in Denmark (see Table 4.4). The excises on other tobacco products are not harmonised. An attempt to harmonise the excise duties on alcoholic drinks failed in 1981. Subsequently, the Commission judged that certain countries use their excises to discriminate against imports and has taken a number of cases to the Court of Justice. Although the Court's ruling has in general favoured the Commission, neither the offending nor the offended states returned to the negotiating table.

Table 4.4: Excise Duties in the Community, 1985

ECUs per	Lowest Country	ECUs	Highest Country	ECUs
1) 20 cigarettes	Greece	0.28	Denmark	1.96
2) 1 litre of beer	Germany	0.07	Ireland	1.14
3) 1 litre of wine	Greece, Italy	0.00	Ireland	2.74
4) 0.75 litre of 40% spirit	Greece	0.16	Denmark	9.58
5) 1 litre premium petrol	Luxembourg	0.20	Italy	0.49

Source: EC, (1985), *Completing the Internal Market*, Document, Luxembourg.

The December 1985 European Summit in Luxembourg, which introduced certain amendments to the Treaty of Rome, changed Article 99 to a commitment to harmonise indirect taxes to the extent necessary to ensure a free internal market. The latter is defined as 'an area without frontiers in which the free movement of goods, persons, services and capital is ensured in accordance with the provisions of the Treaty of Rome'. Completion of the internal market was set for the end of 1992. An internal market free of inter-state frontier controls will not be reached unless indirect taxes among the members are brought more closely into line. It is true that in the USA different states apply different sales taxes without having border controls, but the evidence suggests that tax differences of about 5 per cent is as much as can be sustained without causing large scale tax-dodging.

On similar lines it is argued (by Denmark in particular) that frontier obstacles can be eliminated without aligning tax rates. However, this argument seems to express more the unwillingness of certain members to move forward with the integration of the market than a realistic proposition. If the Community is to be free of customs posts by the beginning of 1993, its members need to agree very soon on target ranges for VAT and excise taxes as the first step towards the equalisation of tax rates. Hence, in July 1987 the Commission presented a proposal for the harmonisation of indirect taxes in the interest of achieving one unified market throughout the 12 countries by the end of 1992. The plan included proposals for the approximation of excise tax rates on tobacco, wine, spirits, beer and petrol. However, no definite time has been set for consideration of the plan by Council.

c) Corporate taxes

Among the EC partners there are considerable differences in the corporation tax. The most important of these concern:

(a) The scope of the tax, that is the liability to corporation tax. All limited companies are subject to the corporation tax, but sole proprietors usually are not liable to it. In the case of partnerships the situation varies from one member state to another.

(b) The basis of assessment, that is the regulations and extent of exemptions, incentives etc.

(c) The tax rate.

(d) The system of taxation. Depending on the extent to which corporation income tax and shareholders' personal income tax are integrated, there are 4 systems of corporate taxation:

(1) The Complete Separation of corporate and personal income tax (the 'classical' system). The corporation is viewed as a separate entity, distinct from its shareholders, and is taxed on its own capacity. Therefore, the distributed corporate income is taxed twice, first as income of the corporation and then again as shareholders' personal income (dividends).

(2) The Split Rate system or Two-rate system. A low tax rate applies on corporate distributions on retained profits.

(3) The Tax Credit or Imputation system. This system is designed partially to avoid the double taxation on dividends by imputing part of corporate profit tax to the personal tax liability of shareholders.

(4) The Full Integration system. In contrast to (1), the corporation is not seen as a separate entity but as a partnership of shareholders. In essence, under this scheme corporation tax does not exist, but instead the shareholders are taxed under the personal income tax liability. Therefore, this system is an extension of system (3) with full imputation of corporate profit tax to shareholders' personal income tax.

Most of the EC states operate at the moment system (3) which is also favoured by the Commission. However, corporation tax is far from harmonised. Differences among the members exist between: (1) The rates of tax imposed on corporations and the rates of tax credit granted to shareholders. Currently, the rates range between 100 per cent in Germany (i.e. full imputation) to 15 per cent in Denmark; and (2) The tax rates themselves, which range from 56 per cent in Germany to 37 per cent in Italy.

Differences in corporation taxation can influence the mobility of capital. In turn, if capital is induced to move by tax considerations and not by financial considerations, the effect is distortive. Harmonisation of the corporation tax aims at integration of the capital markets and therefore optimisation in the allocation of capital and investment in the Community at large. Integration of the market should mean equalisation of corporation tax rates. Then capital would gravitate to where the return on capital employed is highest.

In the Community problems also arise from differences in the basis of assessment for corporation tax and the definition of taxable profits. The member states differ on points of law about how they define and treat the concepts of depreciation, capital gains and losses, reserves and provisions, the valuation of assets and liabilities, stocks, taxation under inflation etc., all of which contribute to the determination of taxable net income.

Another issue of contention is the question of incentives provided by corporation tax. These incentives are introduced with the aim to encourage investment on a nationwide scale or in certain less developed or problem areas (e.g. of high unemployment) and sectors (e.g. energy conservation). Incentives take various forms (e.g. accelerated depreciation, tax relief on investment, tax exemptions on profits, tax concessions on modernisation etc.) and differ in degree from one country to another. An outcome of these differences is that the capital markets of the Community are compartmentalised and, therefore, the allocation of resources within the greater area of the common market is suboptimal. Harmonisation of corporation tax is the first step towards restoring optimality.

The first proposals concerning the harmonisation of the corporation tax in the Community came from the Neumark Committee (1969) which suggested a Split Rate system with taxation of retained profits at one rate and of distributed profits at a lower rate. Distributed profits would also be subject to personal taxation. However, the member states did not accept this proposal. A second committee chaired by Van den Tempel (1970) recommended in its report the Separate system with a single common rate. But this recommendation too did not find favour with the Commission which instead published its first Draft Directive, 1975, recommending the Imputation system of corporation tax and a common system of withholding tax on dividends. The proposal provided that member states would have similar but not identical corporate tax rates ranging between a lower limit of 45 per cent and an upper limit of 55 per cent. What the effect of harmonisation along these lines and rates would be for each member state cannot be easily assessed. In general, harmonisation of corporation tax will affect: a) The use of corporation tax as an instrument for national policy; b) The ratio of distributed over undistributed profits; c) Budgetary revenues; and d) Capital flows among the EC countries and between the EC and the outside world.

However, these Community proposals, which were made at a time of serious economic recession in the world and the EC economies, have not been met with support for immediate implementation, particularly among the member countries which would have to raise their rates. Hence, the proposals have not as yet resulted in significant action.

d) Other Taxes:

Personal Income Tax. The Community members have not included the personal income tax among the taxes intended for harmonisation. In effect, it is tacitly agreed that the harmonisation process should not directly impinge upon this tax which should remain within the sphere of national sovereignty.

Social Security. Personal income taxes and social security contributions and benefits affect the take-home pay and the social insurance of labour. Hence, they are among the factors affecting production costs and prices, as well as the mobility of labour between occupations and countries. Therefore, as in the case of capital and the harmonisation of the corporation tax, there should be a move for the harmonisation of taxes and benefits relating to labour. However, with the exception of certain agreements relating to social policy (see chapter 9), nothing else has happened in this field.

REFERENCES

EC Commission (1963), *Reports of the Fiscal and Financial Committee* (The Neumark Report), Brussels.

EC (1967), 'First and Second VAT Council Directives', *Official Journal*, no. 71.

EC (1980), 'Report on the Scope for Convergence of Tax Systems in the Community', *Bull. EC*, Supplement 1/80.

EC (1985), *Completing the Internal Market*, Document, Luxembourg.

Dosser, D. (1966), 'The Economic Analysis of Tax Harmonisation', in Shoup, C. S. (ed.), *Fiscal Harmonisation in Common Markets*, Columbia U.P.

—— (ed.) (1973), *British Taxation and the Common Market*, C. Knight, London.

Musgrave, R. A. (1959), *The Theory of Public Finance*, McGraw-Hill, Maidenhead.

Prest, A. R. (1983, 'Fiscal Policy', in P. Coffey (ed.), *Main Economic Policy Areas of the EEC*, M. Nijhoff, The Hague.

Schneider, K. (1973), 'Tax Harmonisation Policy from the Point of View of the Commission', in Dosser, D., (op. cit.) (1973).

Tait, A. A. (1972), *Value Added Tax*, McGraw-Hill, London.

Van den Tempel, A. J. (1970), *Company Tax and Income Tax of the European Communities*, EEC, Brussels.

5 Monetary Integration

5.1 PRINCIPLES: ECONOMICS AND POLITICS

The term *Economic and Monetary Union (EMU)* usually defines:

- the free and unrestricted movement of commodities, services and factors of production;
- the existence of a common currency; and
- centralisation of economic policy.

Therefore, Monetary integration is an essential element of an EMU.

Monetary integration has two components (1) exchange rate union, (2) capital market union. Exchange rate union is an area within which the exchange rates of the member countries bear a permanently fixed relationship to each other. Capital market union is an area within which capital can move absolutely freely. Hence monetary integration entails: a) The total and *irreversible* convertibility of currencies; b) The elimination of margins of fluctuation in exchange rates; c) The *irrevocable* fixing of parity rates; and d) The complete liberation of capital movements among the members.

Monetary integration is considered to be a prerequisite for attaining optimal resource allocation within the area of an economic union. As the national economies of the member states in an economic union through trade and factor movement become increasingly more open and more interdependent, two problems may arise: (1) Monetary and fiscal measures taken by a member country to regulate its own economic activity have spill-over effects on other member countries; and (2) Member countries find that it becomes progressively more difficult to cope with economic problems of their own which many times arise from participation in the union, but are no longer subject to treatment by the traditional instruments of national economic policy.

A crucial problem for every country participating in an economic union is how to reach and maintain balance-of-payments equilibrium. For example, a country may face deficits in its balance of payments with its union partners, but be prevented from using protective policies or exchange controls in intra-union trade. In principle, a given position in the balance of payments can be maintained under capital mobility, if the trend in nominal prices follows a similar pattern in the country and its trade partners. This in turn requires that all the members have similar rates of growth of income and productivity. If this condition is not met, then policy intervention for balance-of-payments equilibrium is necessary in one of the following three forms: (1) An exchange rate adjustment; (2) A reduction in real incomes; (3) A compensatory movement in the capital account. However, in an economic union aiming at free trade in commodities, services and factors of production the price level must not diverge between countries; consequently, the exchange rates must remain stable as a *de facto* introduction of a single currency. Therefore, the best solution to this problem is that the member countries ensure real consistency in their development objectives (growth, productivity, etc.) and apply consistent policies to pursue it.

When the members of the economic union pursue consistent monetary policies, they necessarily have to impose constraints on other policies, some of which also have to become consistent between the members of the union. The question now is whether monetary integration precedes or follows the integration of fiscal policies. Three different answers have been provided: The federalists argue that fiscal integration comes first and prepares the ground for the ensuing monetary integration. Others emphasise the political role of monetary integration and advocate its immediate implementation so that fiscal, economic and political unification become inevitable and are imposed next by necessity. Finally, some other observers argue that monetary integration does not require fiscal integration, since monetary and fiscal policies can in principle be exercised separately.

For similar reasons fiscal integration does not have to follow in the steps of monetary integration, since the governments of the member states can finance national budget deficits without recourse to monetary policy, by borrowing in the integrated capital market. However, within the economic union the exercise of national fiscal policy is impaired and therefore fiscal harmonisation is necessary. Needless to say, for those who see economic integration as the means for moving towards political federation, fiscal integration is absolutely essential and it is irrelevant whether it precedes or follows monetary unification.

The enhanced mobility of factors of production within the economic union may make the move towards monetary integration inevitable. Free factor movement may lead to economic imbalance between the members of the economic union. Capital would be much more likely to gravitate to the relatively faster growing areas of the economic union. Sooner or later, labour will follow the same way, migrating where the opportunities for employment and higher wages are present. As a result of these migrations the relatively less developed areas of the economic union will become more impoverished. Imbalance and inequality in sharing the benefits and costs of membership are liable to pose a threat to the cohesion of the economic union and the move towards economic and political integration, which run in parallel lines. If political unification is to be achieved, then inequalities and imbalances among the participants must be reduced to a minimum by application of appropriate measures, such as common monetary and fiscal policies. For these reasons the central authority of the economic union is endowed by the members with the necessary economic and political power to enable it to deal with these inter-state problems.

Monetary integration has immense political and institutional implications. Two of what are generally regarded as the prerogative functions of the government of every independent state—domestic monetary policy and control over the exchange rate—are surrendered to the central monetary authority of the economic union, which takes responsibility for the general running of economic policy. To be able to do so successfully, the authority is also given the necessary instruments of economic policy, which thus cease to be at the disposal of the national governments of the member states. Thus, at the national level governments lose all direct monetary autonomy and the use of the exchange rate as an instrument of national policy.

The transfer of the instruments of economic policy and the authority to use them requires the prior establishment of an appropriate central executive empowered to rule above the strictly national level. This entails the need to provide the central monetary authority with a certain degree of political power, a sizeable central budget and an integrated system of money supply institutions. In most cases the commitment to monetary integration implies explicitly integration of eco- nomic policy, a common pool of foreign exchange reserves and establishment of a Central Bank of the economic union. Any lesser arrangement will not ensure the permanence of exchange rate parities within the union, and will disrupt the process of integration by problems such as currency speculation, balance of payments disequilibria and the need for devaluations etc.

In conclusion, monetary unification cannot proceed without a parallel move towards central fiscal/budgetary unification. This will enable the executive of the economic union to cope with problems concerning the coordination of economic policy at the level of the union, ironing out regional inequality, and fair sharing between the members of the costs and benefits of integration. Hence, the executive of the union must be endowed with economic as well as political power. This implies that economic and monetary integration can be completed successfully only if the members of the economic union have a strong commitment towards political unification.

5.2   OPTIMUM CURRENCY AREAS

Monetary integration cannot be established in a vacuum, even if the will for political unification is very strong. Certain conditions must be met if monetary integration is to be a benefit rather than a burden. Premature moves towards monetary integration may in fact defeat the move towards political unity and undermine the process of economic integration. Historically, the debate about the conditions necessary for efficient monetary integration started with the theory of *optimum currency areas*. This theory attempts to define which countries or regions would combine optimally in a currency union and whether a common currency offers to some group of countries more advantages than either a worldwide fixed or flexible exchange rate system.

The decision to form a currency area is usually based on 'price stability' and a single criterion is selected to decide the suitability of countries for membership. Optimality is then judged with reference to the fixed target of price stability. Consequently, depending on the criteria adopted, different conclusions may be reached. Therefore, not all the theories of optimum currency areas arrive at the same policy recommendations or advocate the same country membership. In general, the conditions stated in the literature as necessary for moving successfully towards monetary integration are based on a single facet of the economies involved or on an evaluation of costs and benefits arising from currency unification. The characteristics most frequently mentioned as necessary are:

(1) *High degree of factor mobility*. In general capital is more mobile than labour, and it is doubtful whether in practice interregional labour mobility within an economic union will be high enough to require (or to cause) the need for monetary integration.

(2) *Openness to trade*. In this case, relatively large surplusses or deficits in the external balance of countries may cause domestic price instability. Monetary integration is thus recommended primarily for stabilisation reasons: countries trading extensively with one another would benefit from forming a common currency area. This recommendation is based on two preconditions, that: (a) The countries trade more with one another and less with the outside world; and (b) The instability they may suffer from is caused by their participation in international trade.

(3) *Low diversification.* The more an economy is diversified in its production and demand, the more independent it is of external influences, and thus the less vulnerable to exogenous fluctuations in income and prices. Hence, monetary integration is recommended if it will result in greater diversification of the economic union. In this context increased diversification is identified with a wide-ranging import-competing industry able to reduce the dependence of the economic union on foreign trade.

(4) *Other.* A number of other criteria have been suggested such as (a) similarity in inflation rates, (b) financial market unification, (c) similarity in general economic policy attitudes, etc. These prerequisites for the formation of successful currency unions may be important in certain cases and for certain economic unions, but they are specific, difficult to assess and do not have general applicability.

(5) *Benefits vs costs.* This approach is based on the evaluation of the benefits and costs of monetary integration for the members. Among the benefits considered are that: (a) Money within an economic union should be a universal measure of value, a universally accepted medium of exchange, and a store of wealth. Hence, a common currency is conducive to allocation efficiency and economic integration; (b) Speculative capital flows are completely eliminated within the area of the economic union; (c) There is a positive saving of exchange reserves.

Among the costs of monetary integration are the following: (a) The loss of autonomy in national monetary policy of the members; (b) The constraints imposed upon the national fiscal policy of the members; (c) The possibility of worsening the existing unemployment/inflation relationships, at least in some member countries; (d) The possibility of increases in regional disparities.

To these pros and cons every member in an economic union attaches its own subjective weights. Complete agreement is not always easy, hence the move towards monetary integration is very slow and very difficult.

In general, the incentive for monetary integration in an 'optimum currency area' comes from the potential improvements of efficiency in resource allocation by the use of a single money in interregional trade. But, in this respect, the theories of optimum currency areas are of little use for the formulation of policy in an economic union. In practice, countries agree to form an economic union for a variety of reasons. If their ultimate objective is to integrate the market for goods, services and factors of production and to proceed with some form of political unification, there are not many valid arguments against establishing a monetary union. It is possible that, according to the criteria for forming optimum currency areas, some countries which ought to participate, are not members of the economic union, while other countries which should not have been included in the currency area, are members of the economic union. But, in the end, when the ultimate goal of the contracting parties is economic unification, there is no market integration without monetary integration.

5.3   THE MOVES FOR MONETARY INTEGRATION IN THE EC

Three decades after the establishment of the EC, unification of the market is still incomplete. Extensive progress has been made as regards the customs union, that is the trade in commodities and services. But, with the exception of the CAP, the integration of economic policy remains 'a desirable objective'. The establishment of Economic and Monetary Union is still a target, but without a specific date for its completion.

The Treaty of Rome declares that the aim of the Community would be pursued 'by establishing a Common Market and progressively approximating the economic policies of Member States' (Article 2). However, while for the creation of the common market there is a detailed timetable of action, the approximation of members' economic policy remains unspecified. This omission probably reflects the prevailing ideas at the time of signing the Treaty, that free trade between the member countries would lead progressively to greater functional interdependence, hence approximation of economic policy will follow automatically. Consequently, the free movement of goods, services and factors of production will inevitably lead to monetary integration. Therefore Economic and Monetary Union is not specifically mentioned as one of the EEC objectives. However, the free trade in goods, services and factors of production, competition on equal terms and the introduction of common policies cannot be sustained until monetary integration comes about, without a transitional period of fixed exchange rates. If a system of fixed exchange rates is not introduced by design, it does not necessarily follow that it will emerge automatically by the introduction of common policies.

The probable outcome is that the common policies themselves will not be sustained, that they will collapse before monetary integration happens. If instead of fixed exchange rates and common polices the members maintain in their trade relations flexible exchanges, then the target of common prices is undermined by changes in the exchange rates which impede the unification of the market, create uncertainty and lead to trade contraction. On the other hand, a fixed exchange rate system requires that the member countries give priority to Community targets and constrain their national objectives by the common pursuit of maintaining the agreed parity of the exchange rates. Fixed parities among the currencies in the economic union cannot be sustained unless the trend in nominal prices and productivities follows the same pattern in all participating countries, and monetary policies converge. This requires coordination of EEC ecomomic policies, including monetary, for convergence of both policies and economic performance.

The Treaty of Rome did not deal with the requirement for monetary integration for two reasons: (1) In the 1950s, when the Treaty of Rome was signed the EEC countries were experiencing similar growth performance, low rates of inflation and satisfactory trends in productivity improvements. The six EEC members also had favourable trade balances and adequate foreign reserves; (2) The international monetary system in operation was that of fixed exchange rates, and this served the EEC's attempts for consolidation of its common policies and progress towards completion of the common market. But in the late 1960s the international monetary system of fixed exchange rates showed signs of progressive instability. The two reserve currencies, the US Dollar and the Pound Sterling, suffered under the strain of deficits in the USA balance of payments during the Vietnam war and bad economic performance in both USA and UK. In 1967 the Pound was devalued by 14.3 per cent.

The weakness of the dollar and expansionary USA monetary policy put the pressure on other currencies including those of the EEC countries. In 1969, France devalued the Franc by 11.1 per cent and soon after Germany revalued the Deutschmark by 9.29 per cent. The last two events changed the intra-Community parity rates, hence the common (mostly agricultural) commodity prices. For the same reasons, the economic performance and inflation rates of the EEC members also started to diverge significantly.

The breakdown of the international fixed exchange rates system meant that countries were no longer subject to a balance of payments constraint, and that they could pursue their national interests disregarding the spillover effects of their policies on other countries. In the EEC, these developments led to the conclusion that market integration cannot be achieved without progress towards a fixed rate, which would consitute the first positive step towards monetary integration. The worry was that a new crisis similar to that of 1967–69 would undermine the Common Agricultural Policy, which along with free trade were the two cohesive Community policies. Changes in members' exchange rates could alter the competitive position of industry in different countries and jeopardise the free trade structure and through it the common market objective. Under this externally imposed pressure the EEC started to consider seriously how to proceed towards closer economic and monetary cooperation.

The first concrete proposal towards monetary integration was the Barre Plan (1969) which called for tighter consultation between member states on matters of economic policy, coordination of monetary policy within the EEC and mutual financial assistance among the members in financial crises. However, the most important development at the time was the proclamation of the EEC heads of state at the Hague Summit in December 1969, that intention of the Community is to proceed gradually towards an Economic and Monetary

Union. In this way Monetary Integration became officially a Community target. Since then, arguments have started to appear for and against this objective.

The arguments against monetary integration in the EEC are both political and economic.

The political argument (1) is that a full monetary union implies the transfer of control of monetary policy from the members' governments to the purposely established Monetary Authority of the EEC. But, since it is considered politically inappropriate to give such control to a supra-national appointed and not elected authority, prior to monetary integration, some form of political integration is required. Political integration involves the transfer of hitherto national power to the executive of the EEC, and it can be accomplished only at the expense of the governments of the member states and of national sovereignty. Even a simple agreement among the member states to *fix irrevocably* the exchange rates entails loss of economic sovereignty. Monetary union, even in its simplest form, reduces national monetary autonomy, imposes constraints on the use of instruments and erodes the ability of national governments to exercise national economic policy.

This argument is correct and, as we have seen, it implies that economic and political unification should be pursued simultaneously. Nevertheless, countries can proceed with economic and monetary unification before moving forward with political unification, if (1) The advantages from it exceed the disadvantages, and (2) It is used purposely as the spearhead for political unification.

The economic argument (2) is that commitment to irrevocably fixed exchange rates, and later complete monetary integration, deprives the participating countries of national control over monetary policy which is an instrument for economic stabilisation. Therefore, monetary integration imposes on the members a costly constraint which weakens national independence and diminishes the ability of governments to exercise economic policy.

The counter argument here is that, first, there are enough instruments left to the government for the exercise of economic policy; and, second, the high degree of economic interdependence within an economic union makes the exchange rate an inefficient instrument of national economic policy. Hence, the commitment to irrevocably fixed exchange rates simply legalises a situation which *de facto* exists already.

With the international monetary conditions worsening, agreement was finally reached that some steps for restoring monetary stability in the Community had to be taken. Disputes then followed regarding what degree of monetary integration was necessary and how would it be implemented. A number of different routes were suggested:

(1) The most radical method advocates the instantaneous establishment of the monetary union by (i) immediate setting up of a Central Monetary Authority; (ii) pooling of the members' reserves of gold and foreign exchange; and (iii) direct replacement of national monies by a common currency.

This method, however, is strongly opposed by the national monetary authorities and governments of the member states, which by losing power become subordinate to the monetary authority of the economic union. Moreover, the less prosperous members of the Community felt that they would suffer most from this procedure because they would be forced to adjust their inflation performance to the lower inflation rates of the prosperous members, with effects on their rate of unemployment and general internal balance.

(2) Currency competition. Under this method all capital controls in the member states are abolished and all national currencies are accepted as legal tender. Free competion between currencies guarantees that eventually one of them will be established by market selection as the currency of the EEC. Thus monetary union will be accomplished by market forces.

The problem here is that the country whose currency will be adopted as the common currency gains, while all other countries lose. Besides the political prestige, the economic gain consists of the *seigniorage*, that is the rent which accrues to a country when its national currency is held by foreigners. The *seigniorage* amounts to the return on the extra assets which the country is enabled to acquire because of the external holdings of its currency, in effect the benefit derived from issuing non-interest bearing debt.

(3) Establishment of a parallel currency to compete with the

national currencies. This parallel currency will be issued by the EEC and it should possess a purchasing-power guarantee to become stronger and stabler than any national currency. Since it will not be the currency of any particular member state, national rivalries are avoided and the economic benefit from *seigniorage* will acrue to the union as a whole.

However, this currency will circulate along with the national currencies of the member states and it is not certain that the market will find it sufficiently attractive to select it as the common currency in preference to any other.

(4) Establishment of the monetary union by steps. This method has the drawback of relying on successive negotiations for defining and implementing each stage in the sequence of steps. If the political will towards monetary integration is at any stage weak, the process will be halted.

The Hague Summit of 1969 finally decided that the Community should proceed towards economic and monetary integration by the stepwise procedure or *gradualism*. Although all the members agreed in principle, differences emerged as to exactly what policies the steps should consist of. Some of the member states (Germany, Netherlands) supported the view that, before attempting monetary unification, it is necessary to reach convergence of economic performance. This should be pursued by setting consistent common targets and co-ordinating national economic policies to meet them. After convergence is achieved, it will be easier to fix the exchange rates and establish the European Monetary Authority. However, other member states (France, Belgium) supported the view that the first step towards monetary integration should involve the narrowing of exchange rate fluctuations. Commitment to this objective would inevitably impose on the members the need for discipline and cooperation in policy and economic performance. Thus, convergence does not precede, it follows the establishment of the European Monetary Authority.

These issues were considered by the Werner Committee which published its Report in 1970. The Werner Report recommended the establishment of the European Monetary Union (EMU) in stages by 1980, with rigidly fixed exchange rates, perfect convertibility of EEC currencies, complete freedom of capital movements, and creation of a Community Central Bank. The Council meeting of February 1971 accepted the substance of the Report's recommendations and attempted to reconcile the different views regarding some isssues which were judged to impinge on national sovereignty. It was thus decided that the first stage should involve the narrowing of exchange rate fluctuation margins, coordination of monetary policies, and the setting up of a European Exchange Stabilisation Fund to provide credit facilities for policies of monetary stability.

But new problems with the US Dollar in the international markets led to the postponement of the implementation of the agreement. At the same time the turbulent international monetary situation convinced the member states that time was running out and steps should be taken towards closer monetary cooperation for the purpose of insulating the Community from the effects of international fluctuations in exchange rates. The Washington (Smithsonian) Agreement on the international monetary system of December 1971 brought some improvement in the international money markets, but was found to be an incomplete answer to the Community's problems. These events finally led the EEC partners to the establishment of the 'European Band', or the 'snake', which combined adherence to international agreements with partial implementation of the Werner Plan. The 'Band' set the permissible margin of exchange rate fluctuations at ± 2.25 per cent against the US dollar, so that the Community currencies could float together. The agreement provided that the central banks of the member states were to take concerted action to keep fluctuations between the Community currencies within the specified narrow band. The fluctuations between any two Community currencies in the band could not exceed 4.5 per cent. The participating countries were allowed to withdraw from the 'snake' if this was deemed necessary.

The narrowing of exchange rate fluctuations was rapidly achieved. In addition to the Six, the UK, Ireland and Denmark also joined the scheme in anticipation of their imminent entry to the Community. Two other currencies, the Swedish krona and the Norwegian krone, also became associated from the outset. However, a few weeks after joining, the UK abandoned the 'snake' when sterling came under pressure, and within days Ireland was forced to follow suit. Thus the attempt to resume progress towards monetary union was undermined right from the beginning. Subsequently, the oil crisis of 1973–4, which affected significantly certain Community countries, made them give priority to national rather than Community policy problems. The currencies in the band came repeatedly under pressure, the market exchange rates changed frequently and for some of the participants made the 'snake' unworkable. The lira was withdrawn in 1973 and the Swedish krona and Norwegian krone in 1977. France abandoned the band in January 1974, rejoined it in July 1975, and left it again in August 1977. Under these conditions, progress towards monetary integration halted and it soon became obvious that establishment of the EMU along the lines and the time table recommended by the Werner Plan was not feasible.

It is important to realise that the Werner Plan advocated the gradual establishment of monetary union within the framework of the fixed exchange rates system, which it was believed would somehow survive the crises. However, in March 1973 the fixed exchange rate system collapsed, and nothing was put in its place. Countries started to pursue domestic objectives by expansionary monetary policies, intervening in the foreign exchange market and, in general, following policies without consideration to their international repercussions. Hence, national policies diverged extensively and the effects of this were reflected in diverging performance and national rates of inflation. From 1973, the differences in inflation and unemployment rates between the members of the Comunnity became so large as to be incompatible with exchange rate stability. The European 'snake' suffered under the onslaught of internal and external events: from April 1972 to March 1979, the 'fixed' parities of the system were altered 31 times, while the band was abandoned and rejoined by committed participants 18 times. By the end of 1977 only the Deutschmark, the Dutch guilder, the Belgian franc and the Danish krone remained in the 'snake'.

In the meanwhile, the international monetary system adopted after the collapse of the fixed exchange rates was that of floating rates. This development, the ensued uncertainties about the stability of exchange rates and the danger of increasing problems over operation of the common market, again showed that the EEC had to move fast towards a monetary system of its own. A new agreement was reached in Bremen (July 1978) and Brussels (December 1978) and the new system came into force on the 13th of March 1979. The UK was not satisfied with the new arrangements and remained outside the exchange rate mechanism of the system. The European Council declared that the new scheme, now called the European Monetary System (EMS), aimed at 'closer monetary cooperation leading to a zone of monetary stability in Europe' which was taken to be 'a highly desirable objective' of the Community.

It must be emphasised that the EMS agreement had economic and political origins and objectives. It would not have been launched without the political commitment towards European integration of France and Germany. It was also an attempt both to revive the process towards politico-economic integration after the 1971–78 stagnation and to establish a limited area of monetary stability in a turbulent world. The long-run viability of the EMS ultimately depends on the political will of the member countries to progress towards European Monetary Unification.

5.4   THE EUROPEAN MONETARY SYSTEM (EMS)

The EMS comprises three activities: (1) The pegging of exchange rates; (2) Credit facilities to help defend these pegged rates; (3) Establishment of a European Monetary Cooperation Fund (EMCF) which would ultimately be replaced by a European Monetary Fund (EMF). These three activities of the EMS we examine in the following:

Pegging arrangements (1) In general, there are two systems of pegging arrangements: (a) The *parity grid*, which ties every currency to every other currency in a system of mutually agreed and consistent rates; and (b) The *basket*, which ties every currency to a common currency unit. Under the system of parity grid, whenever a currency diverges from parity, all other exchange rates would also diverge from the agreed rate. Hence, in this case all countries will respond, that is, assist mutually the re-establishment of parity. Under the basket, a currency can diverge without effect on the parity of other currencies.

The EMS is based on a hybrid system, a parity grid with some features of the basket (see Table 5.2). The central rates of the parity grid are defined in terms of the *European Currency Unit*, the ECU. The ECU is a weighted average basket of all the EC-10 currencies. But the UK, which participates in the credit mechanism and the EMS negotiations, and Greece are not members of the EMS. Spain and Portugal remain outside altogether. The weight of each currency in the basket is determined by its economic strength. If at any time the weights of the currencies in the basket are out of line with the prevailing economic conditions, the agreement provides that they will be amended. The units of national currencies and their weights in the ECU from January 1987 are presented in Table 5.1.

Table 5.1: Composition of the ECU: National Currency Units and Weights, from 1987

National Currency		Units in ECU	Weight in ECU
Belgian Franc	BFR	3.71	0.091
Deutschmark	DM	0.719	0.349
Dutch Guilder	HFL	0.256	0.110
French Franc	FF	1.31	0.190
Danish Krone	DKR	0.219	0.028
UK Pound	UKL	0.0878	0.119
Greek Drachma	DR	1.15	0.008
Italian Lira	LIT	140.	0.094
Irish Pound	IRL	0.0871	0.011
Luxembourg Franc	LFR	0.14	–

Note: The weight of LFR is included in that of BFR.

The ECU is defined in relation to each currency, the *ECU central rate of exchange*. The corresponding bilateral exchange rates between the EEC currencies are determined from these central rates. Thus from Table 5.2 the central rates for 1 ECU are (from 12 January 1987):

Table 5.2: EMS–Bilateral Central Rates, since 12th of January 1987

		Netherlands NL	Belgium B	Germany D	Denmark DK	Ireland IRL	France F	Italy I
HFL	100	100	1830.54	88.7526	338.537	33.1293	297.661	63963.1
BFR	100	5.46286	100	4.84837	18.4938	1.80981	16.2608	3494.2
DM	100	112.673	2062.55	100	381.442	37.3281	335.386	72069.9
DKR	100	29.5389	540.723	26.2162	100	9.78604	87.9257	18894.0
IRL	1	3.01848	55.2545	2.67894	10.2186	1	8.9848	1930.7
FF	100	33.5953	614.977	29.8164	113.732	11.1299	100	21488.6
LIT	1000	1.5634	28.6187	1.38754	5.29268	0.5179	4.6536	1000
ECU	1	2.31943	42.4582	2.05853	7.85212	0.768411	6.90403	1483.58

Note: The pound sterling and the drachma do not participate in the EMS exchange-rate mechanism. Their notional ECU central rates are UKL 0.739615 and DR 150.792.

Source: *Bull. EC* 1–1987.

HLF	2.31943	FF	6.90403
BFR/LFR	42.4582	LIT	1483.58
DM	2.05853	DR	150.792
DKR	7.85212	UKL	0.739615
IRL	0.768411		

The ECU is the *numéraire*, that is the standard of value of the exchange rate mechanism. It also is: (i) The basis for a *divergence indicator*; (ii) A means of settlement between national monetary authorities within the EC; and (iii) A *denominator of operations* in both the intervention and credit mechanisms of the system.

In practice the market exchange rate is fluctuating and is not equal to the bilateral exchange rate deriving from the central rates. The permissible margins of fluctuations are set up to 2.25 per cent either direction around the central rates, except for the LIT which is allowed ± 6.0 per cent margins. For instance, with central exchange rates for the Deutschmark and the F.France 1 ECU = 2.05853 DM = 6.90403 FF, the exchange rate bands of permitted fluctuations between these two currencies are:

$$\text{In Frankfurt} \quad 1 \text{ FF} = \begin{cases} 0.30495 \\ 0.298164 \\ 0.29150 \end{cases} \text{DMs}$$

$$\text{In Paris} \quad 1 \text{ DM} = \begin{cases} 3.4305 \\ 3.35386 \\ 3.2792 \end{cases} \text{FFs}$$

The deviation of a currency's market rate from the central rate is measured in terms of its weight in the ECU, so that the ECU is the basis for determining the *divergence indicator*. The permissive margins of deviation, the 'divergence thresholds', are fixed at 75 per cent of the maximum spread of divergence. For example, the divergence threshold for a currency with 20 per cent weight in the ECU is reached when its market rate deviates from the ECU central rate by

$$([2.25 \times (100-20) \times 0.75]/100) = 1.35\%$$

If the deviation is greater than the 'divergence threshold', it creates the presumption that the country which issued the currency should act to correct it. The government of the country is required to introduce appropriate economic measures to keep its currency within the permitted band of fluctuations (i.e. ± 2.25 per cent of the central rate). Thus, the burden of adjustment falls mainly on the individual country. However, when a currency reaches its trigger point against another member's currency, the central banks of both countries must intervene: the country of the weak currency borrows from the country with the strong currency as required. As a last resort, adjustment of the exchange rates is implemented by *realignment*, that is by devaluations/revaluations of the central rates within the EMS. Hence the EMS is a system of fixed but adjustable exchange rates (in contrast to the Werner Plan which provided only for fixed rates). The decision to realign the central rates is taken by the Ministers of Finance and Central Bank Governors of EEC member countries and the Commission in consultation with the Monetary Committee.

Credit facilities (2) The EMS provides through the European Monetary Cooperation Fund credit facilities, that is loans to member states to enable them to intervene in the foreign exchange market for stabilisation purposes. These loans are: a) Short-term (up to seventy-five days, but renewable for three months) financial facility by which central banks participating in the exchange rate mechanism allow each other unlimited credit in their own currencies; b) Medium-term (nine months) monetary support system of mutual credit among central banks for up to 14 billion ECUs. This facility is funded by quota subscriptions; c) Long-term (five years) mutual financial assistance up to 11 billion ECUs.

The European Monetary Cooperation Fund (EMCF) (3) is the central monetary institution of the Community. It is endowed by the member countries of the Community, members and non-members of the EMS, with deposits equal to 20 per cent of their gold and dollar reserves in exchange for an equal amount of unconditional drawing rights denominated in ECUs. These deposits are not held permanently with the EMCF, but only on three-month renewable swaps.

When the EMS was set up, provision was made that the EMCF would be replaced by the European Monetary Fund (EMF) which, vested with institutional autonomy, would be the central bank of the Community, administering its monetary sector and holding the members' deposits on a permanent basis. These responsibilities are currently assigned to the EMCF and a number of other committees, such as the Monetary Committee or the Committee of Governors of Central Banks. Final decisions are taken by the Council of Economic and Finance Ministers (ECOFIN).

5.5   PERFORMANCE OF THE EMS

When the EMS was introduced many observers found a variety of defects with it and predicted its imminent collapse. However, the EMS survived a number of crises and is still going strong.

For an assessment of the EMS we must examine whether the objectives set by the EC at the time of inception of the system have been approached. Convergence of economic and financial policy among the Community members, and establishment of a zone of monetary stability are the two most immediate objectives of the EMS, while a third objective, that of establishing an Economic and Monetary Union in Europe, is the most important but also the most remote target. All three objectives are interrelated. Convergence of economic and financial policies is required for the creation of a zone of monetary stability in Europe, which could in the longer run lead to a European Economic and Monetary Union.

The EMS has clearly not completely achieved its objectives, but it has led to a significant degree of policy approximation and close cooperation between the central banks of the members. However, the policy approximation is exclusively concentrated in the field of direct monetary policy, with as yet very little coordination in other policies, even such policies as public deficit management which has a direct influence on monetary developments. Therefore, the European economies diverge, less than before 1979 but still very significantly, in a number of important areas, such as inflation rates, unemployment and rates of growth. At the time of the introduction of the EMS a rather higher degree of convergence of economic policy was anticipated which would help the members to manage jointly the movements of the ECU against the dollar. Instead, the exchange rates of the currencies in the EMS continued to diverge, hence the need for periodic adjustments. Although realignments in the central rates were expected, it was believed that they would be infrequent and small. In fact, since 1979, it became necessary to realign the central rates twelve times (the latest one in January 1987), in some cases by a wide margin.

Capital market integration still remains an unfulfilled target. The European countries continue to restrict capital mobility by a wide variety of regulations. These regulations delay the process of monetary integration and create discrepancy between domestic and partner rates of interest which, along with differences in monetary policies, result in asymmetric exchange rate fluctuations. Hence the need for the rather frequent exchange rate realignments.

However, despite these imperfections, the mechanism of the EMS has withstood exceptionally well the realignments which in a way have offered the opportunity for a thorough examination of the operation of the system, and for redirecting national economic policies along paths compatible with convergence.

Another question concerns the operation of the EMS and in particular whether the divergence indicator worked in practice as a reliable early warning signal of potential strains in the system. Critics of the indicator pointed out that under certain circumstances two currencies can reach their intervention limits against one another well before the alarm starts flashing. However, in practice, the authorities recognised that there is no unique standard against which the deviations of all currencies can be measured, and therefore they did not rely exclusively on the divergence indicators for initiating policy changes.

Despite the unstable international monetary environment, the currencies of the countries participating in the EMS were less volatile than they used to be, and than other currencies outside the system; this is true for real as well as nominal exchange rates, and regardless of the measure of variability (Ungerer, 1986 and Artis, 1987). The exchange rates of the participating countries remained fixed, except for *negotiated* realignments. Therefore, the EMS mechanism has worked rather satisfactorily and a zone of relative stability in monetary affairs is in the making. But the EMS is not yet the Community monetary system since the pound sterling and the drachma (as well as the currencies of the new members, Spain and Portugal) remain outside it and the lira fluctuation margin still is 6 per cent. Moreover, the continuing restrictions on the free movement of capital in several member countries mean that complete convergence of monetary policy is still unattainable.

The Single European Act (1986), which envisages the creation of a large internal market comprising all Community countries by 1992, led to the formulation of the Delors plan regarding the liberalisation of capital movements and the integration of financial markets within the Community. A unified financial market area is considered a necessary condition for the strengthening of monetary cooperation and the further development of the EMS. The plan foresees two stages. In the initial stage the aim is to achieve effective liberalisation of capital transactions most directly necessary for the proper functioning of the internal market. In the second stage liberalisation will be extended to all financial and monetary transactions. The proposals for the first stage were approved by the Finance Ministers in November 1986 for implementation before the end of March 1987.

However, recognising the different structural and cyclical conditions prevalent in different member states, the liberalisation measures were accompanied by temporary derogations and safeguard clauses enabling particular members to deal with potential difficulties. Thus current safety measures are valid for Italy and Ireland until the end of 1987, for Greece until end–1988, for Spain until end–1990 and for Portugal until end–1992. The second stage, which will lead to a unified financial market, requires enhanced monetary coordination and harmonisation of the rules of taxation among the member states, with a view to strengthening economic convergence and minimising the possibility of speculative capital movements. In

September 1987, the Council agreed on more measures to strengthen the workings of the EMS. They include increased lending between central banks to allow greater 'intra-marginal' intervention in support of weak currencies before they reach the permitted margins; and more coordination of members' economic policies and performance to improve economic convergence.

Official use of the ECU remains on a small scale. However, a development which had not been envisaged at the time of the introduction of the EMS is the growth of private uses of the ECU. Although this was not much in evidence during the first two years of the EMS, in 1981 it took off. The explanation of this phenomenon seems to be that the ECU as a basket-currency is considered by the market as less risky than other currencies which are subject to national controls. This has been most evident in financial transactions: bonds deno-minated in ECUs have become very popular with both borrowers and investors, within and outside the Community. It is remarkable that the growth in the popularity of the ECU with private transactors is taking place although the use of the ECU by private agents is hindered by official regulations.

The ECU cannot compete effectively with other reserve currencies as long as it is not a recognised foreign currency in all EC countries, and its use is limited by controls on capital transactions. Thus, German residents, including banks, cannot issue ECU-denominated liabilities, because the ECU has not the status of foreign currency, and the German currency law forbids debts whose value depends on other currencies but which are payable in Deutschmarks. Controls on international capital flows impede the purchases of ECU-denominated assets in France, Ireland and Italy. Nevertheless, in Belgium, but above all in France and Italy, buyers are increasingly attracted by the relative protection offered by ECU bonds, against the downgrading of their national currencies. These developments mean that the ECU, having built up a stock of credibility which made it the world's fourth most important bond issue currency, outdistanced only by the Dollar, the Deutschmark, and Sterling, is already firmly established in international banking. It should be stressed at this point that the private ECU is independent of the official ECU.

The ultimate objective of the EC still is Economic and Monetary Union. The EMS, which focused rather on short-term exchange stability, does not seem to be subject to a built-in evolutionary process which would metamorphose it into the EMU. Wider acceptance of the need for European Monetary Union would provide the impetus for further developments of the EMS. Undoubtedly, it would be more efficient for the trading system of the EC, and for the move towards closer economic and political unification, to introduce a single common currency rather than a collection of national currencies, connected by fixed exchange rates. But many problems remain unresolved as a for example: i) The pound sterling, which has 12 per cent weight in the ECU basket, is not subject to the constraints of the EMS and therefore its fluctuations have unfavourable effects on the stability of the ECU; ii) The lira continues to participate in the EMS with the ± 6 margin; iii) The replacement of the EMCF by the European Monetary Fund, which was planned to take place in 1982, has not happened and is now postponed indefinitely. But, taking into consideration that the EC is a group of countries freely electing different sorts of governments which pursue different sorts of economic policies, we should conclude that, till now, the EMS has performed remarkably well.

REFERENCES

Artis, M. J. (1987), 'The European Monetary System: An Evaluation', *Journal of Policy Modeling*, 9, pp. 175–98.

Corden, W. M. (1976), *Monetary Union. Main issues facing the European Community*, London, Trade Policy Research Centre, VI.

EC Commission (1975), *Towards Economic Equilibrium and Monetary Unification in Europe*, Study Group on Optimum Currency Areas, Brussels.

Grubel, H. (1970), 'The Theory of Optimum Currency Areas', *Canadian Journal of Economics*, 3, pp. 318–24.

Ishiyama, Y. (1975), 'The Theory of Optimum Currency Areas: A Survey, *Staff Papers*, International Monetary Fund, 22, pp. 344–83.

Kenen, P. B. (1969), 'The Theory of Optimum Currency Areas: An Eclectic View', in: R. A. Mundell and A. K. Swoboda (eds), *Monetary Problems of the International Economy*, Chicago.

Lomax, D. F. (1983), 'Prospects for a European Monetary System', *National Westminster Bank Quarterly Review*, pp. 33–50.

Mundell, R. A. (1961), 'A Theory of Optimum Currency Areas', *American Economic Review*, 51, pp. 657–65.

Summer, M. and Zis, G. (1981). 'Whither European Monetary Union?', *National Westminster Bank Quarterly Review*, pp. 49–61.

Tsoukalis, L. (1977), *The Politics and Economics of European Monetary Integration*, London, George Allen & Unwin.

Ungerer, H. (1986), *The European Monetary System, Recent Developments*, International Monetary Fund, Occasional Paper No. 48, Washington, D.C.

Vaubel, R. (1978), *Strategies for Currency Unification. The Economics of Currency Competition and the Case for a European Parallel Currency*, Tübingen, J. C. B. Mohr.

Werner Report (1970), 'Report to the Council and the Commission on the Realization by Stages of Economic and Monetary Union in the Community', *Bull. EC*-11, Supplement.

6   Agriculture

6.1 PROBLEMS OF THE AGRICULTURAL SECTOR

In almost every industrial country governments intervene in the agricultural sector, in an attempt to modify its course and to regulate the production and exchange of agricultural commodities. The justification of goverment intervention is based on the principle that an institutional structure rather than the free market will move the agricultural sector towards preferred directions. The specific objectives of government intervention are usually four:

(1) The desire to maintain a certain degree of self-sufficiency in agricultural products, particularly food, because of the risk of interruption or curtailment of foreign supplies.

(2) The saving of foreign exchange arising from the availability of domestic supplies of agricultural products for domestic consumption and exports.

(3) The stabilisation of prices at reasonable levels, for both the consumer and the producer, as the means for reducing hardship and uncertainty, and for encouraging investment and growth in the agricultural sector.

(4) The desire to improve efficiency and productivity in the agricultural sector as the means for raising the level and the rate of growth of agricultural incomes.

The last two of these reasons are used frequently as the dominant excuse for government intervention in the agricultural sectors of developed economies.

The markets for agricultural commodities, free from intervention, possess most of the features of the competitive market model. Namely, the number of firms is large, entry of new firms into the industry is unrestricted, and the output of each commodity is on the whole homogeneous. However, as with most markets, information about the future quantity, prices of output and production techniques is imperfect. But these problems are made more complicated in agriculture than in other sectors by certain features of the short- and long-run demand and supply, in both the markets for agricultural commodities and factors of production. These characteristics of the sector in a way make government intervention in agriculture inevitable.

The most obvious manifestation of the peculiarities of the agricultural sector is that agricultural incomes: (1) are on the whole relatively low, (2) fluctuate widely, and (3) their rate of growth lags behind the national average. Specifically, for these reasons government intervention is often defended on considerations of *relative* national welfare, that is on the premise that the market mechanism does not by itself lead to a 'fair' distribution of national income between agriculture and the other sectors of the economy. Moreover, it is not only that there is an income gap between agriculture and the other sectors of the economy, but also that, in the absence of any positive policy, the process of economic growth tends to make this gap wider. In the following we examine: (1) The determination of prices and quantities in the markets for agricultural products; and (2) The characteristics of factor markets of the agricultural sector.

a) Determination of prices

The supply of agricultural products is characterised by short-run fluctuations and long-run trends which operate against the share of the sector in the production and distribution of national income. The reasons for this phenomenon are that, relative to other sectors of the economy such as manufacturing, the prices of agricultural products are flexible and the quantities of output can vary widely from year to year between gluts and shortages. Moreover in the longer run, technical progress brings about cost reductions which, owing to the competitive structure of the sector and contrary to the experience of other industries, are passed on to the consumer in the form of lower prices.

Short-run fluctuations in production are caused by the crucial dependence of agriculture on natural conditions such as the soil, climate and weather, and on biological constraints which result in the concentration of the flow of output in certain years or seasons within a year. Since in agriculture the output of many subsectors frequently is the input of other subsectors (e.g. cereals as animal feed), generalised fluctuations in the volume of agricultural output are not uncommon. Moreover, the relatively long time-lag between committing resources to production and gathering the output, a process which once started is not easily reversible, also means that the supply of agricultural products is in the short run unresponsive to changes in market conditions. Fluctuations in the short-run supply are therefore common and unpredictable.

In the longer run, modern agriculture is characterised by rapid technical and economic changes, both of which tend to increase factor productivity. Rapid technical innovation in agriculture tends to increase the use of capital, to limit the need for more land, and to decrease the use of manpower. Economic improvement occurs from the move towards more optimal plant size and the realisation of economies of scale, specialisation, and cost-reducing advances in organisation and management. These developments also tend to accelerate the rate of substitution of capital for manpower and thus to decrease the utilisation of labour per unit of output. Hence in the longer run more is produced with less factor input and therefore the cost per unit of output is falling over time. The competitive character of the markets implies that these cost reductions do not in general lead to higher profits per unit of output or to higher rewards to factors of production, but to lower prices for the consumer.

On the other side of the market, the demand for agricultural products is characterised by low price and income elasticities. Consequently, as the economy grows and national income rises, expenditure on food is allocated a declining share.

Low price elasticity of demand means that a fall in the price at a given level of income will induce an increase in the quantity bought but proportionally smaller than the fall in the price. Therefore, producers' revenue from the sale of output will fall. Low income elasticity of demand means that, at given prices, as per capita incomes rise with economic growth, the demand shifts increasingly against the purchases of staples (i.e. resource-based products), so that the share of consumers' spending on purchase of these products, food in particular, falls—and this is known as *Engel's Law*. Therefore, if productivity grows at the same rate in all sectors of the economy, the growth of income will cause the demand to shift against food and in favour of luxuries, or in general, against agricultural products and in favour of manufactures. Consequently, the price of agricultural products falls and that of manufactures rises. These features of the demand in association with the problems of the supply side of the market tend to affect adversely agriculture relative to other sectors of the economy. Rapid technical progress leading to relatively fast growth in the production and supply of agricultural products, combined with a declining demand, exacerbates the difference between the incomes of the agricultural sector and the rest of the economy. Agricultural incomes thus lag behind the rate of growth of national income without prospects of ever catching up.

b) Factor Market Problems

These considerations imply that the agricultural industry is in the short run a relatively risky, and in the long run a relatively unrewarding activity. Since many agricultural products are perishable, it is difficult and costly to build up stocks as a buffer against erratic short-term fluctuations of the supply. In the longer run, any solution to the problems of agriculture would involve the implementation of structural changes which would shift resources—surplus manpower in particular —from agriculture to activities which offer higher rewards. Ideally, this reallocation of resources should be initiated by market forces and be continued until the rewards of each factor are equalised between different uses. But, although following economic growth emigration of resources from agriculture occurs, its pace is frequently slow and unco-ordinated, so that the differentials of factor rewards between sectors persist and widen. The slow mobility of factors of production employed in agriculture is caused by both economic and social reasons. An important economic reason is the high degree of *specificity* of the land, capital and labour that are engaged in the production of agricultural products. This means that these factors are not instantaneously and costlessly adaptable to other uses; structural changes take time and cost money.

Additional problems arise because the transfer of factors of production from agriculture to other sectors is almost always characterised not only by occupational limitations but also by the necessity for geographic mobility. This requirement gives rise to the social causes of relative factor immobility. Farmers in particular will reluctantly abandon their 'way of life' and abode in search for new employment and higher rewards, most probably in an urban environment. They prefer instead to continue living on the land in their traditional ways, frequently reacting to the fall in revenues by attempting to increase their productivity. More often than not, this form of individual behaviour may collectively lead the sector to yet more increases in supply, falling prices, and further erosion of agricultural incomes.

6.2 POLICIES

The preceding discussion shows that an aim of government policy in agriculture should be the optimal allocation of resources, subject to the condition that the agricultural sector remains sizeable, with adequate production of output, and the factors engaged in it receive remunerations comparable to those of other sectors in the economy. These objectives are usually pursued by policies of direct intervention in the markets for factors of production and commodities, which attempt to stabilise prices and minimise unwarranted fluctuations in output. Policies for achieving this objective are many, hence the government has to choose the one it considers most appropriate under the prevailing circumstances.

Optimality requires that each policy instrument is assigned to the target on which it has the greatest impact. But as we have seen, governments in general use agricultural policy to pursue a number of different objectives, some economic and others social and political. Consequently, in the abstract, there is no single policy which is superior or more effective than any other under all circumstances. Depending on the particular problem in hand, the nature of the target in the short and the long run, and other economic, social and political constraints, governments apply to their agricultural sectors not one but a combination of policy instruments to achieve a number of objectives. In general, government intervention takes broadly into consideration the interests of both the consumers and the producers of agricultural products. However, in the field of pressure group politics, especially of developed economies, the farmers' lobby is relatively smaller, more homogeneous, better organised and more vociferous than the consumers' group and it usually wins through.

The policies available to governments differ in effectiveness and implications, particularly with regard to income distribution and resource allocation. The latter as a rule is affected negatively, that is in directions other than those which the free market would have dictated. This is frequently justified as a *temporary expediency* within a spectrum of objectives among which 'efficiency' is not ranked high in the government's list of priorities. The effecs on income-distribution are associated with the financing of the policy. As a rule, policies which raise the market price of the protected commodity directly affect (i.e. are paid for by) the consumer of that commodity, while policies which do not raise the commodity's market price involve budgetary transfers and are paid for by the taxpayer. The two groups, consumers and taxpayers, are not necessarily identical. Significant differences may also exist in the cost of implementation and administration of the different policies.

Two general groups of policies can be distinguished: (1) Price Stabilisation Policies; and (2) Income Support Policies.

a) Price Stabilisation Policies

These policies attempt to eliminate unwarranted price fluctuations and to stabilise prices, usually at a relatively high level. They take the form of (1) price controls, and (2) quantity controls.

Price controls (1) are policies directly applied on market prices for the purpose of changing them, or preventing them from changing by market forces. They include the following types:

(1) Price fixing, which can be sustained only if the government eliminates from the market any disequilibrium tendencies by buying -in for stock all excess supplies and selling -out (from stock or imports) all excess demands.

(2) Tariffs and Levies on imports, which raise domestic prices if the country is a net importer of the relevant commodity. An alternative policy scheme defines a threshold or minimum import price—and hence a domestic price—by the imposition of a variable levy on import price.

Quantity controls (2) are policies which alter directly the quantity of supply in the market as the means for changing market prices. They take the form of:

(1) Building up of stocks as a buffer between production and consumption. The stocks are augmented when, relative to demand, supply is plentiful and reduced when supplies are scarce, so that short-term price fluctuations are minimised.

(2) Quota controls on imports, which reduce the supply and raise prices as in the case of tariffs.

(3) Supply controls, such as the destruction of part of the available output as the means for reducing the quantity entering the market and thus eliminating the pressure on prices to fall.

(4) Production controls, such as acreage quotas, licencing etc., as an attempt to reduce the supply of output at the production stage and thus raise commodity prices.

(5) Export subsidies, which can be included here as an indirect measure for controlling the residual quantity of output remaining available for supply in the domestic market. The subsidy is an inducement to export so that the residual supply for the domestic

market is reduced and the domestic price rises. This policy affects both the taxpayer, who carries the burden of financing the subsidy, and the domestic consumer, who pays higher prices.

b) Income Support Policies.
These policies are distinguished into (1) indirect, and (2) direct:
Indirect (1) income support policies raise the price producers receive for their output as the means for increasing their revenue and income, but without affecting the market price of the product. They take the form of:

(1)   Subsidies at the production stage (input subsidies) or at the output stage. The latter are fixed payments per unit or unit price of output.

(2)   Deficiency payments. The state makes up the difference between a guarantee price and the average price received by the producers from selling their output in the uprotected domestic market.

Direct (2) income support policies are lump sum transfers related to or independent of the volume, price, revenue or income of agricultural activity. Naturally, this policy is the most effective for reaching a target level of income for the agricultural population, but carries high administrative costs.

6.3 THE COMMON AGRICULTURAL POLICY

a) Principles
A recurrent theme in our analysis is that main objective of the EC is the enlargement of the market, preferably in its free form, with market determined solutions to economic problems. However, the market is the means to an end and departures from market determined solutions are not excluded *a priori*. Nevertheless, the principle of competition on equal terms, which common markets adopt, implies that whenever intervention is deemed necessary, it must be general. That is, the interventionist policy must be applied equally to each member state. This rule entails that the national agricultural

policies existing in the member states prior to the formation of the EC had to be dismantled and to be replaced by a Common Agricultural Policy (CAP). Unequal relative size and level of development of the agricultural sector in each member state, different natural environment and different social, political and economic objectives, meant that the countries that formed the EEC pursued in the past different national agricultural policies.

Nature and government policies shaped in turn the structure of agricultural production and prices in each country, in such a way that the members' agricultural sectors collectively were a markedly heterogeneous group. Therefore, when the EEC countries decided to tackle in common the agricultural problem by establishing a Community agricultural policy, they embarked on a task of immense economic and social implications. Despite the difficulties which this has caused from the very start of the Community and the many problems which still remain unresolved, many observers argue that on the whole the EEC has succeeded in establishing the most fully fledged Community policy.

The Common agricultural policy in a way still reflects a balance of interests and a compromise among the original six Community members, all of which were developed and predominantly industrial countries, but continued to have vested social and economic interests in their relatively small agricultural sectors.

The main objectives of the Common Agricultural Policy are defined in the EEC Treaty (Article 39) as follows:

(a) To increase agricultural productivity by promoting technical progress and by ensuring the rational development of agricultural production and the optimum utilisation of the factors of production, in particular labour;
(b) thus to ensure a fair standard of living for the agricultural community, in particular by increasing the individual earnings of persons engaged in agriculture;
(c) to stabilise markets;
(d) to assure the availability of supplies;
(e) to ensure that supplies reach the consumers at reasonable prices.

The particular policies by which these objectives would be attained are also outlined in broad terms in the Treaty (Articles 40–7), but it was left to the institutions of the Community, following prescribed procedures, to work out the details. In general, since its inception the CAP was constructed upon three principles which guide every policy: 1: The single market; 2: Community preferrence; 3: Financial solidarity.

A single market (1) means the free movement of agricultural produce within the Community. This requires the abolition of every distortion on competition (such as barriers to trade, subsidies, etc.) at the member country level. The unification of the market for agricultural products implies central administration of regulations, policies and market organisations, resulting in common prices which are to be administered in such a way that they provide the farmers with remunerations at levels comparable to those enjoyed by other sectors of the economy.

Community preference (2) within an integrated domestic market means protection from external influences, such as competitive imports and price fluctuations in the world markets. Protection is necessary because: (a) Community costs are on the whole above those of other major producing countries; and (b) Community prices are regulated as instruments of policy for the attainment of specified targets. Hence, on the whole Community prices are higher than the prices of the competitive market. Since the aim of the CAP is not self-sufficiency, the principle of Community preference also extends to embrace policies for export promotion.

Financial solidarity (3) means sharing of the cost of the CAP among the member states and centralisation of the necessary funding. This task was allocated to a specially established Community organisation, the European Agricultural Guidance and Guarantee Fund (EAGGF). The 'Guarantee' section of the Fund finances the intervention policies of the CAP, while the 'Guidance' section administers funds intended for policies of structural reform.

During the operation of the CAP, more objectives emerged, reflecting inadequacies of the existing policies or new trends in public affairs. Thus, in recent years more emphasis has been given to problems of regional inequalities in the agricultural sectors of the member states and to concern about the relationship between agriculture, conservationism and environmental protection (*Bulletin EC*, Supplement 4/83). These new issues affect the nature of policies dealing with agriculture in the EEC by introducing additional constraints in the implementation of the CAP.

b) Method

The CAP covers all the quantitatively important agricultural products of the EEC. The actual policy mechanism varies to some extent from product to product. However, we can study most of its important characteristics in the organisation of the market for cereals which, since the inception of the CAP, has been regarded as 'the model'. Cereals occupy a central role in the agricultural sector of the Community, first, as a quantitatively important final product of the sector, and second, as an input to further processes within the sector, e.g. as food for livestock.

The policy and its implications are presented in the following with the help of a diagram which is based on oversimplified assumptions, but at the same time draws attention to the essential aspects of the problem. In Figure 6.1 the EEC supply curve of cereals is upward sloping indicating increasing costs of production, while the world supply is low-priced and perfectly elastic. After taking into consideration local price differentials arising from transportation costs and storage, the EEC Council of Ministers of Agriculture fixes annually a *target price* (P^t) (known as 'guide price' for beef, veal, wine, and as 'norm price' for tobacco). This is the maximum, or the upper limit, of the price, for a standard quality of produce, which is desirable or 'optimum' for the realisation of the CAP objectives. The target price, which is well above the world price (P^w) and the equilibrium market price, E, of the closed economy, is set on an annual basis for each commodity in the '*zone of greatest deficit*' between production and demand. Consequently, at the target price there will be excess domestic supply and threat of competition from imports, both of which will tend to reduce market prices and so to undermine the policy objective of the Community. Hence, both these threats are dealt with by the policy.

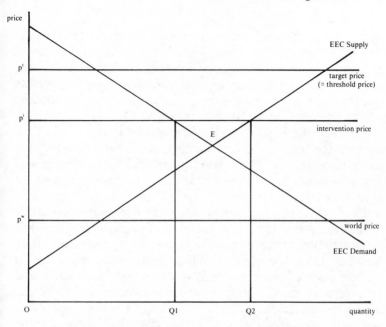

Figure 6.1: Common Agricultural Policy

The permissive minimum, or lower limit, of market price fluctuation is the *intervention price* (P^i) (known as 'basic price' for pigmeat) at which the Community halts the downward pressure of domestic supply on prices by purchasing the excess quantity on offer. Therefore, the CAP fixes a band of permissive price fluctuations which provides the producer with absolute certainty that the lowest price he can expect to receive for selling his output is the intervention price, P^i. The CAP's 'institutional' prices are fixed annually by the Council of Ministers on the basis of proposals by the Commission.

Since the market prices are allowed to fluctuate only within the limits established by the target and the intervention prices, foreign trade is assigned only a supportive role. Thus, the minimum price at which a product may be imported from any non-member country is the *threshold price* (known as 'reference price' for fruits, vegetables, wine and fishery products), which is fixed at or just above the target price. The lowest import price on offer (inclusive of transport, storage and incidental costs) is raised to the level of the threshold price by the imposition of the appropriate *levy* (P^t-P^w), which is calculated on a daily basis and then applies equally to all imports regardless of source and cost of supply. Thus the levy is variable and operates as an equalising tariff, whose variation depends on the difference between minimum current international prices and domestic target prices. However, if for any reason the EEC domestic prices tend to rise beyond the target price, imports become competitive, enter the market and keep domestic prices steady at the threshold price. In this way the consumer is guaranteed that prices will never exceed the threshold price.

By fixing producer prices above the market equilibrium price the CAP induces excess supply. The organisation of the CAP stipulates that the quantities bought by the intervention agencies are to be used as buffer stock for maintaining the market price within the permissible limits of variation. Stocks in excess of this requirement are usually disposed of by sale either in the domestic market at reduced prices for specific purposes, or abroad at world prices as EEC exports. In an attempt to encourage direct exports of the excess supply (and to save on storage costs), the policy provides export *refunds or restitutions*, which compensate the exporters of both basic commodities and processed products derived from them, for the difference between world and Community market prices. Hence the compensation/subsidy per unit of exports varies within the range of (P^i-P^w) minimum and (P^t-P^w) maximum. If for any reason world prices rise above the threshold price, the domestic producers will tend to export their output rather than sell it to the EC intervention agencies. The CAP provides that in this case the export refund is to be converted into an export levy, thus ensuring that domestic supplies reach first the EEC consumer at a reasonable price (the threshold price P^t) and only surpluses are exported. Theoretically at least, Community preference extends to cover both producers and consumers.

Market organisation similar to that described for cereals applies to approximately 70 per cent of the EEC agricultural production (dairy products, meat, sugar, fruits, table wine, etc.). Another 25 per cent of agricultural production (eggs, poultry, flowers, etc.) are covered by a looser organisation confined to external protection without substantial support measures for the internal market. A few other commodities whose production is limited geographically and quantitatively, or for which international agreements prevent extensive protection, get production subsidies (durum wheat, olive oil, tobacco, etc.). They cover approximately 2.5 per cent of total EEC agricultural production. Finally, for certain specific products covering less than 1 per cent of the total agricultural output the CAP provides flat subsidies per hectare or per volume of output.

Common prices policy and common trading policy are the two principal features of the common market in agricultural products which the EEC is implementing through the CAP. The third essential function of the CAP is to shape the future of agriculture within the Community by a common structural policy. As we have seen, structural diversity was, and still is, one of the main characteristics of European Agriculture. This is noticeable at the level of member states, but it becomes more pronounced in comparisons at the EEC interregional level. Under conditions of structural diversity such as that still existing in the Community, a uniform prices and trading policy would take little account of regional disparities. This may lead to the exacerbation of structural differences and the slow-down of the rate of economic growth of the integrated sector. These problems can be solved only by more direct intervention, undertaken by the appropriate EEC organisation, which will aim at the restructuring of the agricultural sector at the level of the Community, for the purpose of increasing efficiency and attaining optimality. This function of the CAP has been assigned to the Guidance Section of the EAGGF with specific objectives: (1) The implementation of technical progress; (2) The modernisation of farms; (3) The rationalisation of production; and (4) The improved processing and marketing of agricultural products. These tasks are pursued by the allocation of capital investments, the provision of grants and aid for agricultural populations. The EAGGF also provides assistance for the relocation of labour migrating from agriculture to other sectors of the economy by financing retraining and related costs.

c) Special Features: Agri-monetary Issues

The Community's common support prices for agricultural products, and the free trade in these products among the member states which still maintain different national currencies (see chapter 5), mean that a common system of price setting had to be devised. Until 1979 this system was based on the European Unit of Account (EUA or ua), a reference price set at 1EUA=1US$. After the introduction of the EMS, the common or 'institutional' prices of agricultural products are denominated in the European Currency Unit, the ECU. For the operation of the CAP, these common prices are next converted into national currency units in each member state. Under a system of fixed exchange rates, prices expressed in accounting units (ua or ECU) will be converted into national currency units of the individual member state by using the market exchange rate. Problems arise when the exchange rate parities are changed.

In the 1960s exchange rate parities did periodically change by policy adjustments. They have changed more frequently since the early 1970s, when the international fixed exchange rates system was replaced by a system of flexible exchange rates. Changes in the value of the market exchange rate would not have implications on the CAP common price policy, if the new market exchange rate is used in the conversions of accounting prices into commercial prices. However, agricultural revenues and farmers' incomes are affected. Devaluation of a currency raises the support prices in terms of that currency; revaluation has the converse effect. For this reason countries whose currency (by either design or the market) depreciated or appreciated were reluctant to apply immediately the same change to the exchange rate used for converting agricultural prices from accounting into national currency units. This problem first appeared in 1969, after the F. Franc was devalued by 11.1 per cent and within two months the Deutschmark was revalued by 9.29 per cent. In order to protect her 'consumers' from the resulting price rise, France was given permission by the Community to carry out a phased devaluation of her exchange rate for agricultural products over a period of two years. Conversely, when Germany revalued, in order to protect her 'farmers' she followed a similar course of action, introducing a phased revaluation of the DM for agriculture over three years. Thus a disparity was introduced between the market (and later, the central) exchange rate, and the exchange rate applied to agriculture which came to be known as the *representative* or *green* rate.

With the frequent parity changes under the flexible exchange rates system and the currency realignments within the EMS, the divergence between central and green rates has persisted, thus becoming a permanent feature of the CAP. In the meanwhile, the inequality between the two exchange rates is driving a wedge between the prices of the same agricultural product in the markets of different members which thus ceased to be 'common'. In this way, market prices no longer reflect actual economic conditions or planned structural changes. Instead, their divergence may give rise to distortive intra-EEC trade flows which clearly have to be stopped. The following example shows why:

Assume that 1ECU=DM2=FF4 and that 1 tonne of wheat is set by the CAP at 200ECU, that is DM400 in Germany and FF800 in France. Now, for reasons unrelated to agriculture, Germany revalues the DM by 50 per cent so that the new central exchange rates become 1ECU=DM1=FF4. If this new exchange rate is to be applied to agricultural prices, 1 tonne of wheat will be valued at 200ECU=DM200=FF800, and the German farmers will lose 50 per cent of their revenue per tonne of wheat sold, and this will be unacceptable to Germany. Hence, by common consent the old exchange rate is retained as the 'green' rate for agricultural prices and the German farmers continue to receive DM400 per tonne of wheat. However, the difference between the green rate and the market rate induces French producers to export wheat to Germany, sell it for DM400 per tonne, convert DMs into FFs at the central/market rate, and thus receive FF1600 per tonne instead of FF800, which they would have received by selling their wheat in France. In general, the producers of every member country would try to sell their output in the German market (or to the EEC intervention agency located in Germany) and pocket the profit.

Consequently, the divergence between the central/market and the green rate causes price differences which can give rise to trade flows unjustified by economic necessity. These trade flows would drain the funds available to the CAP and even threaten its existence. The solution is to stop these distortive trade flows by offsetting the differences between the green and the central exchange rates. This is effected by the imposition of Monetary Compensatory Amounts (MCAs) which are price equalising border taxes or refunds.

The MCAs are calculated on the percentage difference between the green rate and the market rate, and are applied as follows: (1) For members with strong currency, the green rate is below the market rate and the MCA is a levy on imports and a subsidy on exports: Green rate = Market rate – MCA. This is the *positive* MCA which is favourable to the consumer. (2) For members with weak currency, the green rate is above the market rate and the MCA is a levy on exports and a subsidy on imports: Green rate = Market rate + MCA. This is the *negative* MCA which is favourable to the producer. Positive MCAs can be eliminated by revaluation. However, since revaluation involves a reduction in farmers' prices in terms of national currencies, countries with positive MCAs are reluctant to revalue. Elimination of negative MCAs is rather more acceptable to governments because it raises farm prices. In our example above, French producers attempting to export wheat to Germany would have to pay MCA/levy equal to FF800 so that the incentive to export for reasons of currency induced speculation will be eliminated. Similarly, the German producer who will only receive for his sale of wheat in France the equivalent of DM200, will now get an additional DM200 per tonne of exports as MCA/subsidy.

The MCA as a levy is paid to the Community Budget, while as a subsidy is paid from the Community Budget. By this system the principle of common agricultural prices is preserved and trade in agricultural products remains undistorted by the dual exchange rates. However, the prices of identical agricultural commodities, when they are converted to national prices at the central exchange rate, are not uniform throughout the EC. The MCA system creates national rather than EC prices and policies.

Another complication arises because the green rate is used for converting final goods prices only, while the prices of most of the inputs to agricultural production from outside the sector (machinery, fertilisers etc.) are expressed in prices for which the market rate is the relevant exchange rate. This has implications on the costs of production, giving rise to cost differentials between the members of the EEC and thus potentially affecting the allocation of production and the flow of trade.

In conclusion, persistent price distortions arising from persistent differences between the central and the green exchange rates have distortive effects on production and competition, on structural change and the allocation and utilisation of resources, and therefore on economic growth. The MCA system has been justified on the basis that it adds stability to prices and farmers' incomes in periods of widely fluctuating exchange rates. As temporary measures, the MCAs can be defended for as long as adjustments are made to a new exchange rate. But owing to their high cost, and with budgetary crises in sight, the Community decided to eliminate the MCAs by attacking the reasons of their development. From April 1987 changes in central rates under the EMS can no longer lead to the creation of positive MCAs. This is to be achieved by defining a new 'green' ECU, tied to the strongest currency within the Community, and applying a corrective coefficient (equal to the highest percentage revaluation resulting from the realignment) to the EMS central rates for currencies, respecting the ± 2.25 per cent fluctuation margins. Negative MCAs are then introduced for all member states except for the one whose currency has appreciated most. These negative MCAs, which will be larger for countries with weak currencies, will be dismantled, on proposal from the Commission, as and when the economic situation in the various member states permits (*Bulletin EC* 3–1984, p. 46).

In effect the new regulations mean that any new appreciation of the DM (which usually is the appreciating currency) against the other EMS currencies will not be allowed to result in positive MCAs for Germany. It will, however, result in the creation of negative MCAs for the other countries.

6.4 THE EEC AGRICULTURE UNDER THE CAP

We must now examine the main features of agriculture in the Community for the purpose of evaluating: a) The state of EC agriculture under the CAP; and b) The cost-effectiveness of operating the CAP.

The CAP had successes and failures which in a way contributed to the present shape of EEC agriculture. However, it is important to emphasise that not everything good or bad with EEC agriculture can indisputably be attributed solely to the operation of the CAP. It is not always easy to disentangle the complexity of real situations for the purpose of attributing specific outcomes to specific causes. A policy may aim at, or have spillover effects upon, many objectives. But frequently a number of policies are applied simultaneously to achieve a number of different (and sometimes contradictory) primary targets and so cause and effect cannot be easily identified. Finally, changes in the constraints and in the general economic environment within which the policy is applied mean that both the effects and the targets of policy are not fixed but variable.

Three issues are examined in this section: a) Trends, b) Efficiency, and c) Reform of the Common agricultural Policy.

a) Trends in EC Agriculture

As we have seen, the EEC Treaty specifies five main objectives of the Common Agricultural Policy (Article 39). It is therefore opportune to examine the trends in EEC agriculture under five relevant headings, presenting arguments and statistics both in favour of and against particular aspects and features, as they emerged during the operation of the CAP. The discussion is primarily concerned with the EC 9, since for most of the time under consideration Greece, Portugal and Spain were not members of the Community.

1. Structure and Productivity (Table 6.1). The importance of the agricultural sector as a contributor to the Community's gross value-added, and as a employer of factors of production is relatively small and declining. The percentage contribution to Community's GNP at market prices accounted for by agriculture was halved between 1960 and 1980, from about 7 per cent to 3.4 per cent. This is of course due to both the relative contraction of agriculture and expansion of the other sectors of the economy. During the same period, the utilised agricultural area was contracting at an average rate of 0.4 per cent a year, while the work-force employed in agriculture also declined at the drastic rate of nearly 4.0 per cent a year, reducing the manpower to half of what it was in 1960. However, the share of agriculture in total gross fixed capital formation remained relatively stable at 4.0 per cent, suggesting tendencies towards higher capital intensity. But while over the period 1960–1980 the gross value-added of agriculture was increasing at a rate of just 7 per cent a year, the economy as a whole was growing much faster, at the rate of 10.5 per cent annually. Over the period under review, the average labour productivity growth in the Community was about 4 per cent a year, while in agriculture it was more than 6 per cent. But in agriculture it still takes 153 workers to produce the value which in the rest of the economy can be produced by only 84 workers. Thus despite the progress, the productivity ratio between agriculture and the other sectors of the economy is only 1/2. Obviously, more has to be done, if agriculture is to close the gap, and more so after the accession of Greece, Portugal and Spain which have relatively large labour-intensive agricultural sectors. Their addition has raised the contribution of agriculture to GNP to 3.8 per cent, and the employment in agriculture to 8.9 per cent for the Community of 12 member countries (1983).

The data confirm that over a relatively long time period the agricultural sector of the Community is experiencing a remarkable change. However, more is still needed to be done for the realisation of growth rates and levels of development in agriculture comparable to those of other sectors of the Community's economy.

2. Standards of Living (Table 6.2). The second objective of the CAP is to ensure a fair standard of living for the agricultural community, in particular by increasing the earnings of persons employed in agriculture. This objective is pursued mainly by high administrative prices for agricultural products. The outcome of this policy is not an unqualified success. Incomes from agricultural employment have increased less rapidly than other incomes since 1973. In fact, with the exception of only

Table 6.1: Structural Changes in EC Agriculture (Percents)

		B	DK	D	F	IRL	I	L	NL	UK	EC9
Contribution of	1968	4.9	7.7	4.4	7.5	18.8	9.9	4.6	6.9	–	–
Agriculture to GNP	1978	2.7	5.4	2.5	4.8	17.3	7.8	3.1	4.5	2.3	4.0
at factor cost.	1983	2.6	4.7	1.8	4.0	10.7	6.4	3.1	4.4	2.1	3.4
Employment in	1968	5.6	12.8	9.9	15.7	29.4	22.9	10.0	7.9	3.5	12.0
Agriculture over	1978	3.2	8.8	6.5	9.1	22.2	15.5	5.6	6.2	2.7	8.0
total.	1983	2.9	8.4	5.4	7.8	16.8	12.1	4.8	4.9	2.7	6.7
Decrease in	1968–73	0.7	0.2	0.4	0.5	0.0	2.1	0.4	1.2	0.4	0.7
utilised area	1968–83	0.8	0.4	1.0	0.3	1.7	0.1	0.4	0.5	0.2	0.2
Labour productivity	1968–73	8.5	3.7	7.9	7.7	4.9	4.9	2.5	–	–	–
increase.	1973–83	3.9	4.6	5.5	3.9	6.1	4.9	6.1	5.8	5.3	4.7

Notes: In 1983, the contribution of Agriculture to GNP in the new members of the EC was: GR (15.5%), E (5.9%), P (6.5%); and the employment in Agriculture was: GR (28.5%), E (17.9%), P (23.1%). The corresponding averages for EC-12 were 3.8% and 8.9%.

Source: EC Commission: *The Agricultural Situation in the Community*, Annual Report, various issues.

one year, incomes in agriculture for the community as a whole fell throughout the 1975–84 period, reaching in 1984 a level equal to 91.8 per cent of the 1973–75 income level. The exception occurred in 1982, when farm incomes recovered to a level slightly above that of the base period (103 per cent). Relative to the average income of 1973–75, some countries have been consistently above the average (Italy, Greece), other consistently below the average (FR of Germany, France, United Kingdom), while the rest experienced income fluctuations around the average. The observed fall in Community average real farm incomes is in direct conflict with the objectives of the CAP. Two explanations of this paradox are offered: first, it is argued that most incomes in the economy experienced recently stagnation or decline, and that without the support of the CAP, the fall in farm incomes would have been worse; and second, that the price support policy is not an efficient method for improving incomes.

Another drawback of the income objective and the policy instrument by which it is pursued is that they have negative

Table 6.2: *Real Incomes in EEC Agriculture (average 1973–75 = 100)*

Country	1975	1977	1979	1980	1981	1982	Income Disparities 1981–82
B	95	89	91	96	105	113	197
DK	88	107	99	104	118	140	208
D	101	99	91	80	85	99	94
F	90	89	93	80	75	92	118
IRL	107	128	104	89	91	97	96
I	103	104	114	111	105	107	67
L	100	103	104	95	102	141	110
NL	98	101	92	90	111	114	250
UK	94	93	86	79	83	92	173
GR	–	–	113	125	133	134	45
EC–10	–	–	98	92	93	103	100

Note: 1 Based on the index of net value-added at factor cost in agriculture in real terms per person engaged in farming.

Source: EC Commission (1983), *The Agricultural Situation in the Community*, Report, Brussels.

side-effects on other objectives of the CAP. For example, administered prices at levels above those which the free market would have determined tend to distort the mobility of factors of production, to delay the out-movement of labour and to impede the improvement in the allocation of resources between sectors. With relative prices for agriculture above those of the competitive market, the sector tends to attract resources rather than release them to other industries, and thus the policy delays the improvement of labour productivity and efficiency in production. Moreover, when farm prices keep rising, input prices may also rise with the implication that, along with incomes, profits may be squeezed. Low profitability means that capital investment may decline, while land values rise and agrochemical and machinery industries realise higher profits, although they are not those whom the CAP meant to support. This implies that the target of better living standards for the agricultural population can only be approached and maintained if the prices of the sector's final products keep rising well ahead of the increase in input prices. This process inevitably leads to spiral increases of prices and costs (see Table 6.4) which, besides their inflationary effects, do not ensure that in the end the living standards of the agricultural population will actually be improved. Actually, in the Community between 1974 and 1983 the average value of farm input rose by 145 per cent, while the average value of farm output rose only by 121 per cent. Evidence from the UK also shows that while output, input and production levels doubled between 1976 and 1984 and the net rent on tenanted land and interest on capital rose by a factor of four, farm incomes went up by only 42 per cent. At the same time the retail price index rose by 166 per cent.

Another defect of the price support policy for raising living standards is that the actual size of incomes would now depend on the volume of production. Hence the policy provides a strong incentive to the big farmers (and other enterpreneurs in general who take advantage of the certainty of high prices and the opportunity to make a profit by investing in agriculture) to produce as much as possible, irrespective of market demand, which in any case under this sort of policy is irrelevant. A consequence of the dependence of incomes on the volume of output is that higher support prices benefit disproportionately the large producers, who in general are not those in dire need of better living standards. At the same time, the Community accumulates mountains of surplus output which can only be sold at prices vastly lower than the costs of production.

Lastly, a policy for fair standards of living for the agricultural community does not imply these standards of living will converge or that farmers' incomes will be equalised throughout the Community. In fact, a characteristic of EEC agriculture is the marked disparities in farm incomes between the member countries. Table 6.2 shows that the strongest 'average' farmer (NL) has income 2.5 times higher than the Community average, and is more than five times better off than the weakest farmer (GR).

3. Market Stability. An indicator of market stability should be the stability of market prices. However, the prices of agricultural products are themselves administered as the instruments by which the EEC is pursuing its objective of increase in agricultural incomes. Therefore, in the EEC the

Table 6.3: *Increases in the Intervention Prices of Agricultural Products, 1973–86*

Year	Percentage Increase
1973–74	6.7
1974–75	13.5
1975–76	9.6
1976–77	6.5
1977–78	3.5
1978–79	7.0
1979–80	1.0
1980–81	4.5
1981–82	9.1
1982–83	10.1
1983–84	4.1
1984–85	–0.5
1985–86	0.1

Note: Common prices in ECU weighted by agricultural production.

Source: *Bull, EC.*, various issues.

prices of agricultural products should reveal three tendencies:
a) Relatively high levels; b) Relatively high rates of increase,
associated with both the CAP price support system and the
attempt to reach the target of higher farm incomes; c)
Relatively low fluctuations, associated with the market
stability objective of the CAP.

The rate of increase in common support prices has been
rather high. For the period 1973–86 the annual average
increases of the intervention prices (in terms of ua or ECU) are
presented in Table 6.3. The average rate of increase for the
period is about 7 per cent a year with maximum 13.5 per cent
in 1974–5 and minimum –0.5 per cent in 1984–5. Table 6.4
presents price increases of inputs and outputs of the
agricultural sector and of the consumer price index during the
period 1980–85. The data show emphatically that, in
comparison with the Community's inflation rate as reflected in
the consumer price index, the price increases in agricultural
commodities can be considered as moderate. In the majority of
the Community member states the price increases of inputs
(goods and services both directly consumed and contributing
to investment, Table 6.4) in the agricultural sector were

Table 6.4: Price Increases in the EC, 1980–85

Member State	Agricultural Sector			Consumer Price Index
	Commodity Output	Input goods		
		Consumption	Investment	
B	32.6	36.4	48.5	40.5
DK	32.6	42.8	51.3	46.4
D	3.1	14.9	20.4	21.0
F	43.0	52.1	56.9	58.0
GR	154.2	139.1	129.7	156.3
IRL	35.6	47.5	57.3	78.4
I	63.5	63.1	97.3	90.3
L	37.8	36.2	32.5	41.3
NL	14.6	16.5	19.1	22.3
UK	24.0	32.5	38.9	41.5
EC 10	44.1	42.1	60.0	49.1

Source: Eurostat: *Basic Statistics of the Community*, 24th ed., Luxembourg 1987.

significantly higher than the increase in the price of agricultural output. Hence, with higher input costs and higher consumer prices than the prices of the agricultural output, most farmers' welfare has certainly declined over the period under consideration.

Table 6.5 presents the prices of certain Community agricultural products as compared to world prices. Notice that, although the differences between the two prices fluctuate from year to year, for certain highly protected products (Barley, Maize, Beef and Veal, Pigmeat, Butter) there is a steadily ascending trend. In 1979-80 the Community prices were 31-311 per cent higher than the world prices of the same commodities. Although these figures are in themselves impressive, they reveal nothing about relative welfare, that is whether the farmers outside the Community have experienced a deterioration in their standards of living comparable to that witnessed within the Community. However, it is of some importance that these price differences between Community and world prices have occurred at a time of plentiful supplies, and when food continues to take up a small and shrinking share out of consumers's income. Nevertheless, the simple comparison between EC and World prices should be regarded

Table 6.5: *Ratio of Community Farm Prices to World Prices*

Commodity	1973-74	1976-77	1979-80
Common Wheat	79	204	163
Durum Wheat	116	236	159
Barley	96	147	161
Rice	60	166	131
Maize	98	163	190
Sugar	66	176	131
Beaf and Veal	110	192	204
Pigmeat	131	125	152
Butter	320	401	411
Skimmed Milk	156	571	379
Olive oil	96	192	193
Oilseeds	77	121	185

Note: World market prices are based on the lowest third country export offer price.

Source: EC, (1980), *The Agricultural Situation in the Community.*

as an unreliable evidence for the case against the CAP because:
a) The Community's prices of agricultural commodities are
high by design; and b) The world prices (which are not the
domestic prices of any particular country but the offer prices
of exports, i.e. low priced surpluses of countries which in all
probability in their domestic markets follow price support
policies) are low among other reasons because the EEC: first,
is no longer a market participant as a buyer of these products;
and second it is a market participant as a seller of its own
surpluses. What the world prices would have been in the
absence of the CAP, cannot be guessed easily. It is however
certain that, if the Community had continued to be an
important buyer in the world markets for agricultural
products, the world market prices would have been much
higher than they are today.

Implication of the policy of administered prices is that the
Community prices of agricultural products are definitely

Table 6.6: Degree of Self-sufficiency in Agricultural Products, 1984-85

Commodity	Index[1] EC-10	EC-12	Largest producer:	Index[1]
Cereals	128	120	F	220
Rice	67	73	I	206
Potatoes	103	102	N	149
Sugar	132	125	DK	239
Vegetables	101	108	N	202
Fresh Fruit	82	86	I	127
Citrus Fruit	46	72	E	401
Wine	97	98	I	120
Milk powder	133	–	IRL	561
Cheese	108	–	DK	468
Butter	128	–	N	467
Eggs	103	–	N	301
Beef	112	–	IRL	607
Veal	111	–	N	796
Pork	101	–	DK	383
Poultry meat	107	–	N	223

Note: [1]For index = 100 demand equals supply, that is self-sufficiency.

Sources: Eurostat, *Yearbook of Agricultural Statistics*, 1985.
Basic Statistics of the Community, 24 ed.

stabler than the world prices. Thus in the Community price
fluctuation is no longer a matter of concern. However, it is
important to repeat that a degree of stability has been attained
but at a cost, the relatively high levels of prices.
4. *Availability of Supplies* (Table 6.6). Security of supply of
agricultural products in the Community is ensured by the CAP
through the availability of domestic production and imports.
In fact, for a number of products domestic supplies far exceed
the domestic demand of the Community as a whole, without of
course any particular effects on market prices. The long-term
increase in the volume of agricultural production has been 1.5
to 2.0 per cent a year, while consumption has been increasing
by about 0.5 per cent a year. Therefore for the principal farm
products more than self-sufficiency has been achieved, and the
Community has to rely increasingly on exports for the disposal
of excess production.

Characteristic of EEC agriculture is that the demand/supply
relationship is not uniform throughout the Community. The
geographic dispersion of the member countries and the degree
of their specialisation in production means that, for the same
agricultural commodity, some of them produce surpluses and
others experience deficits. For the Community as a whole
problems, of course, arise from the overall surpluses and
deficits in farm products. Despite the increase in agricultural
production and the mountains and lakes of unsold stocks, the
Community remains the world's largest importer of food.
5. *Reasonable Prices for the Consumer.* Consumer prices are
on the whole much higher than producer prices (farm prices at
the farm gate) and there is no close correlation between the
two prices. The increase in consumer prices in the EC over the
last few years lagged behind the inflation rate. Between 1973
and 1980 the prices of agricultural products rose by 7.4 per
cent annually against 11.2 per cent increase in the general price
index. However, as we have seen world market prices for most
agricultural products are well below those of the EC. Hence,
the consumer has on the one hand gained from price stability
and availability of plentiful supplies, but on the other hand he
has lost from having to pay very high prices. Table 6.7 presents
the indices of producers' and consumers' (food) prices for 1985
based on 1980 = 100. The data show that in general producer

Table 6.7: Producers' and Consumers' Prices of Agricultural Products, 1985

Member State	Producers' Prices 1. nominal	2. deflated	Consumers' Prices 3. food	1980 = 100 Difference 3–1
B	132.6	94.4	139.2	6.6
DK	132.6	90.6	147.7	15.1
D	103.1	85.2	114.4	11.4
GR	254.2	99.2	262.7	8.5
F	143.0	90.5	159.1	7.4
IRL	135.6	76.0	155.8	20.2
I	163.5	85.9	177.5	14.0
L	137.8	97.5	143.7	5.9
NL	114.6	93.7	115.9	1.3
UK	124.0	87.6	131.4	7.4
EC 10	144.1	88.6	149.5	5.4

Source: *Eurostat* (1985), *Basic Statistics of the Community*, 24th ed., Luxembourg, 1987.

prices lagged behind consumer prices in every member state, in many cases by a very wide margin. What is most important is that in real terms producer prices (deflated) were in 1985 much lower than they were in 1980. An implication of this is that during the period 1980–5, although the prices of agricultural commodities within the Community did rise, the producers of agricultural commodities were neither solely responsible for the price increase nor did they manage to maintain in real terms the produce prices they enjoyed back in 1980. Therefore, over the last five years the welfare of agricultural producers has worsened.

b) Efficiency of the CAP

The main policy of the CAP, price support, was adopted not because it is considered to be the most efficient for achieving the set objectives, but because it is regarded as less interventionist than other policies, such as subsidies, and therefore politically more acceptable to the public. As we have seen, the objectives of the CAP, to a large extent, have been reached. However, the same or better results could have been achieved by a less expensive and more rational policy. A disadvantage of the current CAP policy is that the impressive increase in agricultural output has led to a spectacular increase in Community expenditure on price support. Table 6.8 shows that the budgetary expenditure of the CAP has grown in thirteen years more than sevenfold, from 3147.2 billion ECUs to 22961.0 billion ECUs, i.e. by more than 16 per cent in every year. Over the period 1973–86 nearly ¾ of the budget have been spent on Agriculture, 95 per cent of it as price support and only 5 per cent on restructuring the sector. The public costs of protection of the agricultural markets seem to increase inexorably, thus limiting the funds available for other competing purposes. Hence, since the mid-1970s mounting criticism has been directed against the CAP because:

- It has kept prices above world prices.
- It has caused significant financial expenditures which required financial transfers between members.
- It has led to substantial intra-Community income redistribution from consumers in one member country to producers in another.
- It has generated surpluses of some commodities.

The surpluses of skimmed milk powder and butter are particularly notorious. At the then current levels of consumption, the 1984 stocks of skimmed milk powder in the Community were equal to 230 days' supply, while stocks of butter to 200 days' supply. These surpluses, besides the initial costs of accumulation and storage, cause new problems by being disposed within the Community or as exports at prices vastly below costs. For example, the export price of skimmed milk powder is three times lower than the support price.

Despite the increases in output, the EC still is the world's largest single importer, but at the same time a considerable exporter, of agricultural products: it accounts for 24 per cent of world imports of agricultural products, and 11 per cent of world exports. In its trading capacity the EC has been accused as being protectionist, while on the other hand it also adds to the instability of world markets by purchasing agricultural products abroad only when domestic supplies are short and

Table 6.8: *Budgetary Expenditure on EAGGF, 1973–1986*

	1973	1974	1975	1976	1977	1978
Guarantee	3174.2	3277.9	4821.5	5365.0	6166.8	9278.6
Guidance	123.7	128.4	184.3	218.2	296.7	323.6
Total EAGGF	3297.9	3406.3	5005.8	5583.2	6463.5	9602.2
Total Budget	4004.6	4515.4	6411.2	7287.6	8704.9	11973.1
Percentage EAGGF	82.35	75.44	78.08	76.61	74.25	80.20

	1979	1980	1981	1982	1983
Guarantee	10462.8	11326.9	11010.1	12424.3	15843.0
Guidance	408.1	601.9	574.7	646.1	749.7
Total EAGGF	10870.9	11928.8	11584.8	13070.4	16592.7
Total Budget	14367.1	16290.4	17792.8	20422.7	24313.0
Percentage EAGGF	75.66	73.23	65.11	64.00	68.25

	1984	1985	1986[1]
Guarantee	19955	22112	22961
Guidance	688	802	966
Total EAGGF	20643	22914	23927
Total Budget	28433	35174	36712
Percentage EAGGF	72.60	65.14	65.17

Note: [1] Appropriations.

Source: EC, *Basic Statistics of the Community*, various issues

selling its surpluses on world markets at subsidised prices. Export subsidies provided under the CAP enable the Community to unload much of its surplus farm produce in other countries, squeezing out more efficient producers. Community exports of surplus dairy products and cereals especially depress world prices and lead to competition with other producers for gaining and holding export markets. These operations cause financial problems to the Community's major trading partners (although some of them, such as the USA, which is by far the most important net exporter of agricultural produce in the world, subsidise their agriculture to a greater extent than the EC) and the LDCs, and complicate international relations within and outside the EC. Recently, there have been many instances of open trade warfare which have led to a demand for liberalisation in the trade of agricultural products under the auspices of the GATT.

c) Reform of the CAP

The first attempt for reform of the CAP was unsuccessful. The Mansholt Plan (1968), which examined the problem of agricultural reform under the general objective of 'reasonable incomes, reasonable prices and increased productivity', proposed a radical restructuring of the CAP followed by trade liberalisation in agricultural products in line with the EEC Treaty. The Plan recommended reduction in agricultural employment by 50 per cent which was to be achieved by offering the farmers alternative employment; reduction in farm area by 7 per cent; reorganisation in large production units for the realisation of scale economies; reasonable incomes for the producers through the market process; and a fairly liberal trade regime in agricultural products. However, political opposition to the Plan, arising from diverse interests among the members, and the concurrent early problems of the forthcoming economic recession, meant that the proposed reforms were not accepted. A second major attempt for reform was presented by the Commission in *Guidelines for European Agriculture* (1981). This plan aimed specifically at a reduction in production by keeping prices down, with the long-run objective of bringing prices in line with world prices. The Community recognised that the agricultural policy required re-examination so that it could fulfil its aims in the changed conditions prevailing at the time, aware of the fact that when financial resources are scarce 'it is neither economically sensible nor financially possible to give producers a full guarantee for products in structural surplus' (*Bulletin EC* 6-1981). Subsequently, on the basis of these guidelines, 'guarantee thresholds' were introduced for a number of products (milk, cereals, rape, and processed tomatoes were added to cotton and sugar which were already covered by a similar policy). Price support was restricted to pre-specified levels of production. When these levels were exceeded then: a) the target and intervention prices were reduced (cereal, milk); b) aid paid under the market regulation was limited (cotton); c) the producers participated in the cost of disposing surplus output (milk) by means of a 'coresponsibility' levy; or d) quotas were introduced at the national or the enterprise level (sugar).

However, these measures did not solve the fundamental problem of agriculture in the Community which is 'how to reconcile the social objectives of the CAP with real market conditions' (*Bulletin EC* 3-1984). Production continued to exceed the level of self-sufficiency with long-run growth for most products at least three to four times higher than the annual rate of increase of their consumption. While the markets within the Community were showing vast supply surpluses, the markets for agricultural exports continued to be unreliable long-run outlets.

The crisis reached a peak in 1984 when, after the failure to bring production under control, the budgetary funds were exhausted and the CAP was threatened with imminent financial collapse. After protracted negotiations a solution was announced at the Agricultural Council of 31st of March 1985. The Council's policy guidelines were later enhanced by parallel measures at the budgetary level which were taken at the Fontainbleau Agreement between Heads of Government. With reference to the CAP, the Agreement included: a) A more realistic policy on prices which were to rise by less than the rate of inflation. It was estimated that in most member countries improvements in productivity would keep farmers' incomes rising. **b) Gradual elimination of the MCAs and** adoption of new arrangements whereby parity changes in the EMS would no longer entail the creation of green rates. c) Control of milk production through quotas.

The milk sector attracted special attention because its output continued to rise by 3.5 per cent per year, while the consumption remained stagnant. Price support and subsidised exports meant that milk products in all forms were taking up more than a quarter of the total EAGGF expenditure. The new policy set national quotas calculated from the 1981 deliveries plus 1 per cent (with certain exceptions for Italy and Ireland). The national quotas were allocated by each member state to its regions and producers. Re-trading of the allocated quotas was not permitted. In addition to the quotas, the coresponsibility levy was raised with quota overruns attracting a 'super levy' of 75 per cent for individual quotas and a 100 per cent for collective quotas. However, a loophole in the system and the unwillingness of the member states to comply with the spirit of the agreement allowed farmers in one region to balance surplus output against under-production in other regions of the same country and thus to reduce the punitive 'super levy' on over-producers. Taking advantage of this, over-production in England and Wales in 1985 was balanced against short-falls in Scotland, so that English farmers paid no more than a token levy.

From the second year of operation of the system quotas became tradable and thus individual quotas can be sold or leased. The system was initially introduced for five years only, but the possibility is that it will not be repealed at the end of the period. But the system of quotas does not constitute a permanent solution to the problems of the CAP. One reason for this is that quota restrictions apply only to the production of milk, while cereals, which create similar problems and take up the second largest share in the CAP budget, are not covered. Another reason is that current quotas are set well above the level of self-sufficiency and surpluses continue to accumulate. Despite the quotas, milk production in 1985 soared to more than one million tonnes above the official quota, and butter stores topped 1.4 million tonnes.

In July 1985 the Commission published one more Green Paper, *Perspectives for the CAP*, reviewing the shortcomings of the CAP and recommending appropriate measures for overcoming them. For the first time in the history of the CAP, this document also stressed the links between agriculture and the protection of the environment. Under the pressure of increasing production and financial shortages, the EC Governments took at the end of 1986 the first significant steps towards reforming the CAP. The Council adopted measures adjusting the system of milk quotas in order to reduce production by 9.5 per cent over two years and to prevent the accumulation of new mountains of surplus butter. In the future the Commission will be empowered to refuse to buy butter when surplus stocks and market prices top fixed levels. Existing stocks of butter will be disposed of in subsidised sales within the Community and abroad over the next two years. It was also decided that the intervention in the beef and veal market will no longer be unconditional but will be limited to certain eligible quantities and qualities.

The Council also decided that in the future the size of the budget should determine the extent of agricultural spending which should grow 'no faster' than the Community's income. But the problems of the CAP continued in 1987, when by the middle of the year the Community agricultural ministers failed in their negotiations to freeze farm prices and implement policy reforms. Their failure to reach agreement threatened once again to deepen the Community's financial crisis, with farm spending set to overshoot the 1987 budget by more than 15 per cent. Behind all these problems is the fact that commodity prices continue to be fixed in response to political as much as economic pressures, and that governments of member states preach austerity by cuts in agricultural expenditures, but at the same time they attempt to secure the best deal for their own farming interests.

The problems of the CAP have become more complicated after the accession to the Community of Portugal and Spain. These two new members brought under the CAP two agricultural systems with production structures in many respects more deficient than those of the other nine (or ten, including Greece) members. After the accession the share of Mediterranean products in the agricultural output of the Community has risen, while the CAP expenditure is still

Table 6.9: Allocation of EAGGF Expenditure: Guarantee Section: ratios per cent.

Commodity	1978	1979	1980	1981	1982	1983	1984	1985
Dairy products	36.5	43.4	42.1	30.5	26.9	27.7	29.7	30.1
Cereals	12.9	15.4	15.3	17.8	15.1	16.0	9.3	11.9
Meat and eggs	7.5	8.9	14.2	17.0	13.1	14.6	17.7	17.6
Oils and oilseeds	6.3	6.9	6.6	10.0	10.5	11.1	9.5	9.1
Sugar	8.3	9.0	5.0	6.9	10.0	8.3	8.9	9.1
Fruit, vegetables, Wine and Tobacco	6.8	6.9	13.3	17.0	11.4	15.8	18.8	15.3
Other products	2.5	3.2	2.8	2.3	4.9	3.2	4.1	5.9
MCAs	19.2	6.8	2.6	2.2	2.5	3.1	2.0	1.0

Sources: *Eurostat Review* 1973–82 and 1974-83
   Bull. EC 4–1986.

dominated by the support to producers of the northern member countries. Table 6.9 presents the distribution of EAGGF expenditure over eight different years. The first three groups of products (dairy products, cereals and meat), which are typically northern ones, absorb between 56 per cent and 72 per cent of the total EAGGF budget. This imbalance is explained by the fact that the CAP was conceived in the early 1960s, when the country composition of the Community was very different from what it is today, and survived in much the same format through three enlargements. With the addition of the agricultural output of Portugal and Spain there is a sharp shift in focus away from the northern producers and commodities to Mediterranean producers and commodities: the Community's production of olive oil has been raised by half, wine by one quarter, citrus fruits by three quarters and fresh vegetables by more than one third.

The latest enlargement also tends to exacerbate the already wide differences in farm structures and incomes between the various regions of the Community. Under the pressure of unresolved and newly instituted problems, the mechanism of the CAP is strained and is in urgent need of radical reform. Adjustments on the same general principles that applied in the past are no longer financially affordable: The Budget has not the required resources to provide support for Mediterranean products similar to that allocated to the products of the northern members. Without reform, the CAP, which in the past was considered to be the main instrument for economic integration, will become a burden and a threat to European unity. The direction of this reform should be 'in accordance with market conditions prevailing in each sector ... [so that] budgetary intervention can be cost-effective' (*Bulletin EC*, Supplement 4/81).

6.5   THE COMMON FISHERIES POLICY

After protracted negotiations, which started in 1966, the Community introduced a Common Fisheries Policy (CFP) in January 1983. The policy aims to ensure 'optimal exploitation of the biological resources of the Community Zone' by improved efficiency in both the structure and marketing of the sector and 'equitable exploitation of these limited resources between member states'. In particular, the objectives of the policy are:

On the Structural Side (1)   a) the rational use of resources; b) the elimination of discrimination among nationals of the EEC member states employed in the industry; c) the conservation of resources.

On the Marketing Side (2)   a) secure employment in the industry, particularly of certain coastal regions traditionally specialising in fishing; b) fair income for those employed in the industry; c) improvement in marketing and marketing standards; d) adequate supply adjusted to market requirements; e) reasonable prices for the consumer.

The necessity for a CFP was enforced by developments in the international field which took place during the 1970s, when many countries introduced 200-mile exclusive fishery zones. The decision to establish a CFP is based on Article 38 of the Treaty of Rome, which deals with Agriculture. This Article was subsequently interpreted to include 'the products of the soil, of stockfarming and of fisheries and products of first stage processing directly related to these products'. Hence, the objectives of the CAP (Article 38–47) apply also to the case of the CFP. The methods for achieving the objectives of the CPF are broadly similar to those of the CAP. Particularly for the fishing industry the instruments of policy are:

Access arrangements, (1)   which determine exactly where fishermen may fish. These also provide 12-mile national fisheries zones for each member country, with limited access for other member countries, and a 200-mile exclusive Community zone with members' quotas of catches. A number of third countries have signed agreements for reciprocal fishing and trade arrangements (e.g. Norway, Sweden, Canada, etc.).

Marketing arrangements (2)   which are designed to promote 'rational disposal' of fishery products and to bring about some degree of stability in the industry and the incomes of those employed in it.

Quotas (3) (total allowable catches, TACs), technical conservation measures (minimum size, minimum mesh size, etc.) and surveillance. These are instruments of policies which aim at the preservation of stocks. The Commission has established a special unit whose specific task is to oversee member states' efforts at enforcement of the CFP regulations (such as mesh size, minimum landing size, closed areas, and closed season areas). However, each member country is responsible for policing the waters under its nominal jurisdiction and for ensuring that the provisions of the CFP are adhered to.

Structural policies (4) which aim at contraction of the industry (which suffers from overcapacity), a better allocation of resources, increased productivity and long-run development. Structural expenditures are financed by the EAGGF.

As in the case of the CAP, for the CFP a target price and a guide price are established annually at the start of each fishing season. A withdrawal price also applies. However, the withdrawals are limited to a maximum of 20 per cent of the permitted annual catch, so that a degree of response, a kind of coresponsibility, is left to the supply. The CFP also provides export refunds and import duties, but the Community is on the whole a net importer of fisheries products. Contrary to the case of the CAP, which is based on guaranteed prices designed to ensure farmers a fair income, the CFP helps to stabilise the market and to shelter fishermen from falling prices. But it does not attempt to regulate the upper bound of price fluctuations, so that fishermen benefit from the peaks of prices and are protected from the troughs.

The Mediterranean member countries are covered by the CFP as regards market organisation, structural change and financial matters. However, there are no 200-mile zones, quotas or TACs established as yet.

The entry of Portugal and Spain has radically altered the structure of the fisheries industry in the Community by: a) doubling the manpower employed in the industry; b) increasing the fishing capacity by 75 per cent; c) increasing the production of the industry for human consumption by 45 per cent; and d) increasing the consumption of fish by 43 per cent. Both Portugal and Spain have accepted the CFP in its entirety. However, transitional arrangements apply to both fish trade between the EEC and the new members and limited access to Community waters. Portugal will become a full member of the CFP by 1995, but Spain not earlier than 2002. For these two countries fisheries are of greater economic and social importance than in the other 10 countries of the EEC. The contributions of fisheries to GNP is 0.12 per cent for the ten members of the Community, while it is 0.90 per cent for Spain and 1.6 per cent for Portugal.

REFERENCES

Buckwell, A., Harvey, D. R., Thomson, K. J., and Parton K. (1982), *The Costs of the Common Agricultural Policy*, Croom Helm, London.
EC (1981), 'Guidelines for the European Agriculture', *Bull. EC*, Supplement 4.
EC (1983), 'Adjustment of the Common Agricultural Policy', *Bull. EC*, Supplement 4.
EC (1983), 'Further Guidelines for the Development of the CAP', *Bull. EC*-6.
EC Commission (1985), *Perspectives for the CAP*, Green Paper, Brussels.
EC (1985), *The European Community's Fishery Policy*, European Documentation, Luxembourg.
Fennell, R. (1985), 'A Reconsideration of the Objectives of the Common Agricultural Policy', *Journal of Common Market Studies*, 23, pp. 257–76.
Harvey, D. R. and Thomson, K. J. (1985), 'Costs, Benefits and Future of the Common Agricultural Policy', *Journal of Common Market Studies*, 24, pp. 1–20.
Josling, T. E. (1979), 'Agricultural Policy', in Coffey, P. (ed.), *Economic Policies of the Common Market*, Macmillan, London.
Marsh, J. S. and Swanney, P. J. (1980), *Agriculture and the European Community*, Allen and Unwin, London.
Morris, C. N. (1980), 'The Common Agricultural Policy', *Fiscal Studies*, 1, pp. 17–35.
Ritson, C. and Tangermann, S. (1979), 'The Economics and Politics of Monetary Compensatory Amounts', *European Review of Agricultural Economics*, 6, pp. 119–64.
Rollo, J. M. C. and Warwick, K. S. (1979), *The CAP and Resource Flows Among EEC Member States*, London, Ministry of Agriculture, Fisheries and Food.
Shackleton, M. (1982), 'The Common Fisheries Policy', in Wallace,

H., Wallace, W. and Webb, C. (eds) *Policy Making in the European Community*, John Wiley, London.

Strauss, R. (1983), 'Economic effects of MCAs', *Journal of Common Market Studies*, 21, pp. 261–81.

7 Trade Policies

7.1 INTRODUCTION

The Treaty of Rome stipulated that 'the Community shall be based upon a customs union' (Article 9), which would involve the gradual elimination of customs duties in trade between the member states, and the establishment of a common customs tariff on trade with third countries. These changes in customs duties were to be completed in three stages over a twelve-year period. In effect, the process was speeded up and the customs union was completed a year and a half ahead of the schedule set by the Treaty. By the middle of 1968 the Six (B, D, F, I, L, NL) had (a) abolished all customs duties, charges of equivalent-discriminating effect and quantitative restrictions on trade between them, and (b) applied a common customs tariff (CCT, also called common external tariff, CET) on trade with non-members of the Community.

The three new members of the first enlargement (DK, IRL, UK) dismantled their tariffs on intra-Community trade and adopted the CET during a transitional period which ended on 1st July 1977. Greece, Portugal and Spain were given a seven-year transitional period, starting from the date of their entry, to phase out their tariffs and adopt the CET. By 1st January 1993 the process of tariff cuts and adoption of the CET will be completed and the Community will become a customs union of twelve full-member countries. In the meanwhile, the Community is also attempting to reduce by harmonisation, and ultimately to eliminate the existing national non-tariff barriers on internal trade and the internal frontier controls.

Harmonisation of indirect taxes is also pursued as discussed in chapter 4. Table 7.1 presents the direction of EC internal and external trade in 1985. Trade between the members of the Community accounts for more than half of their total trade.

The Community has been expressly provided with powers by the EEC Treaty to conduct common external policy in the field of tariff and trade (Articles 11, 113), with regard to relations with international organisations (Article 229) and with regard to the conclusion of association agreements (Article 238). Article 3 of the Treaty states that the objectives of the Community require the establishment of 'a common commercial policy towards third countries'. Article 110 confirms that the member states 'aim to contribute, in the common interest, to the harmonious development of world trade, the progressive abolition of restrictions on international trade and the lowering of customs barriers'.

The Common Commercial Policy (CCP) began operating with the end of the transitional period in 1968, after the introduction of the Common External Tariff, when the member states passed to the Community the power to enact foreign trade policy, that is to negotiate international trade agreements, fix customs procedures and determine export and import policies (including measures to be taken in cases of dumping or subsidies) (Article 113). However, the members still retain some measure of autonomy in external-trade policy by operating (with Community authorisation under Articles 115) their own lists of specific products subject to national import restrictions from within or without the Community.

Article 116 specifies that the members shall act in common in respect of all matters of particular interest to the common market arising in international organisations 'of an economic character'. Decisions on Common Commercial Policy are taken by the Council, on proposals from the Commission, by qualified majority vote. Article 228 states that agreements between the Community and third states or international organisations are negotiated by the Commission and concluded by the Council by a unanimous decision. A similar procedure is followed in the case of application for membership in the Community by any European state (Article 237). Article 238 states that the Community may conclude with a third state, a union of states or an international organisation agreements 'creating association embodying reciprocal rights and obligations, joint actions and appropriate forms of procedure'.

The Treaty pays special attention to a group of non-European countries which are the subject of favourable trade and aid arrangements. These are 'countries and territories' which had dependency and colonial ties with some of the Six. Part VI of the Treaty (Article 131-6), and subsequent agreements based upon it, granted to these now independent countries associate membership from the start for the purpose of promoting their economic development and establishing close economic relations between them and the Community as a whole. The association agreement involves rules regulating their trade with the Community and the supply of aid for the 'economic, social and cultural development to which they aspire' (Article 131).

On the basis of the relevant provisions of the Treaty of Rome, the Community has negotiated three enlargements and many association and trade agreements with third countries. As a result, the Community has become one of the most important trading blocs in the world and has affected both the volume and the direction of international trade. In the process, the Community faced criticisms from advocates of a more liberal economic order with regard to its position towards tariff preferences. Problems have also arisen in the Community's relations with other trading countries, some of which welcome the EEC as a large trading partner predisposed toward trade liberalisation (for manufactures), while others saw in the EEC the emergence of an adversary who does not always play the international trade game according to the rules, particularly so in the trade of agricultural commodities. In the following sections of this chapter we examine the relations between the GATT and the EEC, and between the EEC and non-member countries.

7.2 THE GATT AND THE EEC

The General Agreement on Tariffs and Trade (GATT) was

signed in 1947. It has been updated since in order to adapt to major changes in the international economic order. The GATT is a voluntary agreement providing a code of rules for the conduct of world trade and a forum for the resolution of disputes and the reduction of trade barriers. The Agreement is based on the free market, fair competition, and free trade and specialisation according to comparative advantage. The contracting parties of the GATT have agreed to two main principles:

(1) Trade liberalisation through the reduction of customs tariffs and the general elimination of quantitative restrictions and other non-tariff barriers to trade.

(2) Non-discrimination in trade through the application of the most-favoured nation (MFN) clause, with the derogations and flexibility necessary to accommodate regional economic integration and special and more favourable treatment for developing countries.

Principle (1) aims at 'transparency' in the conditions in which world trade is conducted. Free trade is regarded as the best policy for the contracting parties and trade liberalisation is the main objective of the GATT. However, given that free trade cannot be achieved in the short run, the tariff, which affects trade indirectly by its effects on prices, is considered as the least evil of the instruments of trade restrictions because it is transparent, easy to negotiate and fully compatible with the market.

Principle (2) fosters a multilateral approach to trade liberalisation. However, three exceptions have been recognised. First, the less developed countries, which as a group may be subject to more favourable treatment. Second, trade preferences already in existence between countries before the formation of the GATT were excluded from the MFN extension, so that discrimination continued under the GATT. Third, by Article XXIV the GATT specifically allowed mutual preferences for free-trade areas, customs unions and interim agreements leading to economic integration provided that: (i) The tariffs of the customs union must not be higher than those of the member countries prior to union; (ii) The arrangements must involve 'substantially all the trade' between the parties; and (iii) The customs union or free-trade area must be completed 'within a reasonable length of time', that is within a relatively short period.

Article XXIV has been invoked several times since the signing of the GATT due to the growth of regional economic integration. As we have seen in chapter 1, Regional Economic Associations (REAs) combine trade liberalisation between the members with trade discrimination toward nonmembers. In effect, Article XXIV conflicts with the general principle of non-discrimination, since the abolition of tariff barriers between countries forming a customs union is necessarily regional and preferential and does not extend to all contracting parties of the GATT. The first two conditions attached to this exception attempt to direct countries to the formation of *trade creating* customs unions which can be regarded as a step towards free international trade. Nevertheless, even with a common external tariff limited to the level of the tariff prior to the formation of the customs union, some of the members could well experience trade diversion.

The EEC's Common External Tariff was set by the Treaty of Rome 'at the level of the arithmetical average of the duties applied in the four territories comprised in the Community' (Article 19). The six founding members comprised the four customs territories Benelux (B, L, NL), France, Germany FR, and Italy. The resulting average CET was approximately 11 per cent, much lower than the tariff of most of the important trade partners of the EEC, such as the USA and Japan. However, the GATT considered that the method of calculation of the CET contravened the rule 'that the duties shall not on the whole be higher or more restrictive than the general incidence of the duties prior to the formation of such union' (Article XXIV). Despite representations by the GATT, the EEC refused to discuss the best method of calculation, maintaining that Article XXIV did not demand any special method of calculation. Later, after enlargement of the EEC to countries which were more protective than the original Six (such as Greece, Spain and Portugal) and had to adopt the CET, the GATT arguments became irrelevant. Moreover, under the GATT negotiations for tariff reduction of 1960–2 (Dillon Round), 1964–7 (Kennedy Round), and 1973–9 (Tokyo Round) in which the EEC participated as a single unit (although not the Community as such, but its members are contracting parties of the GATT), the CET was reduced further and it is today approximately 7.5 per cent. The Uruguay Round of trade liberalisation, which got under way in February 1987, is expected to reduce further tariff and non-tariff barriers to international trade. However, despite the repeatedly emphasised commitment of the Community to an open world trade system (European Economy, 1984), the CET applies only to trade of manufactures. The Common Agricultural Policy (CAP), which is based on high protection for the domestic market and on the granting of subsidies to exports, clearly is at odds with trade liberalisation. Trade in services virtually remains outside the GATT.

Introduction of the CET and subsequent reductions in it do not mean that the EEC has completely abstained from using other forms of protection. During the course of the ongoing economic recession and the rising level of unemployment, the lowering of tariffs under the GATT has been followed at a worldwide scale by proliferation of protection by non-tariff barriers. For example, in the steel industry the EEC operates volume controls and Voluntary Export Restraints (VER). The latter are quantitative restrictions on exports of a product, agreed bilaterally between governments or industries and usually administered by the exporting party. Under the Multi-Fibre Arrangement (MFA), which limits the imports of competitively priced textiles from developing countries, the EEC has negotiated Voluntary Export Restraints with 25 states. Similarly, in trade with Japan, which shows a large deficit for the EEC countries, a mandate has been given to the Commission by the Council to negotiate VERs; in the meanwhile the member states apply import ceilings bilaterally agreed with Japan or they even resort to unilateral implementation of non-tariff barriers. Both VERs and MFAs are formal derogations from the GATT, although MFAs are usually negotiated under the auspices of the GATT.

Another issue of contention and criticism by the GATT was the Association System of the EEC. The preferences between France, Belgium, Italy, Netherlands and their dependencies were permitted under the GATT rule, since they existed prior to 1947. Objections were raised when it was decided that association between the dependencies (listed in Annex IV of the Treaty of Rome) and the EEC implies that preferences will extend to all the members of the Community, including those who had no historical ties with overseas territories. This was regarded as constituting the establishment of new preferences on a bilateral basis, thus contravening the spirit of the GATT which favours the multilateral approach to trade liberalisation. The EEC maintained that its Association system constitutes an interim agreement for the formation of a customs union and therefore it is permitted under the GATT (Article XXIV). However, Article 133 of the Treaty of Rome stipulated that the associate overseas territories 'may levy such customs duties as are necessitated by their need for development and industrialisation', and this seemed to violate the GATT condition that the establishment of a free-trade area or customs union should include abolition of customs duties 'on substantially all the trade in products originating in such territories'. This issue was examined by a working party of GATT and EEC representatives which concluded that 'if at any time, contrary to their expectations, damage to the interest of third parties could be proved, the EEC would take steps to mitigate it' (Barnes, 1967, p. 13).

In 1965 the GATT enunciated a new rule, that 'the developed contracting parties do not expect reciprocity for commitments made by them in trade negotiations to reduce or remove tariffs and other trade barriers to the trade of less-developed contracting parties' (GATT, Appendix E, Article XXXVI). This rule implied that the EEC's Association System, which is based on 'reciprocity' in tariff concessions, was in effect illegal and that the EEC policy of 'reverse preferences' in her trade agreements with less-developed countries constituted an infringement of the GATT. The EEC maintained that her trade agreements with less-developed countries are based on Articles XXIV of the GATT which permits the establishment of free-trade areas based on the reciprocity of trade concessions. Therefore, if there is a problem, it clearly arises from contradictions between different GATT rules. The official view of the GATT has been that the free-trade areas between the EEC and less-developed countries are more fictitious than real, and that 'the creation of preferential trade links between a few developed and one, or few, developing countries here and there through new discriminatory agreements for which no historical justification can be claimed' (GATT, 1972) violates the spirit of the GATT and should be deplored. Nevertheless, the association agreements between the EEC and other developed and less developed countries have proliferated. Taking a pragmatic point of view, most members of the GATT have accepted that in all these agreements the EEC has kept within the letter, if not always within the spirit, of the GATT. One can conclude that to the extent that the GATT objective is to help its less-developed members, association with the EEC is advantageous; the benefits received by the less-developed associated members clearly outweigh those received by the EEC. This has lately prompted some observers to claim that, with its network of preferential trading agreements, the EEC has created a privileged group of client states with which it dominates the process of decision making in the GATT, thus rendering the organisation a 'paper mouse'.

7.3 THE LOMÉ CONVENTION

Under the Treaty of Rome, Part IV, Article 131–6, the EEC granted associate membership to certain overseas territories (listed in Annex IV of the Treaty) which were still dependencies of Community members. The Association agreement entailed 'reciprocal rights and obligations' emanating from the establishment of a free-trade area with two-way free access for each other's products. It also included the granting of Community aid to the associate states by the purposely established European Development Fund (EDF). Under the terms of the Treaty, this association system had to be reviewed after four years of operation. Soon after 1960, most of the EEC associate overseas territories gained their national independence and started negotiations for a new agreement with the Community. This led in 1963 to the conclusion of the Yaoundé Convention, an agreement between the Community and eighteen African States. In contrast to the first agreement which provides for the abolition of customs duties between all the contracting parties, the Yaoundé Convention excluded the abolition of tariffs in inter-associate trade, establishing in effect eighteen free-trade areas, between the EEC and each of the eighteen associates. The second Yaoundé Convention was signed in 1969 and was extended to Mauritius in 1972. After the first enlargement which increased the full members of the EEC to nine, it became necessary to reconsider the Community's Association System for possible inclusion of developing countries which had close ties with the UK through the Commonwealth. A new five-year association agreement, the Lomé Convention (1975–80), was signed in 1975 by the EEC nine and forty-six African, Caribbean, and Pacific (ACP) countries. This agreement was succeeded by the Lomé II Convention (1980–5) which was signed by sixty-three ACP countries. The Lomé III Convention (1985–90) was signed by sixty-six ACP countries in December 1984. As Table 7.1 shows, the share of the ACP group's trade with the EEC is from the Community's point of view relatively small.

Three institutions are involved in administering the Convention: (1) The Council of Ministers consists of the Community's Council, the Commission and a member of each ACP government. (2) The Committee of Ambassadors oversees the running of the Convention on a day-to-day basis. (3) The Consultative Assembly consists of members of the European Parliament and of representatives elected or appointed by ACP States, and deals with and expresses opinion on matters related to the Convention.

The main provisions of Lomé III are:

Tariff preferences: (1) almost all present ACP manufactures enter the Community at zero or very low tariffs. The Community, in return, gets 'most-favoured-nation' treatment from the ACP states and an undertaking that they will not discriminate between member states of the EEC.

Agricultural exports (2) from ACP countries competing with Community products are subject to CAP regulations. However, such products enjoy a preferential arrangement which includes levy rebate or exemption for out-of-season products. Special provisions exist for sugar, beef and rice which are subject to annual quotas. Agricultural exports which do not compete with Community products have preferences over third-party supplies.

Table 7.1: Community Trade by Partner Countries, 1985, Percentages

Country	Import Origin					Export Destination				
	EC-12	USA	Japan	ACP	Other	EC-12	USA	Japan	ACP	Other
B/L	68.6	6.0	2.2	2.9	20.4	70.1	6.3	0.8	1.7	21.0
DK	50.7	5.5	3.5	0.8	39.5	44.8	10.2	3.0	1.5	40.5
D	53.1	6.5	4.2	3.2	33.0	49.7	10.3	1.5	1.1	37.3
E	37.9	10.8	3.1	6.5	41.6	53.4	10.2	0.9	2.6	32.9
F	59.4	6.4	2.2	4.7	27.3	53.7	8.7	1.2	4.3	32.1
GR	48.1	3.1	6.4	1.1	41.3	54.2	8.2	0.9	1.1	35.6
IRL	71.7	14.4	2.9	1.1	9.9	68.9	9.8	1.6	1.7	18.0
I	47.1	6.0	1.6	3.4	41.9	48.2	12.3	1.2	1.8	36.6
NL	55.8	8.4	2.5	3.2	30.0	74.6	5.1	0.5	1.4	18.3
P	45.7	9.8	3.0	6.3	35.2	62.4	9.3	0.8	1.6	25.9
UK	47.3	13.0	5.1	2.9	31.8	48.8	14.9	1.3	3.2	31.8
EC-12	53.4	7.9	3.3	3.3	32.2	54.9	10.1	1.2	2.1	31.7

Source: Eurostat, *Basic Statistics of the Community*, 24th ed., Luxembourg.

Aid: (3) Under Lomé III and in contrast to previous practice, aid is directed towards programmes rather than projects. The aid budget amounts to ECU 8.5 billion, the bulk of which is provided by the European Development Fund in the form of grants, soft loans and the financing of two institutions, the Stabex Fund and the Sysmin Scheme. The ACP countries also have access to funds from the European Investment Bank (EIB).

The Stabex Fund (4) provides EEC funds for the stabilisation of earnings from the exports of mainly agricultural products. In order to qualify for a transfer from the Fund, the product must over the previous five years account for 6.0 per cent of the country's total export earnings which must have fallen by more than 6.0 per cent below the average. In the case of least developed, landlocked and island states the activation thresholds are reduced to 1.5 per cent. As a general rule, states that have benefited from transfers help to replenish the Fund to the extent of their receipts, but only if their export earnings have improved.

The Sysmin Scheme (5) supports mineral production and provides financial assistance to ACP countries which are heavily dependent on mineral exports. The Scheme is designed to help countries to cope with serious temporary disruptions affecting their export earnings from mining sectors. In order to qualify for a transfer from the Scheme, the disruption must reduce capacity by at least 10 per cent and the country must be earning at least 15 per cent of export receipts from the exports of the product concerned. Lomé III has extended the Scheme's objectives to include investment for restoring a mining industry's viability or for economic diversification. The list of eligible products comprises copper, bauxite, iron ore, phosphates, manganese and tin.

Criticisms against the Community's Association Scheme have been raised by ACP members and third countries. ACP members argue that the aid provided by the EEC is insufficient and non-increasing in real terms or per head of population. For example: (i) The aid budget for Lomé III represents in real terms little increase over that of Lomé II (ECU 8.5 bn vs. 5.5 billion); (ii) During 1981, claims from the Stabex Fund exceeded available funds, so that drawing rights had to be reduced by 40 per cent in the case of poorer associate states, and by 52 per cent in the case of richer ones. The granting of preferences by the EEC to the ACP countries has been looked upon with distrust and criticism by those countries, mostly Latin American, which were not included in the arrangements. They considered the Association Scheme discriminatory and divisive for the group of less-developed countries. Under pressure from them the United Nations Conference for Trade and Development instituted in 1968 (UNCTAT II) the Generalised Scheme of Preferences (GSP) whereby developed countries give preferential treatment to exports of finished or semi-finished manufactures and processed agricultural products from developing nations. To its credit, the EEC became the first major trading entity in the world to implement the GSP scheme. The beneficiaries of GSP are mostly Latin American and Asian countries which are not EEC associates and therefore they would otherwise have to face the full Common External Tariff.

7.4   TRADE RELATIONS BETWEEN EEC AND EUROPEAN COUNTRIES.

Besides the European Community (EC), two more integration schemes exist in Europe: the European Free Trade Area (EFTA) and the Council for Mutual Economic Assistance (CMEA or COMECON). In this section we examine the trade relations between the EEC and other European countries, members of these organisations.

EFTA began life in 1960 by the Stockholm Convention. Its objective of trade liberalisation in industrial products between the members was virtually completed by December 1966. Agricultural products were excluded from tariff-free trade, and this raised questions about infringement of GATT's Article XXIV. The six EFTA countries are: Austria, Finland, Iceland, Norway, Sweden, and Switzerland. From the original members of EFTA Denmark and the UK left to join the EEC in 1973, and Portugal in 1986.

Proximity and historical ties meant that the Community was by far the principal trade partner of EFTA. As members of the EFTA, Denmark and the UK already had free trade in manufactures with the other member countries. Therefore, when they applied for membership in the EEC, an opportunity was presented for negotiating the reduction of the barriers that divided Western European trade. Given that certain of the EFTA countries (e.g. Sweden, Switzerland, Austria) for political reasons did not want to join the Community, a merger of the two organizations was not considered. It was decided that instead negotiations should start over the future of their mutual trade arrangements. The bilateral agreements between the EEC and each of the EFTA countries were concluded in the early 1970s and put into effect from the date of the first enlargement, 1 January 1973. Collectively, these agreements constitute the establishment of a free-trade area for industrial products throughout Western Europe. The elimination of tariffs on mutual trade was completed in July 1977. Rules of origin have been introduced to prevent *trade deflection* (imports from non-member countries entering the free trade area through a low tariff member), as well as safeguard arrangements permitting countries to introduce special protective measures in case of balance-of-payments crises. Each free-trade agreement is administered by a joint committee, consisting of representatives of the EEC and the relevant EFTA country.

Further integration between the two organisations was envisaged by the Luxembourg Declaration of April 1984, which calls for the creation of a 'dynamic economic space in Western Europe'. This is expected to be achieved by reduction in non-tariff barriers to trade, such as border formalities, harmonisation of standards, improvement in the rules of origin, and application of fair competition rules. However, the tendency towards closer economic cooperation in Western Europe did not receive unqualified approval by the advocates of the multilateral approach to trade liberalisation, who accused the EEC of violation of the GATT by treating differentially the EFTA group of countries from the rest of the non-EEC industrialised world.

The Council for Mutual Economic Assistance (CMEA) was founded in 1949. Among its members are included the following European countries: Bulgaria, Czechoslovakia, the

German Democratic Republic (GDR), Hungary, Poland, Romania, and the USSR. Most of these countries are not members of the GATT. Trade between the CMEA members and between the CMEA and non-member countries is usually conducted by barter on a balanced-trade basis. There has not been any trade agreeement between the EEC and CMEA, among other reasons because the latter does not recognise the EEC as a trading entity, while on the other hand it is the Community that has the power to negotiate and conclude international trade agreeements on behalf of its members. However, after unsuccessful attempts in the 1970s, the two organisations re-opened the dialogue to establish official relations. Two rounds of meetings in 1986 and 1987 have brought progress in the process of *rapprochement* of their negotiating positions and an agreement is expected soon.

In the meanwhile, agreements between the EEC and individual members of the CMEA have been concluded on a year-to-year basis. These include bilateral trade and cooperation agreements with Romania and Czechoslovakia, while negotiations are going on for similar arrangements with Poland and Hungary. In addition, a number of agreements exist between individual EEC and individual CMEA countries. Under the Treaty of Rome special arrangements apply to trade between the Federal Republic of Germany and the German Democratic Republic. The lack of a formal agreement between the USSR and the EEC does not mean that trade between the two does not take place. In fact the USSR is one of the top ten trade partners of the EEC and one of its most important customers for agricultural surpluses, such as butter.

7.5   EEC AND THE MEDITERRANEAN COUNTRIES

After the accession to the Community of Greece, Spain and Portugal, the term Mediterranean countries refers to the following non-member countries of the Mediterranean basin: (1) The Maghreb group: Algeria, Morocco and Tunisia. (2) The Mashreq group: Egypt, Jordan, Lebanon and Syria. (3) Turkey. (4) Israel, Cyprus, Malta and Yugoslavia. Albania and Libya have no trade agreements with the EEC.

For historical, strategic and economic reasons the EEC countries always had close relations with the countries bordering the Mediterranean. Today, approximately 10 per cent of EEC exports are directed to these countries. They in turn sell 50 per cent of their exports to the EEC.

Establishment of the EEC, introduction of the CAP and restrictions on imports of agricultural commodities meant that many of the Mediterranean countries could lose their most important export markets. In an attempt to maintain access to these markets, they asked for special trade relations with the Community. The Community responded favourably, and from early on trade agreements were concluded with individual members of the Mediterranean basin. These agreements were different in legal structure from country to country, some taking the form of association under Article 238 with a view of eventual membership (Greece and Turkey), others aiming at establishment of free-trade areas (Tunisia, Morocco), and others offering only most-favoured-nation (MFN) advantages (Israel, Lebanon).

Since the Mediterranean countries produce and export a broadly similar range of commodities, there was no economic rationale for this multitude of different trade agreements. Some of the countries concerned were in the past protectorates or dependencies of Community members and perhaps one reason for their preferential treatment could have been the historical and political ties. However, the most convincing explanation is that in its relations with neighbouring developing countries, the EEC had not developed coherent plans, the various agreements were uncoordinated and their terms were determined *ad hoc* as they came along with a view to current events and the lobbying activity of individual countries. The final outcome was a 'mosaic' of Mediterranean trade agreements openly contravening the MNF principle of the GATT.

The concept of the EEC's 'Global Mediterranean Policy' was developed in 1971–2, when the Community was preparing for its first enlargement and the Tokyo Round of GATT negotiations for tariff cuts. The Commission proposals, which were presented in September 1972, were based on rational differentiation and envisaged the establishment of a free trade area for industrial products by 1977, with exports of agricultural commodities to the Community based on specific quotas. However, with objections from the southern parts of the EEC, who would have to carry the burden of concessions on the trade of agricultural commodities which they are producing themselves, the negotiations dragged on. Finally, a diluted 'Global Mediterranean Policy' was put into effect only by the end of 1978. The trade agreements are still bilateral between the EEC and each of the Mediterranean countries, and differ substantially in their details. However, the following general principles can be discerned:

(1)　For the Arab Mediterranean countries and Yugoslavia the agreements are based on non-reciprocity, that is on Most-Favoured-Nation terms. For Turkey, Malta, Cyprus and Israel partial reciprocity applies.

(2)　Free access for exports of industrial commodities to the EEC. Exceptions apply to certain sensitive commodities, such as textiles, clothing and refined petroleum for which exports are determined by quota allocation. In general terms the quotas for textiles and clothing are larger under the bilateral agreements than under the restrictions which the EEC would have imposed on the basis of the Multi-Fibre-Arrangements. For the Arab Mediterranean countries the benefit from free access for industrial exports is minimal because their industrial production of exportables is insignificant.

(3)　(a) Agricultural commodities for which the EEC is a producer but has not reached self-sufficiency are exported in quantities determined by licences, quota allocation or tariffs. Off-season supplies are treated more liberally. (b) Agricultural commodities which are not produced on any scale in the EEC are either subject to very low tariffs or have free access to the Community. The clauses concerning agricultural exports are being renegotiated in the light of Spanish and Portuguese accession to the Community.

(4)　Aid in the form of loans from the EIB and technical **cooperation agreement.**

With the exception of the agreement with Yugoslavia, which is limited to five years, all other agreements are unlimited. The agreements with Cyprus and Malta provide for future negotiations for setting up a customs union. The trade and cooperation agreement with Israel provides for the establishment of an industrial free trade area. The agreement with Turkey established a customs union with potential full membership in the Community after the end of a lengthy association period.

7.6 TRADE AGREEMENTS WITH OTHER DEVELOPING COUNTRIES

The Community also has non-preferential agreements with Argentina, Brazil, Mexico, Colombia, Guatemala, Haiti, Uruguay, Bangladesh, India, Pakistan, and Sri Lanka. Under the revised Multi-Fibre-Arrangements (extended to the 31st July 1991), agreements concerning textiles have been concluded with India, Hong Kong, Korea, Pakistan, Thailand, Macao, Malaysia, Singapore, The Philippines, Sri Lanka, Bangladesh and Indonesia. A second five-year (1985–90) trade and cooperation agreement has been negotiated with China. Cooperation agreements have also been concluded between the Community and Yemen AR, and the Andean Group of countries (Bolivia, Colombia, Ecuador, Peru and Venezuela).

7.7 RELATIONS WITH THE USA AND JAPAN

The EEC's trade relations with non-European industrial countries, that is Australia, New Zealand, Japan, South Africa, Canada and the USA, are supposed to be conducted under the GATT rules and regulations. But relations are frequently strained, mostly because of the effects of the CAP on world markets and the discriminatory trade policies of the EEC with non-member countries. Consequently, disagreements occur frequently which are usually resolved by recourse to the multilateral GATT dispute settlement procedure.

The problems created by the impressive rise of Japanese

exports to the Community are rather more difficult to resolve. The Community has frequently disputed the pricing of Japanese exports and in some cases resorted to the use of anti-dumping duties. Japanese firms then reacted by setting up assembly plants in Europe. But a new EC law was specifically set up in June 1987 to stop these 'screwdriver' operations. Accordingly, if the assembly plants have been set up as a result of previous infringement and more than 60 per cent of the finished product consists of components shipped from Japan, penal and anti-dumping duties would apply to the imported components.

Relations with the USA seem to be negatively correlated with the strength of the Dollar in international money markets, improving when the competitiveness of USA improves, and deteriorating when the deficit in the USA balance-of-payments worsens. Over recent years the trade relations between the Community and USA have become very tense on a number of issues relating to both imports and exports of agricultural and industrial products:

Agricultural Trade (1)   The USA objects to the EEC's Common Agricultural Policy on three issues: (1) Protection of the European market which affects USA exports to the Community; (2) CAP policies of subsidised exports which compete with USA production and exports in the markets of third countries; (3) Bilateral agreements of preferential trading with third countries and enlargement of the Community, both of which discriminate against USA exports. On these issues the USA lodged complaints under the GATT concerning many sectors (poultry in 1962, citrus fruit in 1983, pasta in 1983, sugar, poultry meat and flour in 1981, etc.), and retaliated by both levying protective taxes on her imports from the EEC and underbidding EEC export prices by increasing the subsidies to her exporters. The EEC's response is that her policy of subsidies is not different from the open and hidden subsidy policies which the USA government has been following, that the EEC share in the export trade of agricultural commodities is relatively to that of USA very small, and that despite the CAP the EEC is the biggest market in the world for imports of agricultural products (see also chapter 6).

Although in certain cases GATT dispute panels ruled that the EEC's CAP and preferential trade arrangements indeed hurt American interests, the GATT council (which takes decisions on the unanimity principle) rejected the call for further action. When in retaliation the USA set up the Domestic International Sales Corporation (DISC) and the Bonus Incentive Commodity Export Programme (BICEP) which provided subsidies to exports to help them compete with foreign suppliers, it was the turn of the Community to file a complaint with the GATT. A similar procedure was followed by the EEC when the USA imposed restrictions on imports of wine from the Community. Similarly, when objecting to the Community's trade agreements with Mediterranean countries the USA raised its customs duties on imports of pasta products from EEC by up to 40 per cent, the Community retaliated by taking counter-measures affecting imports of citrus fruit from USA. This dispute was settled by an agreement, a key provision of which was that the United States accepted the consistency of the EEC's Mediterranean trade policies with Article XXIV of the GATT. On the whole, this hidden/open trade war is usually contained by mutual threats of actions and counter-actions which lead to a negotiated settlement rather than to escalation and economic sanctions. However, no permanent solution has been contemplated.

The most recent dispute concerns the effects of the latest enlargement of the EEC to Portugal and Spain on USA exports of agricultural and industrial products. Community preferences indicate that intra-Community trade will displace competitive imports from non-members, such as the USA. The problem was particularly important for USA agricultural exports because, first, of a serious crisis in the domestic and exports markets of agricultural commodities, and, second, the Iberian markets for cereals, particularly maize and oilseeds, prior to the enlargement had been dominated by USA suppliers. The dispute reached a peak during 1986, with threats and counter-threats of retaliation and the publication by both USA and EEC of hit lists of commodities which were to be subject to import tariffs of up to 200 per cent. Finally, the dispute was settled on 29th of January 1987, again by a bilateral agreement which provides for a specific volume of cereals to be imported from non-member countries (and this in effect means the USA) in the markets of Portugal and Spain.

Steel (2)   The effects of the current economic recession had particular repercussions on the world demand for steel. The USA and EC steel industry also suffered additional blows from the onslaught of steel exports at competitive prices from Japan and newly industrialising countries, such as Korea, Mexico, India, and Brazil. Under the Davignon Plan, the Community introduced a policy which aimed at capacity reduction and modernisation of the steel industry (see chapter 11). The Plan introduced voluntary agreements on production ceilings and minimum prices, supplemented by a code on state aid in the form of subsidies to producers who would agree to reduce capacity. Imports were also contained by voluntary restraint agreements and import levies. Under USA law, firms which can sustain a claim that their products face competition from subsidised imports have recourse to automatic anti-dumping action in the form of countervailing import duties. These are import tariffs levied against users of export subsidies and are equal to the foreign subsidy, as assessed by the USA authorities. If the injured party can prove that the export subsidies paid have no adverse effect on the economy of the importing country, then the countervailing duties are lifted.

The procedure for levying countervailing duties was invoked in January 1982 by USA steel manufacturers on imports of steel from the Community, which amount to approximately 6 per cent of total USA consumption. The USA official investigation estimated that the Community subsidises steel production by 20–40 per cent, and announced the introduction of appropriate countervailing duties. The Community's reaction was to object to the method used by the official USA investigation which did not distinguish between operating subsidies and grants for modernisation. The two parties agreed to discuss their disputes in an attempt to resolve their differences. However, a problem appeared for the Community side: the Treaty of the European Coal and Steel Community (ECSC) specifies that commercial policy for the products covered by it is exercised by the governments of the member states and not by the Community. Consequently, the ten Community governments first had to agree to joint negotiations with the USA. These negotiations led to the conclusion of a voluntary export restraint (VER) until the end of 1985. A similar dispute broke out in 1983 and in 1984, when the USA announced a restriction on imports of special steels. The Community responded by unilaterally adopting counter-vailing measures against certain American exports and filing a claim for compensation under GATT rules. An agreement was finally reached on the 5th January 1985 which determined a market share of 7.6 per cent for Community products, excluding products the American industry cannot supply.

7.8 CONCLUSIONS

With the implementation of a Common Commercial Policy the Community has become a large economic unit with a unique, and potentially very strong, trading position *vis à vis* all other countries. However, in certain respects the commercial policy of the member states is not as yet fully integrated. Many barriers to trade exist because the member states still have substantially different legal, tax and administrative systems. There is no common commercial policy *vis à vis* CMEA or Japan and, because of conflict between the EEC and the ECSC Treaties, steel is not covered by the Common Commercial Policy. Moreover, within the Community, national non-tariff barriers to trade have not as yet been eliminated nor has harmonisation of taxes been completed. The intra-Community trade in agricultural commodities is still affected by price differentials arising from 'green currencies' and Monetary Compensatory Amounts.

Over the years the Community has concluded a number of agreements with developed and less developed countries. A common characteristic of these agreements is the discrimination which the EEC has introduced in its trade in different commodities, and in trade relations with different countries.

First, the CAP discriminates by restricting trade in agricultural commodities. The declarations of the Treaty of Rome regarding free trade, and the frequently repeated commitment of the Community to an open world trading system apply only to industrial commodities. The CAP constitutes a serious departure from the principles of free trade, causing misallocation of resources in the Community and at a world wide scale.

Second, the agreements which the Community has concluded with different countries are not based on the GATT principles of multilateral trade but on bilateral concessions which discriminate not only between developed and less-developed countries but also within these groups between countries. These agreements have conferred privileges selectively, resulting in a ranking of countries according to their place in the Community's 'pyramid of preferences'. Among the less-developed countries, the ACP associate states are placed higher than the Mediterranean countries which are placed above the non-associate countries of Asia and South America. Among the developed countries, the EFTA group are placed above the non-European industrial countries and the CMEA countries.

However, it can be argued that the lack of a consistent direction in the Common Commercial Policy of the Community is justifiable during a period of economic recession and turbulence in the world economy, when many developed and less-developed countries have started to advocate the doctrine of 'new protectionism'. Moreover, after three enlargements the Community has become a common market of heterogeneous countries which are characterised by divergence in economic performance and domestic economic policies. Therefore, the incomplete state and the contradictions of the Common Commercial Policy should not be unexpected. However, it is not yet clear whether the European Common Commercial Policy will be more or less liberal in the future. The current economic recession has brought a number of problems to the economies of the EC countries which simultaneously face unemployment and contraction in their industries and loss of competitiveness in international markets.

An approach for solving these problems advocated by some members is to combine liberalisation of the internal market with a common industrial policy based on protection from foreign competition. The argument of the proponents of these measures is that the European industry has fallen so far behind the USA, Japanese and newly industrialising countries' industry that only protection can revive it. Protection is also needed for the establishment of advanced-technology industries on infant industry grounds (Richonnier, 1984). These arguments have found more favour among experts and officials responsible for the industry rather than foreign trade. But whether neo-protectionist arguments will prevail and the European Community will become generally or selectively more protectionist in international trade, is a matter for conjecture.

REFERENCES

Barnes, W. G. (1967) *Europe and the Developing World*, PEP European Series No. 2, Chatham House, London.

EC (1979), *25 Years of European Community External Relations*, European Documentation, Luxembourg.

EC (1984), *Opinion to the Council and the Commission on the Issue of Protectionism*, Economic Policy Committee, No. 19.

EC (1985), *The European Community and the Mediterranean*, European Documentation, Luxembourg.

EC Commission (1984), *Agriculture in the United States and the European Community: a Comparison*, Agricultural Information Service of the Directorate General of Information, No. 200.

General Agreement on Tariffs and Trade (1972), *GATT Activities in 1970/71*, Geneva.

General Agreement on Tariffs and Trade (1982), *GATT: What It Is; What It Does*, Geneva.

Hine, R. C. (1985), *The Political Economy of European Trade*, Wheatsheaf Books, Brighton.

Long, O. (1985), *Law and Its Limitations in the GATT Multilateral Trade System*, Martinus Nijhoff Publishers, Dordrecht.

Paarlberg, R. L. (1986), 'Responding to the CAP: Alternative Strategies for the United States', *Food Policy*, pp. 157–73.

Richonnier, M. (1984), 'Europe: Decline is not Irreversible', *Journal of Common Market Studies*, XXII, pp. 227–43.

Shlaim, A. and Yannopoulos, G. N. (eds) (1976), *The EEC and the Mediterranean World*, Cambridge University Press, London.

8 Regional Policy

8.1 THE NATURE OF REGIONAL PROBLEMS

Regional problems are the disparities in the levels of income, rates of growth of output and employment, and in general in levels of economic inequality between the geographic regions of a country. They arise from unequal growth rates of economic activity. Higher income areas are invariably those where the centres of population, government and industry are to be found.

According to the neoclassical theory of regional development, free competition and factor mobility will tend to equalise factor returns across regions within a state and therefore regional differences in economic development cannot be sustained. However, in practice the conditions of the neoclassical theory are not always fulfilled. For instance, capital and labour may not be completely mobile and persistent disparities among regions may exist in production functions, economies and diseconomies of scale, and obstacles to the market mechanism. Consequently, it is possible that the process of development may tend to favour certain regions within a country by a cumulative gravitation mechanism. Thus, new industry and trade will be attracted where industry and trade already exist, and the necessary infrastructure, associated services and the market for selling output are relatively more readily available than in other areas.

This gravitation process leads to the phenomenon of intra-country polarisation, by which areas which are relatively developed continue to grow fast, while the relatively backward areas experience cumulative economic decline. Regional growth thus tends to be concentrated in 'poles of development', that is in geographic areas that provide new investment with economies of scale, thus making possible for them to gain an initial headstart and to continue to grow at the expense of other regions of the economy. These scale economies are both external and internal, and are usually specified as economies of localisation and economies of urbanisation. Economies of localisation arise from the geographic concentration of plants in the same industry and the advantages gained by linkages between them and the potential for increased efficiency through specialisation. Urbanisation, or agglomeration, economies arise from the geographic concentration of a large number of economic activities served jointly by different facilities, such as transportation, availability of a skilled labour force, financial institutions, proximity of markets for their output, etc. Polarisation causes a vicious spiral of economic growth which may assist the relatively more developed regions in a country to grow at the expense of the less developed regions. Hence, the regional problems are both causes and effects of the problems of unbalanced growth within the borders of a country.

Regional inequalities have economic and social implications and costs. The extensive trade and factor movement links between the regions of a country entail that the economic problems of the regions tend to be transmitted into other regions, and to affect the overall economic activity of the country. Regional unemployment, economic imbalances and inequity, and excessive concentration of residential, industrial and commercial activity in major conurbations cause severe costs to society. Hence, policies are introduced to deal with them.

Regional policy at the national level attempts to reduce the socio-economic disparities between regions. It is based on the principle that market forces cannot be relied upon to produce the necessary degrees of interregional balance in economic growth. This economic argument in support of regional policies is always supplemented by political and social considerations. The political argument asserts the importance of equity as an essential element in the cohesion between the regions of a country. The social argument stresses that, if the national economy grows, all citizens wherever they happen to live and work within the country, should be provided with a reasonable share of the country's increasing prosperity.

8.2   REGIONAL PROBLEMS WITHIN ECONOMIC UNIONS

Once the process of economic integration is in progress, it is likely that already existing problems of regional disparities will intensify. The reasons for this are two.

(1) Labour productivity and wage differentials between independent states are taken care of by adjustments in foreign exchange rates which restore export competitiveness. In effect, foreign exchange policies provide the depressed areas with a measure of protection by reducing domestic prices, and hence real wages, relative to foreign prices. But, with economic integration, free trade, enhanced competition and freer mobility of factors of production will tend to equalise commodity and factor prices (wages, rent of capital, etc.) between the participating states. However, productivity differentials will continue to exist and they will favour the technologically advanced firms of the developed areas within the economic union. With progressive integration of monetary policy and, at a later stage, monetary unification, the low productivity regions will no longer be protected by exchange rate adjustments. At the same time regional money wage differentials will tend to be eliminated and therefore the low productivity regions will face progressive comparative disadvantage.

(2) Economic integration may encourage concentration of new industry and relocation of existing industry in certain areas of the economic union which afford superior infrastructure, lower transport costs and availability of skilled labour. With enlargement of the market and enhanced competition, the most efficient enterprises will expand by the integration process, while the less efficient will contract or even be driven out of the market. It is not uncommon that the

enterprises at the periphery are on the whole less efficient, with lower productivity than those at the developed centre. Therefore, economic activity at the periphery of the economic union will be affected negatively and disproportionately from the effects of integration.

As a consequence of (1) and (2) above, the rates of growth in the developed centres will be higher than those in the less developed regions of the economic union. Different rates of growth will in turn induce a substantial degree of geographic relocation of industry and migration of capital and labour from the underdeveloped periphery to the developing centres. Peripheral regions, which before integration relied for their growth on small scale production units, may become unable to reach the scale advantages of integration or to face the competition with large industry. Thus with progressing economic integration, the economic and social life of the underdeveloped regions will tend to lag behind the growth levels of the developed regions. This is not a remote theoretical possibility. Actual cases of the decline of regions after (economic and political) integration abound, as for example the economic decline of Southern Italy after the unification of the Italian States in the 1860s.

The question then is, if economic integration tends to accentuate regional problems, whose task should it be to take appropriate policy measures to redress the decline of the regions?

During the process of integration regional economic problems undergo changes in dimensions and severity. Economic integration tends to exacerbate regional inequalities and to induce tendencies for polarisation at the larger scale of the economic union. It internationalises the problem of regional inequality by adding to the already existing trends of national regional inequality the more powerful gravitation of the developed centres of the economic union which can very well be outside the borders of the country. Hence areas which were considered relatively prosperous before integration, may turn into backward regions of the economic union. Obviously, this aspect of integration is not conducive to the furtherance of economic and political cohesion within the economic union. Therefore, under economic integration the purely national regional economic problem of the member states is transformed into a community problem. Regional inequality thus becomes the subject of a common regional policy.

This is necessary, among other reasons because many of the policies which a member country will be advised to adopt for its regional problem may already be incompatible with the integration agreement or ineffective under the increased interdependence between the members of the economic union. For example, subsidisation, differential taxation, the granting of development grants, and other similar instruments of national regional policies operate in principle against the unification of the market and are incompatible with competition, the free market and the convergence of intra-union economic policy. National regional economic policies, which might had been effective for ameliorating regional disparities at the national level, may become ineffective within the integrating area, while at the same time the regional problems are exacerbated by structural changes brought about by the economic integration. A possible way out from this conundrum would be to respond collectively to the regional problems by integrating the regional economic policies. The effectiveness of national policies can be restored by coordination at the level of the economic union or by the inauguration of common regional policies aiming at a common objective. As a first step towards this direction, the regional economic policy of the member states should be supplemented by union regional policies.

In conclusion, coordination and ultimately integration of regional economic policy at the level of the economic union is required in order to ensure that:

(1) The national regional economic problems of the member states are not aggravated by the dynamic process of integration.

(2) The policies undertaken with regard to regional economic development are equitable between the members and compatible with the integration agreement.

(3) The costs and benefits of integration are properly shared between the member countries and the regions of the economic union as a whole.

8.3 REGIONAL PROBLEMS IN THE EC

Regional disparities exist in every country of the EC, although the regional problem differs between countries in nature and intensity. In general, four main types of regional problems are found in the Community: (1) Rural underdevelopment; (2) Industrial decline; (3) Congested cities; and (4) Frontier regions.

Underdeveloped rural areas (1) depend primarily on agriculture for both employment and production. But farming in these areas is usually based on very small holdings of relatively infertile land, with low capitalisation and application of technology, low productivity, low participation rate, and high incidence of disguised unemployment. Therefore these areas lag behind the more prosperous areas in both income and employment.

Farming areas in developed countries also suffer from regional problems. But in contrast to the case of over-dependence on uneconomic agriculture, the problems of these agricultural areas have come about from the application of modern technology, which led to fast increase in productivity causing rapid decline in the employment of labour. Over the post-war years the reduction of labour employment in agriculture has been pronounced in every European country, both developing and developed. This has forced rural labour to seek employment in other occupations and other locations. Large scale migration has occurred from rural areas to developing industrial and urban centres, both domestic and foreign. However, the decline in agricultural employment: (i) has not spread evenly among the regions of every country, and (ii) has tended to encourage the migration of the relatively employable younger section of the population, with the consequence that those who were left behind were the older and the less productive. Moreover, in the less developed European countries, neither the expansion of employment in urban sectors and industrial regions has been sufficient to offset the decline in agricultural employment nor has the released agricultural labour had always had the necessary skills to be easily employable in other occupations. Hence, despite the outflow from the problem regions, surplus labour and chronic unemployment still exist.

Such problem areas abound at the periphery of the European Community, the west of Ireland and the southern member countries, Portugal, Spain, Italy and Greece. Similar but less severe problems are found in regions of the more developed member countries (North Netherlands, Western France, South Belgium) but in most cases expanding alternative opportunities have kept the unemployment rate at bay. In general, over the 1960s the dispersion of income and unemployment among the regions of countries tended to decline by the migration of labour. But since the early 1970s the gap between the prosperous and declining regions has either increased (Italy, Spain) owing to the general economic recession and the upward shift in unemployment at the national level, or, at best, it has remained static. In certain areas the problem has recently been accentuated by the current recession which in some cases has caused reverse migration, the return of unemployed migrants from the urban centres to the rural areas of their origin where they swell the numbers of regional unemployment.

Decline of existing basic industries (2)   located in certain areas within a country is experienced, while wage levels have remained relatively rigid. Hence problem areas have emerged which still are predominantly industrial but face increasing unemployment and de-industrialisation (southern and eastern Belgium, Ruhr and Saar in Germany, northern and eastern France, and in the United Kingdom: west-central Scotland, South Wales, north and north-west England and Northern Ireland).

For historical and economic reasons certain industries (e.g. textiles, steel, coal, shipyards, etc.) have been concentrated in the same area over long periods of time. But, in recent years, shifts in technology, decreasing demand for output, and increasing international competition have led to a declining demand for labour and the emergence of severe regional unemployment. These problems have been aggravated by the ongoing recession. In a way, the problems of these industrial regions are structural. The existing industry is under threat because of rising costs associated with near exhaustion of stocks (such as coal), the emergence of more competitive

reasons for decline

alternative sources of domestic supply, and the increasing competition from imports originating in newly industrialising, low labour-cost countries (NIC, such as Korea, Hong Kong, etc.). Moreover, while in these declining regions the existing infrastructure seems to be adequate for the development of alternative industry, the new industry tends to be located nearer to demand centres and away from traditional industrial poles. Therefore, industrial change and renovation which would have kept these areas prosperous has not happened and it seems that it will never happen by market forces alone. The uncontrolled expansion of the past and the current industrial decline combined to produce only environmental degradation and desolation. The introduction of labour saving technology and the overall problem of economic recession mean that the industrial decline of these regions cannot be compensated by the growth of new industry, which is unable to absorb the available labour surplus.

Regional imbalance (3) means that within the same country regions of excess supply of labour may coexist with regions experiencing excess demand for labour. The latter, which are called 'pressured' or 'congested' regions, display the reverse characteristics of those found in backward rural areas and areas of industrial decline. In contrast to the underdeveloped regions, the congested areas offer a very high degree of agglomeration economies which are causing excess concentration of capital, labour and industrial production to the detriment of the declining areas. This concentration of economic activity is considered excessive, because it combines the social benefit of increased economic activity with rising social costs associated with overpopulation, congestion, pollution, noise and other urban problems. These problems are a manifestation of market failure arising from interdependence, negative externalities and the divergence between private (firms) and social (public) optimum. Market failure due to externalities leads to misallocation of resources and welfare waste. A degree of optimality can be restored only by government intervention in the form of regional policy. In many cases, the benefits from high growth rates of income and employment in highly industrialised congested conurbations coexist with inner-city decay and pockets of poverty, general decline in the environment, and deterioriation of the quality of life.

Major conurbations in both the developed and the less developed members of the Community attract very large proportions of the population and of economic activity. The Paris region, which is just 2 per cent of French territory, contains 20 per cent of the population and 23 per cent of the total employment, and produces 30 per cent of the national output. The Randstad region in the Netherlands which has four major centres (Amsterdam-Utrecht-Rotterdam-The Hague) comprises 46 per cent of the national population. London and the South-East region of England are only 12 per cent of the national territory and comprise 30 per cent of the population. Similar congested regions are the Rhine area of the FR of Germany, greater Copenhagen, Glasgow and Liverpool, and in the Mediterranean countries, Greater Athens, Naples, Barcelona and many more.

The regional problem of the congested areas consists of: (a) How to divert activity away from them in order to reduce congestion and stimulate growth through renewal of the existing industry; and (b) How to stimulate enough growth in other regions to attract economic activity from the congested regions.

Frontier areas. (4)   As a result of reduction of barriers to trade and factor movement, regions across the internal frontiers of the Community face a re-orientation of their economic activity resulting from changes in their comparative advantage. They will develop closer economic links, trade and factor movement with regions of neighbouring member states and in the process some of them will benefit while others will lose. On the whole, regions across internal frontiers are handicapped by inadequate cross border infrastructure associated with the historical separation of national states. In this case, regional policy is required to promote the necessary infrastructure and to encourage the border regions to exploit the opportunities offered by integration. In contrast to the internal border regions, a different kind of problem arises from the external border regions of member states, and therefore of the Community. These are the geographically peripheral regions for which economic integration may induce reorientation of trade from their natural outlets in neighbouring states to other regions within the common market (e.g. the Zonenrandgebiet along the West German/East German border). Regional policy in such cases attempts to protect and cushion the impact of integration on the economies of these border regions.

8.4 REGIONAL ECONOMIC POLICY OF THE EC

The Treaty of Rome does not specifically deal with regional economic problems, though in the Preamble it does mention the need to reduce regional disparities. References to regional problems are also found in the Articles dealing with the European Investment Bank (EIB) which is authorised to grant loans for 'projects for developing less developed regions' (Article 130), the Common Agricultural Policy (Article 49) and the European Social Fund (Article 125). In practice, the Community from early on recognised that the problem of regional disparities between the richest and the poorest areas threatened to disrupt the convergence of economic performance inside the EC and to delay the progress towards integration. Many areas, particularly in the south of Italy and France, lagged well behind the average level of European income and displayed the characteristics of rural unemployment and outward migration from subsistence farming. Other areas in the industrial north suffered inner city degradation and industrial decline.

From the start, it was acknowledged that the process of integration could itself accentuate the regional problems of some areas as the Community's competition rules promoted freer trade and factor mobility. During the 1960s the range of economic disparity between the regions of the Community narrowed somewhat. Hence, when in 1969 the Commission submitted its first set of proposals for the introduction of a common regional policy, the Council took no action. It was envisaged that the regional problem was a subject of national policy, and that growth and the positive impact of economic integration on the general prosperity of the Community would assist in bridging the gap between developed and less developed regions by national regional policy.

It was also expected that various Community funds and common policies which, though not exclusively regional, had been designed to function with regional problems among their objectives, would have a positive impact on the development of the regions. Institutions and funds, such as the *European Coal and Steel Community (ECSC)*, the *European Investment Bank (EIB)*, and the *European Social Fund (ESF)*, finance regional projects for modernisation of the industry, investment for job-creation, and training and retraining schemes in problem regions. The Common Agricultural Policy also has regional implications, positive and negative: the *Guidance Section* of the *European Agricultural Fund* (EAGGF) aims at restructuring and modernisation of agriculture, and can be considered as an instrument of regional policy; but on the other hand the Guarantee section of the EAGGF (a) pays out vast amounts in support of agricultural production in rural areas which are not backward regions of subsistence agriculture, and (b) takes up the largest share out of the Community Budget, so that there is not much left for use by other common policies, including the regional policy.

Regional policies usually take the following forms; 1) Government assistance for investment in new and existing industry which is expected to help solve problems such as regional unemployment, decentralisation, slow growth, etc. The assistance provided consists of outright grants, special depreciation provisions, tax allowances, cheap loans for investment, and so on; 2) Public expenditure on infrastructure, roads, ports, housing etc; 3) General subsidies to reduce the cost of production, such as subsidies to the use of labour which encourage adoption of labour intensive techniques contributing to the reduction of unemployment; 4) Negative inducements, such as controls over industrial location in an attempt to deter industry from concentrating in prosperous areas or areas of high congestion, etc.

Obviously, if the members of a common market follow different subsidy policies, and in general have different degrees of government intervention in regional policy, the outcome will be unfair competition. In the EEC, state aid which destroys competition is incompatible with the Treaty of Rome, but a special dispensation is provided for 'aid intended to promote the economic development of regions where the standard of living is abnormally low, or where there exists serious under-employment' (Article 92). This means that member states' plans for regional development require Community approval and, therefore, national regional policies are *a priori* subject to harmonisation.

After prolonged negotiations the Community moved, in October 1971, towards adopting a set of general principles which were to apply at the level of national regional aid schemes. These principles were that: a) There should be an upper limit of permissive investment aid for the development of the regions; b) All aid should be 'transparent', so that its extent could be easily calculated; c) Regional aid should be region-specific and must not cover the entire national territory.

Although agreement on these issues provided some degree of uniformity among the members in the exercise of regional policies, it did not in itself constitute the inauguration of a common regional policy. But, from the beginning of the 1970s with the prospect of enlargement to nine members, two of which suffered from chronic regional disparities (UK and IRL), the problems of the regions could no longer be ignored. At the Paris Summit of 1972 it was agreed that the Commission should report on the regional problems of the Community, taking into account the forthcoming accession of three new members. It was also agreed that a special fund should be established, the European Regional Development Fund (ERDF), to assist financially the development of the regions. The *Report on the Regional Problems of the Enlarged Community* (the Thomson Report) was published in 1973. Under the assumption that the Community regional problem is the aggregate of the regional problems of the member states, the Report recommended that the common policy should be one of coordination of the member states' national regional policies and of common policies with a regional impact, rather than of direct intervention by a Community regional policy.

Within a few months from the publication of the Report the first oil crisis necessitated revision of the members' and the Community's expectations of economic growth. With the recession deepening, unemployment started rising and the disparities among regions were aggravated. It then became clear that the recession would obstruct and delay the convergence of members' economic performance, and that under the prevailing conditions progress towards integration would require a different and more active regional policy at the level of the Community.

The European Regional Development Fund (ERDF) was finally set up in March 1975 under Article 235 of the Treaty, and started operating in the same year. Its initial allocation was only 960 million EUA for 1975–7, much smaller than the 3000 million EUA proposed to Council by the Commission. The Regional Policy Committee, a consultative body composed of senior policy officials of the member governments and the Commission, was also set up to advise the Commission on research programmes and general intercountry coordination in the regional development field.

From the start, problems were encountered with the definition of a region and the eligibility of regions for financial assistance and grants for development. Evidently, the relative terms 'developed region' and 'less developed region' are defined with reference to a single member state. In contrast, the Community regional problem has to be defined by interregional comparisons at the international setting of the EC, and therefore it is not identical with the sum of the regional problems of the member states. For example, within Germany there are more and less prosperous regions which give rise to a national regional problem, but in the Community context the less prosperous regions of Germany are actually better off than many of the prosperous areas in other member states. The 1973 Report used the regional subdivisions existing in each member state as the basis for analysing the Community regional problem. Two types of regions were recognised: Level I are those regions which are subject to European regional policy. Level II are smaller regions which constitute basic administrative areas within member states. The same classification of regions is in use today: the Community of 12 member states has 64 Level I regions (Table 8.1) subdivided into a number of Level II regions (e.g., the UK has 11 Level I and no Level II regions; Denmark constitutes one Level I region comprising 3 Level II regions).

Eventually, the member states settled for a political

compromise rather than for radical solutions to the regional problem. The Fund was to function as an instrument of the Community designed to help the efforts of national governments to assist the development of their problem regions. It was decided that eligible for assistance were the regions where: (i) The GDP is consistently below the national average; (ii) There is above-average dependence on agriculture or on a declining industry; (iii) There is a consistently high rate of unemployment or net migration; (iv) Community policies, in particular free trade, had an adverse effect. It was also agreed that the disbursement of funds from the ERDF would be based on national quotas which would take account of the relative gravity of each country's regional problem. Although this arrangement was changed in 1979 by dividing the Fund in two sections, 95 per cent of it continued to operate under the national quota system. This meant that in effect the ERDF had no say in the choice of regions deserving financing; this was decided by the government of each member state. The Fund would finance expenditure directed towards improvements in transport and telecommunications, water and electricity supplies, the building of industrial estates and the development of social services. It is worth observing that from the amounts committed by the ERDF from 1975 to 1985 Italy received 37 per cent and the United Kingdom 24 per cent (*Bulletin EC* 12–1985).

Under the original Regulation establishing the Fund, the Commission was required to review its activities and to produce proposals for the future of regional policy after the initial three-year period. Following proposals made by the Commission, in May 1984 the Council adopted a Regulation reforming the European regional policy and the Fund and introducing provisions for integrated operations and coordination of national regional policies. The Regulation specifies that the common regional policy will consist of three elements: (1) Periodic analysis of the socio-economic situation of the regions; (2) Coordination of national regional policies; and (3) Assessment of the regional impact of all major policies. The Community shall support the achievement of the objectives of regional policy by the action it takes through the structural Funds. The ERDF in particular 'is intended to help redress the principal regional imbalances in the Community through participating in the development and structural adjustment of regions whose development is lagging, and in reconversion of declining industrial regions' (*Bulletin EC* 11–1985). Since 1985, all the resources of the 'new' European Regional Development Fund (new ERDF) are allocated on the basis of 'ranges', that is a minimum and a maximum for each member state. In contrast to the old system of national 'quotas' which the member states effectively regarded as 'drawing rights' which they could use to replace sums they would otherwise have provided themselves to their regions, under the new system the requests for funding must conform to common specific criteria and are not satisfied automatically. Therefore, the lower limit of the 'range' is not a 'guaranteed' minimum of finance from the Fund. With the accession to the Community of Spain and Portugal, the new ERDF 'ranges' have been defined as follows:

Belgium	0.61 to 0.82%	Ireland	3.81 to 4.61%
Denmark	0.34 to 0.46%	Italy	21.59 to 28.79%
Germany	2.55 to 3.40%	Luxembourg	0.04 to 0.06%
Spain	17.95 to 23.93%	Netherlands	0.68 to 0.91%
Greece	8.35 to 10.64%	Portugal	10.65 to 14.20%
France	7.47 to 9.96%	United Kingdom	14.48 to 19.31%

These 'ranges' apply for a three year period. The total of all the minima equals 88.5 per cent, which means that the Commission now has at its disposal at maximum 11.5 per cent of the ERDF finances available for regional development. In general, the Regional Fund helps to finance Community programmes, national programmes of Community interest, projects and studies, by providing supplementary aid to that allocated by a member state for the development of beneficiary regions. The rates of Regional Fund assistance are 50 to 55 per cent of the total expenditure. Community programmes concern the territory of more than one member state, e.g. inter-country infrastructure. The priority areas within a country are still nationally defined, but the member states undertake to communicate to the Commission their regional development programmes and to report on the progress of their implementation. National programmes are eligible for financial assistance from the Community if they serve national and Community objectives and policies. In principle, aim of the ERDF is to make the sum available for investment in the regions larger by supplementing the regional development expenditures of the member states.

Along with the reform of the ERDF, the Council also considered the regional implications of the structural Funds, and decided to improve their allocation by coordinating their activities in the form of Integrated Operations. These consist of a number of investment projects in a region of a member state which are financed on a complementary basis by national and local authorities and the Community.

Among the Community instruments for regional development are also included the Integrated Mediterranean Programmes (IMPs). These are limited duration projects designed to assist the disadvantaged regions of Greece, Southern France and Italy to cope with the consequences of the latest enlargement of the Community to Portugal and Spain. The IMPs were launched in 1985 for a six year period, but the Commission has proposed that they should become a fourth 'structural fund' (in addition to ERDF, ESF, and EAGGF), for advancing the development of the weaker regions. The accession to the Community of Portugal and Spain increased the number of poor agricultural regions, which are located in the southern members, and placed further demands on the ERDF.

Table 8.1 shows in very broad lines the extent of the regional problem of EC-12 at the Level I classification of the regions. The disparities within and between countries are very substantial. Germany, Denmark, France and Luxembourg have no regions with GDP per head below the EC average. Greece, Ireland, Portugal and Spain have no regions with GDP per head above the EC average. Of the remaining four countries, Belgium, the Netherlands and the United Kingdom have national average GDP per head above the EC average, but some of their regions lag behind the EC average. Italy has national average lower than the EC, with some regions above and some below the Community average. In general, 43 per cent of the EC population live in regions which display average GDP per head below the Community average. The poorest

Table 8.1: Main Regional Indicators

Country	Main Regions	Unemployment % (1985) Total	Unemployment % (1985) Highest	Unemployment % (1985) Lowest	GDP per head index (1983) Total	GDP per head index (1983) Highest	GDP per head index (1983) Lowest	Population[1]
B	3	11.3	13.2	10.1	105	164	87	67
DK	1	7.9	–	–	142	–	–	100
D	11	7.3	12.7	4.2	138	230	115	100
E	7	21.9	29.1	14.5	54	64	42	0
F	8	9.9	13.1	7.5	122	175	101	100
GR	3	7.8	9.1	4.3	46	48	42	0
IRL	1	18.3	–	–	67	–	–	0
I	11	9.2	19.3	6.2	80	103	56	22
L	1	3.0	–	–	120	–	–	100
NL	4	10.3	12.0	9.3	119	157	98	80
P	3	8.6	:	:	28	:	:	0
UK	11	10.7	16.7	7.8	104	118	85	56
EC–12	64	10.6	29.1	4.2	100	230	28	43

Notes: [1] Per cent of total population in regions with GDP per head above EC average.
       : not available

Source: Eurostat, *Regions, Statistical Yearbook, 1986*, and *Basic Statistics of the Community*, 24 ed., Luxembourg, 1987.

member country is Portugal with average GDP per head
(equal to 28 per cent of the EC average) 202 percentage points
below the regional highest (Hambourg in Germany with 230
per cent of the EC average).

8.5 EVALUATION

The Community's commitment to a more active regional
policy as the means for promoting economic convergence for
the development of the internal market has been repeated once
again in the agreement reached at the Luxembourg Summit
(December 1985) which states: 'In order to promote its
harmonious development overall, the Community shall
develop and pursue its actions leading to strengthening its
economic and social cohesion. In particular, the Community
shall aim at reducing disparities between the various regions
and the backwardness of the least favoured regions.' But,
despite all these very promising declarations, the Community's
regional policy remains inefficient and weak. This results, first,
from the fact that the Community regional policy has to
function as a supplement of the national regional policies of
the member states; and, second, from the relatively small
financial resources allocated by the Community to the
common regional policy. Under the national quota system,
these resources were not only small but also widely dispersed,
so that their impact was insignificant: in the eleven years of its
existence (1975–86) the ERDF committed the sum of ECU 14
billion, spread over some 25,000 projects in ten countries. With
the limited resources available for an effective common policy
for regional development, concentration of expenditure would
have had a larger impact.

Table 8.2 presents the 1983 distribution of grants for
structural purposes. The total sum from every source of
finance amounts to 5122 million ECUs, that is approximately
0.2 per cent of EC–10's current GDP. Expenditure under the
Regional Fund amounted in 1985 to 5.7 per cent of the
Community budget, or approximately 0.05 per cent of EC–
10's GDP. Clearly, the sums involved are small in every
respect, and in particular, relative to the expenditure needed

Table 8.2: *Distribution of Grants for Structural Purposes, 1983 (in million ECU)*

Country	Agricultural Fund (EAGGF)	Social Fund	Regional Fund	European Coal & Steel Comm.	Total	Per cent
B	16.0	32.7	8.9	10.9	68.5	1.3
DK	21.1	42.1	22.4	1.6	87.2	1.7
D(a)	113.0	110.6	43.8	53.0	320.4	6.3
F	186.6	277.6	285.4	10.8	760.4	14.8
GR	85.1	114.0	355.4	–	554.5	10.8
IRl	101.4	182.0	106.5	0.1	390.0	7.6
I	232.4	534.0	818.9	2.0	1587.3	31.0
L	1.5	0.9	0.0	0.2	2.6	0.1
NL	29.3	24.2	20.1	1.2	74.8	1.5
UK(a)	157.3	558.0	459.9	101.2	1276.4	24.9
EC-10	973.7	1876.1	2121.2	181.0	5122.0	100.0

Note: (a) Excluding special and supplementary measures.

Source: EC (1985) *Grants and Loans from the European Community*, European Documentation, Luxembourg.

for an effective common regional economic policy: the macroeconomic impact of such small amounts is bound to be insignificant. The membership of Spain and Portugal brought to the Community more regional problems, without provision for an equiproportional expansion in resources, and aggravated the north-south tensions. Both countries have serious regional problems of their own, Portugal in particular has a very low standard of living. On equity considerations, both countries qualify for Community assistance to regions dependent on declining industry or agriculture and for investment in infrastructure. Before Spain and Portugal joined the Community, one European in eight had an annual income 30 per cent or more below the Community average the figure in 1987 is one in five (EC, 1987).

Completion of the single internal market renders inevitable that 'resources, both of people and materials, and of capital and investment, flow into areas of greatest economic advantage' (EC Commission, 1985). This means that, unless appropriate measures are taken at the national and the Community levels, either the internal market will not be completed according to schedules or the regional problem will worsen. Unless the regional policy of the Community changes, the limited funds of the ERDF, as shared among 12 member countries, will not be sufficient even for alleviation of that component of the regional problem which has arisen from the process of integration, with the implication that the disparity between the richer and poorer regions of the EC will widen. This would mean that convergence of economic policy and performance, which is an essential adjunct to the development of the internal market, will not occur, to the detriment of European unity.

REFERENCES

Armstrong, H. W. (1985), 'The Reform of the European Community Regional Policy', *Journal of Common Market Studies*, 23, pp. 319–43.
Armstrong, H. and Taylor, J., (1985), *Regional Economics and Policy*, Philip Allan, Oxford.

EC Commission (1969), *A Regional Policy for the Community*, Brussels.

EC (1973), *Report on the Regional Problems in the Enlarged Community*, (73) 550, (Thomson Report), Brussels.

EC (1985), *Grants and Loans from the European Community*, European Documentation, Luxembourg.

EC Commission (1985), *Completing the Internal Market*, Document, Luxembourg.

EC (1987), 'The Single Act: A New Frontier', *Bull. EC.,* Supplement 1.

McCrone, G. (1969), 'Regional Policy in the European Communities', in Denton, G. R. (ed.), *Economic Integration in Europe*, London Weidenfeld and Nicolson, London.

Vanhove, N. and Klaassen, L. H. (1980), *Regional Policy: a European Approach*, Gower, Farnborough.

Yuill, D., Allen, K. and Hull, C., (eds), (1980) *Regional Policy in the European Community*, Croom Helm, London.

9 Social Policy

9.1 INTRODUCTION

The Treaties of the three communities comprising the European Community refer to social policy. The ECSC Treaty includes provisions on wages and mobility of workers in the coal and steel industry. The Euratom Treaty deals with the health and safety of workers in the atomic energy industry. But the most comprehensive reference to social policy is provided in the EEC Treaty: Part Three, Title III (Articles 117–28) of the Treaty of Rome is devoted exclusively to social provisions. Among the objectives outlined in the EEC Treaty are:

(1)   The improvement in the living and working conditions of workers (Article 117).

(2)   Close collaboration between the member states in matters relating to employment, labour law and working conditions, vocational training, social security, prevention of occupational accidents and diseases, occupational hygiene, and the rights of association and collective bargaining (Article 118).

(3)   The introduction of equal remuneration for the same work between men and women (Article 119).

(4)   The establishment of a European Social Fund to promote employment opportunities and labour mobility between professions and countries of the Community (Articles 123–8).

In addition to this specific section, Article 104 of the EEC

Treaty states that the maintenance of a high level of employment is one of the prime economic objectives of the Community.

The references above show clearly that the relevant section of the EEC Treaty, 'without prejudice to other provisions of this Treaty', identifies social policy with issues most relating to the employment of labour. Some more general provisions are found in Articles 48–66 which deal with the commitment to achieve within the Community free movement of labour with guaranteed eligibility for social security benefits (Article 48–51), the right of establishment (Articles 52–8), and the freedom to provide services (Articles 58–66). In practice, the Community coverage of social policy has been widened by subsequent legislation and policy action in a number of other fields, but it still is much narrower than the social policy of member states. Some observers define as Community social policy the work that is carried out by the Directorate-General for Employment and Social Affairs (D-G V) which, in addition to the specifications of Article 118, includes among its terms of reference general social policy guidelines, the migrant workers, the employment of handicapped persons, and the

Table 9.1: *Social Security Expenditures as a Percentage of Gross Domestic Product*

Country	1970	1975	1980	1983
B	18.5	24.2	28.1	30.9
DK	19.6	26.9	29.7	30.6
D	21.4	29.7	28.6	29.1
F	19.2	22.9	25.9	29.0
IRL	13.2	19.7	20.6	23.9
I	18.4	22.6	22.8	27.1
L	16.4	22.4	26.4	26.5
NL	20.8	26.7	30.4	33.9
UK	15.9	20.1	21.4	23.8
EC–9 (Means)	(18.2)	(23.9)	(26.0)	(28.3)
(s.d.)	(2.6)	(3.3)	(3.6)	(3.3)

Notes: s.d. = standard deviation.

Sources: Eurostat, *Social Protection Statistics*, 1970–80.
            Basic Statistics of the Community, 24th ed., 1987.

European Social Fund. Some of these areas have been regarded as marginal, and more appropriate for consideration by the social policy of the member countries, while others have received more attention by the Community.

The common social policy is part of a coordinated Community approach which also includes economic, industrial and regional policies. Besides the general interest for improved social conditions which 'will ensue not only from the functioning of the common market ... but also from the procedures provided for in this Treaty' (Article 117), an objective of the Community is the harmonisation of social policy among the member states. Given that the member states for a number of ideological, political, economic and institutional reasons had given different priorities as to who and to what extent should be covered by social policy, and what share of the national expenditure should be directed to it, the differences among the members are very significant. If these differences remain unharmonised, they may cause serious distortions in the pattern of competition and resource allocation within the common market.

Table 9.1 presents as an example the social security expenditures as a ratio of national income (GDP) for the Community as a whole, and for each of the EC-9 member countries. The figures reveal that over recent years these ratios have been rising very fast in every country. This increase was caused by expansion of both the coverage of state social security programmes and the eligible (beneficiary) population, as a consequence of growth in state care and in the problems brought about by the contemporary economic recession. In 1983 the ratio of social security expenditure on GDP for the Community as a whole was 28.3 per cent, with Netherlands at the top of the table (33.9 per cent), UK at the bottom (23.9 per cent), and dispersion among the member states higher than in 1975 (standard deviation 3.3 against 2.6). After enlargement of the Community to 12 members, it is estimated that the average ratio for the Community as a whole has fallen and its dispersion has risen (in 1980 the relevant ratios were: for Portugal 14.4 per cent, and for Spain 16.1 per cent).

Significant differences also exist among the members in the way social security programmes are financed. Table 9.2 shows the relative shares of contributions to current social security receipts by employers, employees and the government. The lowest contribution of employers and employees is in Denmark (14.4 per cent) and the highest in France (75.8 per cent) and the Netherlands (68.3 per cent). Hence government/general tax financing of social security is highest in Denmark (78.1 per cent) and lowest in France (20.5 per cent) and the Netherlands (18.3 per cent), which rely more on earmarked taxation for the financing of social security expenditures. The three countries with the largest government contribution, Denmark (78.1 per cent), Ireland (64.3 per cent) and the United Kingdom (42.6 per cent), are in fact those where the state maintains a basic social welfare system by financing directly (from general taxation) the major part of social security.

Table 9.2: Contributors to Social Security Receipts, per cent 1984

Country	Employers	Employees	Government	Other
B	41.5	19.8	33.6	4.8
DK	10.4	4.0	78.1	7.5
D	40.5	29.8	26.3	3.4
F	52.8	23.6	20.5	3.1
IRL	21.7	13.2	64.3	0.8
I	53.3	13.9	30.6	2.2
L	33.1	25.5	32.6	8.6
NL	32.0	36.3	18.3	13.4
UK	30.8	16.9	42.6	9.7
EC-9 (Means)	(35.1)	(20.3)	(38.5)	(5.9)
(s.d.)	(13.9)	(9.7)	(20.2)	(4.1)

Source: Eurostat (1987), *Basic Statistics of the Community*, 24th ed., Luxembourg.

In general, the EC partners display many differences in national social policy but have also achieved some success in common. A major driving force for the harmonisation of social policy in the Community is the differential social cost of production among the member states, and its implications for competition and the allocation of resources within the common market. Changes in the social security contributions, brought about, for example, by a policy of harmonisation, would lead to changes in the marginal cost of labour differentially across the member states of the Community. In principle, this would affect investment patterns between the members and cause capital (and perhaps labour) migration, and capital substitution leading to reallocation of productive resources within the economic union.

Although the national social policy programmes of the EC countries differ in scope and detail, their basic characteristics are substantially similar. All member countries to a greater or lesser extent use (payroll) tax contributions of the current year to finance current year benefits. These tax-transfer arrangements from tax payers in the labour force to beneficiaries outside the labour force have income redistributional effects which affect labour supply decisions by changing the relative price between work and leisure. However, this particular issue, and the question of income redistribution in general, have created little interest in the Community, do not constitute an activity area of D-G V, and will not be examined here.

In the following sections of this chapter we review the basics of the Community's social programme and the attempts for coordinated action in certain areas of social policy.

9.2   THE EUROPEAN SOCIAL FUND (ESF)

Article 123 of the EEC Treaty defines as an objective of the European Social Fund (ESF) 'to increase the possibilities of employment for workers in the Common Market and to contribute thereby to raising the standard of living' by 'rendering the employment of workers easier and increasing their geographical and occupational mobility within the Community'. For this purpose the Fund makes available financial assistance to training, retraining and job creation projects for the unemployed, underemployed and handicapped persons.

However, the ESF had three major weaknesses: (1) The rule that the Fund would reimburse 50 per cent of the expenditure incurred by a member state's public authorities in providing vocational retraining to workers obliged to change jobs. The

Fund resources, which from the beginning were small, proved increasingly inadequate for fulfilling this objective as with the recession, unemployment started to rise fast. (2) The Fund could only intervene retroactively, that is when the worker who had already received vocational training had been productively employed for six months. (3) By statute, intervention of the Fund in a particular country or region depended crucially on the scale of structures and funds available there for vocational retraining and resettlement (EC, 1983). A consequence of the latter provision was that, while the intention of the relevant clauses of the Treaty was to help eliminate unemployment in the least developed regions, such as southern Italy, the main beneficiary of the Fund was actually Germany.

The Treaty provided that after the transitional period, the Council could 'unanimously determine the new tasks which may be entrusted to the Fund' (Article 126). Accordingly, a reform was implemented in 1971 which divided the Fund into two sections, one operating in response to current changes in employment and the other being used to help eliminate long-term unemployment and underemployment. The new Fund was endowed with a larger budget and became: (1) more flexible, by financing more projects directly chosen by the Community; (2) more effective, by deciding in advance how to allocate its own resources; and (3) more comprehensive, by opening up its operations not only to public bodies but also to private bodies and even business firms. For public projects the Fund would still provide up to 50 per cent of eligible expenditure, while in the case of private sector projects the amount of Fund assistance would be equal to whatever aid was contributed by the public authorities. Most of the new Fund appropriations (90 per cent) continued to be directed towards training and retraining of workers in backward areas and regions where the predominant industry was in decline, and to certain occupational (agriculture, textile and clothing industry, etc.) and social categories (migrant workers, handicapped persons, etc.).

However, despite the extensions, the ESF's statutory coverage limited its ability to aid the really needy regions, industries and population groups. During this time, the nature of the social problem had been changing with the effects of the recession, which had led to unprecedented levels of unemployment, particularly among the young. Hence a second reform of the Fund was adopted by Council and entered into force in January 1978. Under the new regulations, a larger share of the Fund's appropriations were designated for unemployment assistance to less-developed areas of the Community (55 per cent). A further regulation was issued in December 1978 which introduced a new form of aid from the ESF to promote specifically the employment and the geographic and occupational mobility of young people.

The next major reform of the Fund was approved by Council in October 1983 and the new provisions took effect from January 1984. The system of giving aid to public and private undertakings remained the same. The main changes are:

(1)   The appropriations of the different operations of the Fund are entered under separate budgets for: aid for the under-25s; aid for the over-25s; less-favoured regions and other regions of high unemployment; specific actions on pilot projects.

(2)   The major emphasis is in the financing of operations carried out by private or public operators, concerning the training and employment of young people. Approximately 75 per cent of all the Fund's appropriations in any one year are allocated to projects to help the young. The aid granted by the Fund to these groups amounts to 15 per cent of the gross average industrial wage.

(3)   Geographic concentration of assistance: 40 per cent of the total appropriations available for operations within the framework of labour market policies go to Greece, the French overseas departments, Ireland, Northern Ireland and the Mezzogiorno.

(4)   Up to 5 per cent of all the available appropriations are reserved for specific operations aiming at the implementation of innovatory projects, e.g. experimental training schemes. For specific operations carried out on the initiative of the Commission, the Fund covers the total of eligible expenditure.

(5)   The operations must concern the following target
groups: young people under 25; the unemployed, and
the long-term unemployed in particular; women
wishing to return to work; handicapped people;
migrant workers; and the retraining of workers
employed in small and medium size firms.

With the economy in recession and only 4.9 per cent of the
total Community Budget (1985) allocated to social policy,
applications to the Fund for assistance far exceed the available
appropriations. Hence, each year the Commission adopts
Fund-management guidelines which serve to determine the
types of operations regarded as reflecting Community
priorities. New guidelines for management of the Social Fund
were adopted in 1985. These clarified the rules for ESF
intervention and introduced stricter criteria for the assessment
of applications for priority financing.

9.3   THE SOCIAL ACTION PROGRAMME

The Social Action Programme (SAP) was drawn up by the
Commission in 1973 in response to the declaration of the Paris
Summit in October 1972, after the first enlargement, that the
European Council 'attached as much importance to vigorous
action in the social field as to the achievement of the economic
and monetary union'. The form of the Programme finally
adopted by Council in January 1974 included three main
objectives: attainment of full and better employment;
improvement and upward harmonisation of living and
working conditions; and greater involvement of employer and
employee organisations in the economic and social decisions of
the Community, and of workers in the life of their firms.
Although the economic and social conditions within and
outside the Community have changed significantly since 1974,
the Social Action Programme has continued to provide a
reference point for a number of measures which the
Community implemented in the field of social policy. The
most important of these measures are described below.

Unemployment (1)   Following the first oil crisis of 1973, the
rate of unemployment in the Community started to rise. The

ascent continued through the 1970s and early 1980s, with unemployment reaching in 1985 nearly three times the level of 1975 (Table 9.3). Certain of the member countries (and regions within countries, see Table 8.1) were particularly hard hit: Ireland with an unemployment rate 18.3 per cent tops the league of the old members of the EC, while a new member, Spain, with an unemployment rate 21.9 per cent holds the overall record of unemployment rate in the Community (1985). Two groups of persons have fared significantly worse than any other population category: women, which display much higher unemployment rates than men in every member country except the UK; and the young, who on average are twice as likely to be unemployed as the adults; nearly one quarter of the under-25s were unemployed in the Community in 1985.

Table 9.3: Unemployment Rates (Percentage of Civilian Working Population)

Country	Unharmonised Data			Harmonised Data, 1985			
	1975	1980	1985	Total	Men	Women	Age <25
B	5.3	9.1	13.6	11.3	7.4	17.8	23.5
DK	4.6	6.7	8.7	7.9	6.7	9.2	12.2
D	4.2	3.4	8.4	7.3	6.3	8.7	11.2
F	3.9	6.4	10.3	9.9	8.1	12.3	24.3
E	2.3	14.0	22.1	21.9	20.6	25.1	48.1
GR	1.1	1.2	7.8	7.8	5.6	11.7	23.8
IRL	8.5	8.2	18.0	18.3	17.8	19.5	26.0
I	5.3	7.2	12.9	9.2	6.2	15.0	31.7
L	0.2	0.7	1.7	3.0	2.2	4.3	6.5
NL	4.0	6.2	13.3	10.3	9.2	12.3	17.2
P	3.2	5.3	8.6	8.6	6.2	12.1	19.9
UK	3.8	6.0	12.0	10.7	11.3	9.9	18.7
EC–12			12.0	10.6	9.4	12.5	23.2

Note: The unharmonised data are not comparable between countries.

Source: Eurostat (1987), *Basic Statistics of the Community*, 24th ed., Luxembourg.

These extremely bad figures do not reflect lack of concern or inefficiency of Community policy to combat the problem of unemployment. Instead, they demonstrate the confined role which has been assigned to the common policy for the unemployed. From necessity the function of Community social policy is limited to coordinating the work of various national employment services, rather than solving centrally the problems of unemployment. The Community decided from early on that the problems of recession and unemployment required active participation and shared responsibility of the two sides of the industry, management and labour. Accordingly, it set up a consultative body, the Standing Committee on Employment, whose main task is to facilitate joint appraisal by employers' and employees' representatives and by the members' Ministries of Employment on current problems relating to employment and labour policy, and measures contemplated by the Community. At the Community level, these areas of activity were pursued which aimed at: improvement of knowledge of the labour market; development and coordination of placement services; and concerted forward-looking management of the labour market. In May 1982, the Council adopted a resolution on Community action on unemployment and asked the Commission to submit proposals for an overall employment policy at the level of the Community. The Commission's proposals were published in 1983 and among other novelties they include the financing of small scale local employment initiatives and schemes for the employment of women.

The Community has paid particular attention to the problems of the unemployment of the young, who were caught in a vicious circle: because they have not vocational training they cannot find a job, and because the have not a job they cannot acquire in-job vocational training. Under the SAP, in 1975 the Council adopted a proposal of the Commission to set aside appropriations for the financing of the geographic and occupational mobility of persons under 25, with priority for first-time job-seekers. In 1976 a resolution was adopted concerning measures to improve vocational education and in 1977 general guidelines were issued for a common policy on vocational training. In the same year the Council established in Berlin the *European Centre for the Development of Vocational Training*, which was entrusted with the promotion of vocational education and planning for the harmonisation of national standards and training qualifications. In 1979 the

Council adopted a resolution which advocated the development of closer links between work and training and, for the
first time, it directed the ESF to provide financial
contributions for the creation of new jobs. This was followed
in 1983 by a resolution pledging support over the next five
years for an active vocational training policy at member state
and Community level, including guarantee of training for a set
period for unemployed school-leavers (this in the UK took the
form of the Youth Training Scheme, YTS).

The equal treatment of men and women in matters of
employment, according to Article 119, was dealt with in a
number of directives during the period 1976-8. Accordingly,
the member states were required to: (1) Repeal all laws,
regulations and administrative provisions incompatible with
the principle of equal pay; (2) Abolish all statutory provisions
and terms of collective agreements prejudicial to the
employment of women as regards access to employment,
vocational training, promotion and working conditions; (3)
Extend progressively the principle of equal treatment for men
and women in matters of social security, the obligation to pay
contributions, and the calculation of benefits and allowances.
The integration of these directives into national legislation is
monitored by the Commission. If a member fails to act, the
Commission can bring infringement proceedings before the
Court of Justice. Private individuals may claim their rights by
bringing action before their national courts, and as a last resort
before the European Court of Justice. However, in practice
disguised and open sex discrimination persists, in some
instances becoming more acute by the adverse economic
situation. Sex discrimination is not confined to the southern
less developed members of the Community: in 1985, Court
proceedings were brought by the Commission under Article
169 of the EEC Treaty against Denmark, Germany FR and the
Netherlands.

In 1982 the Council adopted a new action programme
(1982-5) on the promotion of equal opportunities for women,
and in 1983 produced a communication on women's
employment which contains suggestions for action on job
creation and recruitment, vocational training, improvement in
market opportunities, information campaigns and the

adoption of measures to promote equal opportunities in practice. In 1986 the Council adopted recommendations presented by the Commission on equal treatment for women in self-employed occupations, including agriculture. Discussions have also started on a memorandum presented by the Commission on equal income tax treatment for men and women.

Working Time (2) With the unemployment situation deteriorating, the Paris European Council in 1979 requested the Commission to consider the social and economic implications of a concerted reorganisation of working time. The Commission's proposals led to a 'Resolution on the Adaptation of Working Time' which was adopted by Council in December 1979. This was followed by the Commission launching a number of initiatives which aimed at increase in the supply of jobs by a co-ordinated reduction and reorganisation of the current volume of working time, and by limiting systematic paid overtime. In 1982 the Council adopted a recommendation on the principles of a Community policy with regard to flexible retirement, that is a reduction in total working life with entitlement to retirement pension. The Council also adopted an amended version of the Commission's Directive on part-time and temporary work designed to give greater protection to and provide minimal guarantees for persons engaged in this sort of employment. Discussions were also initiated on memoranda dealing with a reduction in annual working time (entailing a cut in weekly working hours, longer annual holidays and more training leave), overtime and shift work.

In the 1950s the average working week was forty-eight hours in nearly every European country (except France which already had the shortest working week). By 1960 the working week had been reduced to forty-five hours or less in Belgium, Germany, Ireland, Luxembourg, the Netherlands and the United Kingdom. In 1975 the Council established by regulation the *European Foundation for the Improvement of Living and Working Conditions* which opened the following year in Dublin. Its objective is to research on shift work and the organisation of working time, the impact of technological change on work organisation, and the psychological effects of work conditions. In the same year (1975) the Commission forwarded to the member states a recommendation for harmonisation advocating a forty-hour week with four-week paid holiday for full-time workers. Accordingly, towards the end of the 1970s the forty-hour week was applied to nearly all industrial workers of the Community. Greece, which joined the Community in 1981 agreed to comply with the recommendation, and to cut the working week to forty hours on 1 January 1983. In the same year, Denmark, France and Luxembourg followed Germany and extended the basic annual holidays to five weeks.

Industrial Democracy (3) In most members of the Community industrial democracy, which means employee participation in the management of companies, is limited to consultation on matters relating to personnel, improvement of working conditions and safety standards. The Community has felt that industrial democracy has to expand particularly under the current difficult conditions for both management and employees. Two Commission proposals have been issued to this effect. One concerns companies established under the proposed European Company Law. These companies will have a dualistic board structure, comprising a management and a supervisory board of which one third of the members will be workers' representatives. Workers employed in establishments belonging to a European company will be able to enter into European collective agreements and will belong to a European works council. However, the European Company Statute has not as yet proceeded further than the draft stage (see Chapter 11).

The second proposal was included in a directive on approximation of member states' company law, which was submitted by the Commission to the Council in July 1983, eleven years after it was first drafted (*Bulletin EC.*, Supplements 10–72 and 8–74). For companies with more than 500 employees, the proposal provided for a two-tier board structure with a management and a supervisory board; of the latter's members one third will be workers' representatives. Following lengthy discussions at the European Parliament and the Economic and Social Committee, this proposal was radically amended by the Commission. The new directive, which will now apply to firms employing more than 1000 employees, recommends a more flexible board structure, allowing companies to choose either a dualistic or a unitary system, with a unitary board consisting of executive and non-executive members. Depending on the system chosen, four different structural forms of employee participation in the supervisory board are permitted.

Another proposal was the *Vredeling Directive* (submitted in 1980) which dealt with large national and multinational companies, and the rights of workers to be consulted and informed on matters of the company they work for. The draft directive advocated: (1) Consultation between management and employees on all major decisions (closures, dismissals, restructuring, etc.): and (2) Disclosure of comprehensive information concerning company operations, in particular transnational undertakings. The directive attracted strong opposition from employers on the grounds that its acceptance would increase costs, inhibit management, damage confidentiality, and reduce foreign investment in the Community. After consultations and discussions in the European Parliament the Commission produced a watered-down modified version of the directive in July 1983. This has been condemned by both the European Trades Union Confederation (ETUC), which supports the Commission's initiatives and the original version of the Vredeling Directive, and the European employers' organisation (UNICE), which opposes both versions of the Directive. Some member states also expressed concern at the possible disincentives offered by the Directive to investors from within and outside the Community. The issue of the form and extent of industrial democracy in the Community remains unresolved.

Handicapped Persons (4)   One of the priority tasks of the SAP was to help disabled people integrate into the life and work of the Community. To this effect, the ESF made available financing for pilot projects aiming at the rehabilitation of handicapped people, and the Commission prepared in 1981 an action programme for their employment in a free economy. The programme covers: (1) The establishment of a Community-wide network of *demonstration projects* aiming at improvement of the quality of vocational rehabilitation facilities currently in operation; (2) Improved exchanges of *information and experience* between rehabilitation and training bodies; (3) Studies and conferences aimed at drawing up *Community Guidelines* for longer term projects and policies; (4) More financial assistance for the existing Community network of *Rehabilitation Centres*; (5) Further development of the Community's scheme of *pilot housing actions* for the handicapped. A Community network of model projects was set up, and later on the initial phase of a computerised Community database on the handicapped (Handynet project) was launched.

Migrant Workers (5)   There are six million migrant workers resident in the Community; with their families the figure is twelve million. Approximately 75 per cent of them come from countries outside the Community. In general the majority of the migrants are unskilled workers who take up rough, poorly paid jobs which the local workers refuse to do. In addition to poor housing and inadequate training and education facilities, the migrants face specific problems, such as linguistic difficulties and religious differences, which adversely affect their social integration in the community.

Community policies have been directed towards improving the social conditions for the migrant workers and their families, as part of the overall social policy programme. The basic policy rules were outlined in a 1971 regulation on *social security for migrant workers* which specified that, under the Community arrangement for free movement of labour, workers who are nationals of one member state and work in another have total access to social security in the state of their work on the same basis as the nationals of that member state, and that they can accumulate employment insurance and pension rights in one state and export them to another. This scheme was extended to the self-employed from 1st July 1982. An *Action Programme for Migrant Workers and Their Families* was adopted by Council resolution on the 9th February 1976. The Programme introduced specific measures relating to language teaching, vocational training, social security, housing, social services, schooling, and economic political and trade union rights, all of which aim at obliteration of the discrimination against migrant workers and their dependents.

Poverty (6) Most national social policies include measures aiming at income maintenance of people living in poverty, especially the old, sick or disabled, unemployed, one-parent families, the homeless and vagrants. The policy objective is to bring these people up to some poverty line, expressed as a percentage of the national average income. The problem is that no two states in the Community have similar poverty lines. Moreover, while in some countries poverty is alleviated by a system of non-contributory supplementary benefits, either general (UK, IRL) or means-tested (DK, NL), most Community countries operate a contributory insurance system which leaves out those poor who have not contributed to the system. Therefore, it is not surprising that international studies, which used standardised data, have shown that even in developed countries, despite the existence of extensive welfare programmes, a large section of the population continued to live in poverty (OECD, 1977). A relevant example is Belgium, where approximately 20 per cent of the population were below the poverty line before welfare benefits, and 6.1 per cent remained there after welfare benefits.

The Social Action Programme did not include any reference to poverty. However, the Commission at a later stage did put forward a proposal making the fight against poverty a priority. The Community anti-poverty programme consisted of twenty-nine pilot schemes and projects to be mounted in various member states, and two cross-national studies on the general issue of poverty. The proposal was adopted by Council in 1975 and ran until the end of 1980, with the cost shared on an equal basis between the Community and the participating member states. On the basis of these studies the Commission prepared an assessment report which was forwarded to the Council in 1981. The report confirmed that, despite the unprecedented growth in national incomes and in the welfare state since the mid-1950s, poverty had not declined and the gap between the standard of living and opportunities enjoyed by the average man and the poor had not closed: in EC-9 approximately thirty million people were under the poverty line. However, the pilot studies had shown that action against poverty was possible and effective, and that at the national level the costs need not be high. The Commission's conclusion was that action against poverty needed to be given high priority and that a major strategy for combating poverty is to reduce unemployment by creating new jobs and sharing existing jobs. The Council noted this report on the 10th December 1982, agreed that more action by the Community was necessary and laid down certain guidelines for such action.

9.4 EVALUATION

The Community Social policy is supplementary to that pursued by the member states. Its main objective is harmonisation in an upward direction. However, with the members at different levels of economic development and with unequal growth potential, the progress towards a uniform system of national social policies will necessarily be slow. The expectation that market integration and economic progress will automatically lead to convergence of the social policies of the member states has not been realised. In recent years the situation has become even more difficult, since recession and slow growth have caused grave financial problems and, in an attempt to reduce inflation and large budgetary deficits, many countries have resorted to drastic cuts in public expenditure, including social services outlays. These measures, coupled with demographic changes, which have already reduced the birth rate and increased the number of pensioners, have had a regressive effect on social policy provisions.

In the EC, the countries which have least developed social policy sectors are the less developed, the newest members of the Community (Greece, Portugal and Spain) which, with per capita income well below the EC average, cannot afford to raise their social policy expenditures to match the level of the most developed members. Hence, they will depend heavily on Community guidance and financial assistance to help them bring their national social legislation and policies in line with those of the developed member countries. Social policy harmonisation has thus become a larger issue for the Community after the latest enlargements. Under the prevailing conditions existing problems have become more intense and therefore Community action should be expected to continue in areas already pursued actively (unemployment, pay, working conditions, vocational training, migrant workers, industrial democracy, etc.). At the moment, the development of Community initiatives in other areas, or the adoption of more radical solutions, are severely constrained by the small amount of the Budget devoted to social policy. Compared to the social policies expenditures of the national governments, the size of the Community social budget is minimal. Financial constraints dictate that the Community can do very little on its own to solve social problems, such as youth unemployment, by direct social policy. What it can do well is to organise coordinated action by the social services of the member states. In general, the Community can expand its operations in what it can do effectively within the financial means available to it, that is 'act in close contact with the member states through the promotion of studies, the giving of options, the organising of consultations both on problems arising at the national level and on those of concern to international organisations' (Article 118). In general, the Community can coordinate the search for a solution to social problems, which may differ in extent but otherwise are common to all countries, by guiding the member states towards harmonisation of social provisions and by showing the direction that social policy in the member states should take.

REFERENCES

Collins, D. (1975), *The European Communities. The Social Policy of the First Phase, Vol. 2*, Martin Robertson, London.

EC Commission (1974), *Social Action Programme*, Luxembourg.

EC (1983), *The Social Policy of the European Community*, 3rd ed., European Documentation, Luxembourg.

EC Statistical Office (1980), *Social Indicators for the European Community*, Luxembourg.

OECD (1976), *Public Expenditure on Income Maintenance Programmes,* Studies in Resource Allocation, Paris.

Shanks, M. (1977), *European Social Policy Today and Tomorrow*, Pergamon Press, Oxford.

Watson, P. (1980), *Social Security Law of the European Communities*, Mansell, London.

10 Transport

10.1 THE PROBLEM

The Treaty of Rome provides separate Titles, that is chapters, only for two economic sectors, agriculture and transport. In fact, with 3.5 per cent agriculture's, and 6 per cent transport's contributions to the Community's GDP, transport is much more important than agriculture.

Transport is a service sector with many cross-links with other sectors. In the Community, expenditure on transport is estimated to represent 11 per cent of total private investment and 40 per cent of public investment. Many sectors of the industry (e.g. motor, aircraft, shipyards, road building, steel production, etc.) depend on transport. The sector accounts for 25 per cent of total energy consumption. Approximately 45 per cent of oil consumption is used by Transport, 85 per cent of that by road transport alone. Expenditure on road, rail, waterways and transport infrastructure in general constitutes a major component of national expenditures on regional development. Transport is also a major sector of manpower employment: approximately one in ten of the working population work in transport.

Two of the most important problems of the sector are investment and resource allocation. Both of these problems are connected with the issue of government intervention in transport. With reference to the latter, two attitudes exist which have resulted in two approaches, the 'commercial' and the 'social', each with different policy implications. The 'commercial' approach tends to regard transport as a service.

The objective of government transport policy is to help the market forces to operate efficiently. Government intervention aims at improvement of the structure and organisation of the market, so that supply matches the market demand in both quality and quantity, and at the lowest possible cost. The 'social' approach holds that transport does not only serve the existing centres of social and economic activity, but it also affects trade and industrial development, the distribution of employment, population, and land use, as well as the quality of life of the community. Consequently, under the second approach transport policy is an instrument for pursuing wider economic and social goals, such as growth, allocation of production, energy conservation, quality of life, the environment and so on. Therefore government intervention is more widespread and active under the 'social' rather than the 'commercial' approach to transport policy. Clashes between advocates of the two different views occur frequently, whenever a major transport project comes under discussion, for example, the building of new motorways or airports, closure of rail lines, bus services, etc.

Whatever the approach, 'commercial' or 'social', a characteristic of the sector is extensive state intervention. The government is omnipresent in transport, first as investor in infrastructure and then as provider of services directly to the public or indirectly by subsidising other carriers, as recipient of transport taxes, and as legislator of numerous regulations concerning the operation of the industry. In general, governments attempt to control the quality, quantity, organisation, and resource allocation of the sector. The first three of these objectives are usually pursued by regulation and appropriate legislation, the last one by economic management. Quality controls are mostly regulations dealing with safety aspects (speed limits, minimum standards, working conditions, qualifications of operators, pollution, congestion, etc.). Quantity controls attempt to match the (usually public) supply with the requirements of the market. The organisation of the sector is concerned with the ownership of the industry, which in most countries is partly public enterprise, and the structure of the market (monopoly, oligopoly). Economic management for the objective of resource allocation aims at the attainment of efficiency.

Transport is characterised by high *individisibilities* which impinge on both pricing and investment. Many investments in the sector, which are usually large, have a long life-span and are infrequently made, e.g. infrastructure, are undertaken by the public sector. Therefore problems arise with the financing of transport projects and the allocation of costs. A far more complex problem is the pricing of the output of the sector, and the relationship between the prices of public and private transport. In its turn, pricing affects directly the resource allocation and the efficiency of the sector. Efficiency is here taken to mean the benefit to the community derived from the goods and services that transport produces. Optimality implies the derivation of maximum benefit from transport at the least possible cost.

Additional complications arise from the multiplicity of modes, that is of forms of transport, which contribute to the total output of the sector. Production by different forms entails a multifarious sectoral output which is heterogeneous and cannot be easily aggregated, evaluated or compared between different modes. Therefore, it is also difficult to devise and implement comprehensive transport policies which would encourage fair competition between different modes of transport.

10.2 COMMON TRANSPORT POLICY

The reason customs unions require a common transport policy is that transport constitutes an important production input and thus transport costs fall on the pricing of output. It is estimated that on average 25 per cent of final costs are accounted for by transport costs. Therefore, transport directly affects the degree of competition in the market. Hence, a determined country can alter its comparative advantage and its trade flows by policy-induced changes (subsidies, taxation) of transport costs. Therefore, within a common market trade liberalisation and a common transport policy should be implemented simultaneously.

However, the cross-links between transport and other sectors of the economy mean that common transport policies at the level of the Community will have implications for a number of other economic sectors. This characteristic, combined with the fact that a considerable section of the sector is not directly involved with inter-state trading and is therefore considered to be exclusively in the domain of a state's domestic policy, implies that agreement on common transport policies cannot be reached easily. On the other hand, if a common transport policy is ever devised, it would constitute a major step towards the integration of a large section of the members' economies.

Transport cost is an important component of the final price, and therefore transport affects relative prices and trade. Since a major objective of the Community was to promote inter-state trade by tariff elimination, transport was to be given an important role. It was therefore crucial to harmonise national transport policies with the view to advancing a coordinated and efficient Community transport system, which would reduce costs and assist the development of inter-state trade on the basis of comparative advantage. For this reason the Commission endeavoured from the start to introduce a common transport policy in step with trade liberalisation. But the six original members of the Community had diverse interests and priorities in their national transport sectors. What all of them had in common was that for both economic and social reasons they exerted state quality and quantity controls over transport in the form of rates, quotas and licensing.

State intervention in individual member countries took the form of differential taxation, or the granting of subsidies and the enactment of regulations to protect national carriers in general from foreign competition. A second source of important differences between the Community states was the preference which individual countries placed on the various modes of transport, some of them (France, Germany) departing from free market principles discriminated in favour of the railways, while other (Netherlands) by a policy of impartiality created a competitive environment that actually assisted the development of road haulage. The inter-links between transport and other sectors were exploited by different countries to various degrees by using transport as an instrument of policy to further objectives in the fields of regional development, social policy, industrial policy, etc. Consequently, the quality of transport, the degree of government interference, and the objectives of government policies differed among the Community partners to a very large extent. Moreover, in some of the member countries, transport had been manipulated to serve external trade in a role similar to that of tariffs and subsidies, promoting exports and inhibiting imports. Since state intervention in transport was dissimilar between the members, trade liberalisation would bring forward cost distortions and price differentials emanating from different transport policies.

For all these reasons, the field where the common policies were to be applied was very uneven, had varying implications on the prices of traded goods and different social effects on the community at large. This made the search for common transport policies a difficult and lengthy enterprise. However, the importance of transport as a complement to the liberalisation of trade and integration of the market was recognised early on. Transport is one of the three sectors specifically mentioned in Article 3 of the Treaty of Rome (external trade and agriculture are the other two) for which the Community intended to develop common policies. These policies were to serve a dual objective: first, to establish an integrated and efficient transport sector able to serve the intregration of the market; and, second, given the involvement of transport in every other economic sector, to use transport as an instrument designed to further the attainment of the general aims of the Treaty. The general framework of Community policy is presented under a separate Title of the Treaty, Articles 74–84. These Articles outline the basic principles for the development of a more detailed set of policies. The actual design and implementation of the common transport policy were left to the discretion of the Council and other Community institutions.

In Articles 74–5 the member states agree to pursue the objectives of the Treaty with regard to transport by a common transport policy and by a specified institutional procedure. Article 84 states that this common policy would apply to transport by rail, road and inland waterways, but also to shipping and aviation, provided this extension is decided by the Council 'acting by means of a unanimous vote', which was duly done. Among other general policy guidelines, Article 75 prescribes common rules for frontier-crossing traffic within the Community, and for opening up national transport markets to intra-Community competition. Agreement on these two issues constituted a fundamental prerequisite for achieving the short-run objective of the EEC, establishment of the customs union. The remaining articles of the Title contain particular rules for removing the discriminatory practices of member states against carriers of other member states, for relating charges levied at frontier crossings to actual costs, and for regulating state financial assistance at the level of the Community. Article 83 sets up a consultative committee of experts, usually drawn from the Transport Ministries of the member states, to give the Commission advice (technical, financial, legal, etc.) on the formulation of common transport policy.

In fact, the formulation of a common transport policy proved to be a difficult and slow process. The first proposals for common action were presented by the Commission in the Schaus Memorandum (April 1961). A central theme of the common policy was to be the introduction of measures for banning discrimination and for coordinating investment particularly on 'trunk routes of Community importance'. The guiding principle of transport policy was taken to be the gradual implementation of free market competition subject to consistent arrangements in line with social and economic requirements. Consequently, more emphasis was placed on the 'commercial' rather than the 'social' approach to policy orientation. The transport market was to be organised in accordance with the general principles of the market economy: free competition; free choice of means of transport by users; equality of treatment for modes of transport and for carriers as regards taxation, social charges and subsidies; financial and commercial independence for the operators; and coordination of transport infrastructure. Public intervention was not excluded *ad hoc*, but the understanding was that, whenever it would occur, it was expected to be minimal and discreet, having as its main function the supervision of the market for the attainment of operational efficiency.

The Council of Ministers found the Schaus Memorandum too general and took no immediate action for implementation of its proposals. However, in the general spirit of the Schaus Memorandum and in an attempt to refashion the transport services of the Six, the Commission produced in 1962 an ambitious Action Programme for the common transport policy. The Programme provided for: (1) liberalisation of the national markets on the basis of commercial criteria as a prerequisite for the integration of members' transport sectors; (2) organisation of the market with reference to competition and control of carriers' charges; and (3) harmonisation of state intervention in the fields of fiscal, technical and operational measures as a step towards removal of discrepancies between the transport sectors of the Six. However, these liberalisation proposals, which were not confined to inter-state transport but extended over the national transport system within the member countries, faced from early on a hostile reception.

An area considered by the Community in need for change was the road haulage issue. This is a private enterprise system in every country of the Community subject to rules and regulations of national nature. Domestic road haulage is usually administered by licensing. This the Community considered that it could continue to be, subject to national rules which, however, should be harmonised between the members of the Community. Complications arise from inter-state road haulage which was governed by licensing and quotas agreed between states on a bilateral basis. The Commission took the view that, following the formation of the common market, inter-state trade would grow and inter-state transport should be subject to common policies. The first problem was that the quota system by which each state regulated the number and load capacity of foreign vehicles in its own territory would have to expand in conformity with the growth of trade. This could be done by progressively liberalising the existing system, first, by expanding the existing bilateral quotas and, later, by replacing the bilateral quotas by Community (multinational) quotas which would grow in pace with the growth in intra-Community trade.

Another important element in the Commission's plans for the liberalisation of transport was the proposal for immediate introduction of *forked tariffs*, that is establishment of a minimum (floor) and a maximum (ceiling) of charges determining the range within which carriers would be free to charge what they liked. The preference for forked tariffs rather than complete equalisation arose from necessity, that is from the fact that the national regimes for carriers' charges were widely different between the member states, and within each state between modes of transport. The introduction of a common legal maximum charge aimed at prevention of monopolistic exploitation of the market, while the common legal minimum charge was needed to prevent the development of destructive and socially detrimental competition. The idea behind this arrangement was that the characteristic inflexibilities of the short-run supply, and the seasonal fluctuation in demand created price fluctuations in the sector. Hence, the forked tariffs proposal was seen as no more that a device to build into the system some degree of stabilisation. However, in reality the forked tariffs represented a sort of political compromise between the two extreme systems then in force in member countries, the fixed rates of Germany and the completely free pricing of the Netherlands.

Implementation of the common transport policy started with a Regulation issued in 1960 prohibiting discrimination in transport on grounds of nationality (in accordance with Article 79). However, progress was slow. The Community quotas system was partially implemented by adapting the existing bilateral quotas, contrary to the Commission's proposal which envisaged complete elimination of bilateral quotas. Discussion on the forked tariff proposal dominated the scene for more than five years, the issues raised being related to technical difficulties in the implementation of the proposal, the width of the fork, permitted exemptions, rules of enforcement, administrative costs, etc. Finally, the Six reached agreement on a watered down version of the forked tariffs, but due to more general differences concerning the desirable degree of market regulation, the Council reached a stalemate and the forked tariffs proposal was not implemented.

In the end, under pressure from the governments of the member states, who repeatedly demonstrated their unwillingness to introduce changes in the status quo of their transport sectors, the Commission's Action Programme was abandoned as unrealistic. Instead of an all-embracing and general transport programme, a series of *ad hoc* policy measures were introduced (e.g. normalisation of railways accounts, Community quotas for road haulage, etc.), known collectively as the 'mini-programmes'. Among them, a mini forked tariff measure was introduced, imposing mandatory maximum and minimum of 11.5 per cent around the basic rate on frontier crossing road haulage. This regulation was introduced in 1969 for an experimental period of three years. The Council also adopted a regulation in 1969 concerning the normalisation of railway accounts under common rules for granting state subsidies. Hence, in the 1970s, a certain degree of cooperation in transport was achieved, but not to the extent envisaged in the Action Programme. In the meanwhile, the forthcoming enlargement of the Community to three new members (two of which are islands), which was expected to add more problems to the search for a comprehensive common transport policy, also contributed to the final demise of the Action Programme.

10.3 NEW DIRECTIONS

The functionalist school of thought believed that with the liberalisation of trade and the free exchange of goods, the transport system that carried these goods would be liberalised by the market process. However, this did not occur automatically or otherwise, among other reasons because of the unwillingness of the members to cooperate in the search for, and the application of an all-embracing common transport policy. Nevertheless, active state intervention in transport continued in every member state. With expansion of the Community to nine member states, some of which appeared to oppose the principles of the common transport policy plans of the 1960s, the need for a new approach became apparent. It was thus realised that a common transport policy cannot start before harmonising the intervention policies of the member states. Thus from necessity, a change in direction took place. This change was manifested by the early 1970s, when the emphasis shifted from the attempt to regulate transport operations and pricing towards the development of a common infrastructural policy.

The idea behind this change in strategy seems to be that, if by common policies a compatible infrastructure of the appropriate level and type is achieved, then coordination of transport policies affecting the users will not be difficult. Long-term investment harmonisation coincided also with a change in attitudes towards transport in general and the role of transport policy in modern society. Contributing factors were the rapid increases in the cost of fuels and energy caused by the first oil crisis, and the greater awareness of the environmental and ecological implications of unrestrained transport growth. Unrestrained growth of transport and development of transport infrastructure have implications on energy consumption, transport safety, land use, and environmental pollution.

The reorientation of Community policy towards the development and coordination of transport infrastructure was also prompted by the growth rate of traffic between member states, which was twice as rapid as that of the volume of purely national traffic. The problem was that the demand for international transport could not be satisfied with the existing networks, which were designed to cater mainly for domestic traffic.

Investment in inter-state infrastructure is not subject to cost-benefit assessment on a purely national basis, because it does not provide benefits only to the country in which the investment is undertaken. The need for inter-state infrastructure thus becomes a supra-national issue with benefits and costs accruing to the Community as a whole. However, Community action is not a substitute for the action of the member states which will continue to be responsible for the maintenance and development of the transport infrastructure within their frontiers. Hence, in this function the Community principally operates as the coordinator, who will guide the national authorities in such a way that the national transport networks combine to meet the Community's present and future needs. Infrastructure projects of importance to the Community as a whole receive Community financial support. In particular, the Community provides aid for transport infrastructure which aims specifically at: (a) elimination of notorious bottlenecks within the Community or straddling its external frontiers; and (b) improvement of major traffic links between member states. The financial support granted by the Community from this scheme is limited to a maximum of 25 per cent of the cost of the project, provided that the total contribution to this project by all Community sources does not exceed 50 per cent of the total cost of it.

Development of transport infrastructure will of course have implications both economic and social. New investment will constitute additional expenditure, for which the required financing has to be raised. In turn, besides the availability of infrastructure ready to accept the increasing inter-state traffic, these investment expenditures will have positive effects on the rate of growth of the member countries. Positive and negative effects will also occur in the social field, in the effort for regional development, environmental protection, etc. For example, new transport infrastructure will induce changes in the location of housing and economic activity and, although these and associated developments are expected to cause considerable beneficial effects on the organisation of production and distribution, they may also have negative social implications by inducing 'enforced mobility' of labour which may bring forward changes in the 'quality of life'.

With these ideas as background, and after the accession to the Community of three new members, the Commission presented in October 1973 an updated version of its 1971 plan for a common transport policy. The revised plan was based on the following basic principles: (i) Gradual implementation of the principles of market economy with free competition in the transport market and approximation of the starting conditions as between states; (ii) Coordination with regard to national taxation of commercial vehicles; (iii) Approximation of national provisions governing relations between the railways and the state; (iv) Harmonisation of social legislation, improvement of working conditions, transport safety regulations, etc.; and (v) Coordination for the development of common transport infrastructure.

The Commission's transport policy programme was considered over the following two years by the European Parliament and the Economic and Social Committee, and was approved without substantial changes in the line of its recommendations. However, the Council of Ministers did not commit itself by adopting the programme as a whole. The Commission was instead asked to define the priority problems for another working programme, covering the timetable for implementation of common transport policy over the next three years. At the end of 1977 the Commission presented a new document based on the fundamental ideas of the 1973 plan in which it listed the priorities for implementation of a common transport policy. The Council took note of these and agreed to act upon them when the situation should permit it. In October 1980 the Commission submitted its proposals to the European Parliament which approved in principle the transport programme. Finally in March 1981 the Council adopted the Commission's Draft as a Decision laying down the new principal points for the 1981-3 programme, but it again refused to commit itself by adopting the Commission's list of priorities. Thus, once again, we observe the fundamental difficulty of establishing and implementing a common transport policy: the Commission, either on its own initiative or sometimes after a request from the Council, presents proposals for the liberalisation of the market, but the Council does not take the necessary steps for the transformation of these proposals into active policy. In the meanwhile, the enlargement of the Community to twelve members has introduced new difficulties by widening the heterogeneity of the already heterogeneous transport sector of the Community. Consequently, the introduction and implementation of common policies were again postponed till another day.

10.4   RECENT DEVELOPMENTS

All these setbacks do not mean that nothing has happened in the field of common transports. By 1985, the Community had adopted some 200 pieces of transport legislation. But this record of legislation, which was approved after many years of effort, constitutes only a minor contribution towards establishing a Community transport policy. For example, it took nearly fifteen years of protracted negotiations, to reach agreement on two long-running issues. In June 1983, the Council agreed on a maximum axle weight for tracks of 11.5 tonnes for continental Europe and 10.5 tonnes for Britain and Ireland. It also decided to open up the road haulage market by issuing more Community quota licences permitting firms to pick up goods anywhere in the Community. It is estimated that at the moment, after many expansions in the Community quotas, up to 30 per cent of the EEC trucks on international journeys are empty on the return leg. The agreement provides that the system of Community quotas, which currently amounts to 15 per cent of the total, and are still arranged bilaterally between member states, will expand progressively by 40 per cent each year, so that by 1992 freight movement in the Community will be completely liberalised. A degree of harmonisation was also reached in the social field, concerning periods of rest of those engaged in road transport, the introduction of tachographs and mutual recognition of qualifications.

Agreement on a common shipping policy narrowly failed to be reached in June 1986. Of the four questions considered, that of coastal shipping remained unresolved owing to the unwillingness of the Mediterranean member states to open their markets to intra-Community competition by admitting other members's boats to ply for trade in their coastal waters. However, with the exception of Greece and Spain, all other members agreed on the other three issues: (1) Common rules applying to competition in maritime transport; (2) Coordin-ated common response to third countries which reserve part of their trade to their own shipping; and (3) Common response to unfair competition in maritime transport, allowing the Community to impose anti-dumping levies against third countries whose shipping lines practise predatory pricing policies.

Air transport is another area of contention. In general, every member country agrees that regarding air fares within the Community the situation is chaotic. The market is carved-up among the state-owned European flag-carriers, who fix fares and capacity by bilateral agreements and prevent any new airline from competing. Pooling arrangements, whereby revenues are split 50–50, are typical, cushioning the most inefficient carriers and and making Europe's air fares among the highest in the world. Ultimately, the aim of Community policy in air transport is to liberalise the industry by removing the plethora of bilateral and complex arrangements which maintain the high cost of intra-European air travel. But repeated attempts to raise the issue of air transport liberalisation in the Council of Transport Ministers did not succeed. Apart from the Commission only two member states, the UK and the Netherlands, are convinced advocates of freer air fares. The other states favour the status quo.

After many years of sterile discussions, the Commission finally initiated action by recourse to the interpretation of the Treaty's competition rules. Subsequently, the Court of Justice ruled on the 30th April 1986 that the competition rules are applicable to air transport, and member states had an obligation under the Treaty of Rome not to approve fares if they know they result from an agreement or concerted practices between airlines. Under Articles 88 and 89 of the Treaty of Rome, competent bodies for deciding whether violation of the competition rules has occurred are the Commission and the anti-trust authorities of member states. Hence, the Commission, through the competition or transport commissioners, can initiate legal proceedings to enforce competition in air transport. In June 1986, the Hague Summit also declared that the Council of Transport Ministers, which was in session at the same time, 'should without delay adopt the appropriate decisions on air tariffs, capacity and access to markets, in accordance with the rules of competition of the Treaty'. However, the Council again failed to reach agreement and the meeting ended in total disarray.

In an attempt to force a resolution, the Commission decided to act directly in the market by sending letters to ten leading European airlines presenting evidence of infringement of the competition rules by bilateral agreements on fare fixing and capacity sharing, fare structure, and other restrictive practices. The airlines were asked to reply indicating how they proposed to comply with the competition rules. In the case of positive evidence of infringements and unsatisfactory reply, the Commission could declare such agreements null and void and thus the airlines would be liable to prosecution. Moreover, under Article 169, a member state which abetted infringement of the competition rules by an airline could itself be brought by the Commission before the Court of Justice. In June 1987 the Commission reached agreement with the airline industry on a package of liberalisation measures sufficient to grant it a *block exemption* from direct application of the competition rules (see Chapter 11).

Another positive step for opening up air transport was taken in June 1987 when the Council of Transport Ministers were set to agree on a fiercely bargained package involving four main components: (1) Fares: discounts between 65 and 90 per cent of the economy class fare and deep-discount between 45 and 65 per cent of the reference fare for advanced booking, off-peak travel, group travel and age qualifications; (2) Capacity: reform of the way routes are carved up, with the size of the market 'reserved' for a country's national airline falling to 45 per cent, then to 40 per cent in three years; (3) Market access: more airlines allowed to compete on the busiest routes; (4) Application of the Community competition rules to air transport. However, at the last moment the deal was delayed because of a conflict between the Spanish and British Governments on the problem of sovereignty over Gibraltar airport. The agreement was finally signed in December 1987.

In conclusion, the transport sector of the Community is not liberalised and a Common Transport Policy does not as yet exist. The reasons for this lack of success is to be found in the intransigence of member states towards establishment of common policies which will open their transport sectors to competition by firms of other member countries, and will restrain their power to interfere in their national transport sectors. However, the search for a common transport policy is reaching a crucial point with the coming into force of the Single European Act in 1992. The abolition of frontier controls means that the transport quotas will have to be progressively relaxed until they are abolished all together. This will require the adoption of common safety standards which will enable hauliers to operate freely throughout all the member states. There is more real chance for opening up the market and remove restrictions in every mode of transport, road, air, rail and marine.

REFERENCES

Bayliss, B. T. (1979), 'Transport in the European Communities', *Journal of Transport Economics and Policy*, 13, pp. 28–43.

Button, K. J. (1979), 'Recent Developments in EEC Transport Policy', *The Three Banks Review*, 123, pp. 52–73.

Despicht, N. (1969), *The Transport Policy of the European Communities*, London, Chatham House: PEP.

EC Commission (1961), *Memorandum of the General Lines of a Common Transport Policy* (Schaus Memorandum), Brussels.

EC Commission (1962), *Action Programme of the Community for the Second Stage*, Brussels.

EC (1979), *A Transport Network for Europe: Outline of a Policy*, *Bull.-EC* (1979), Supplement 8/79.

EC Commission (1981), *Civil Aviation Memorandum No. 2, Progress Towards the Development of a Community Air Transport Policy*, Brussels.

EC (1984), *The European Community's Transport Policy*, European Documentation, Periodical 3.

EC (1987), *Europe Without Frontiers – Completing the Internal Market*, European Documentation, Periodical 4, Luxembourg.

Swann, D. (1984). *The Economics of the Common Market*, 5th edition, Penguin Books, Harmondsworth.

11 Industrial and Competition Policies

11.1 INTRODUCTION

In every country there is a preference for industry over other sectors of the economy. In developed countries this preference arises from the fact that industry already is a high priority sector of the economy for production, employment and growth. In less developed countries the preference for industry is often based on the alleged dynamic effects of industrialisation which are associated with technology and the capacity to raise productivity and the rate of growth of national income.

In the European Community, the structure of labour employment and production differ considerably between the member countries. While on average in the Community of twelve, industry employs 34 per cent of the labour force and contributes 38 per cent of the GDP, the corresponding figures in Germany are 41 per cent and 40.9 per cent, and in Greece 27 per cent and 28.5 per cent (see Table 2.2). Where sectors of the industry are concerned, the disparities between different countries are even greater. These disparities are a consequence of differences among the member countries in the level of economic development, the degree of specialisation, and other geographic, historical and economic reasons. Most of these reasons have been inherited from the past when the countries of the Community were separate and relatively small economic units. However, with enlargement of the market within the Community, new opportunities have appeared which favour changes in the structure and scale of production, specialisation according to comparative advantage and reallocation of

227

production and employment in such a way that they make the Community industry compete effectively with that of its trade partners.

Countries in general intervene in their industrial sectors for a variety of social, economic and political reasons. Many decentralised market economies, such as those of the EC countries, follow mixed industrial policies, actively promoting structural change in some sectors and simultaneously submitting other sectors to the free market forces. In the latter case, responsibility for production, investment and technical innovation rests essentially with firms, while the role of the state is to supervise the orderly functioning of the free market.

In the countries comprising the EC, different attitudes towards the free market have led to different degrees of government intervention, with the implication that industrial policies at the national level of the Community members have been diverse. Membership in the Community means that many industries, which in the past were cushioned by interventionist policies, will be exposed to increasing competition through the enlarged market, and in the process some of them will perish. Under these circumstances it is likely that governments will attempt to protect threatened industries and jobs. Therefore integration may itself induce a tendency for more intervention at the level of national industrial policy. This danger calls for coordination and harmonisation in the field of industrial policy during the process of market integration. A common industrial policy is also needed if Community industry is to take advantage of the opportunities for rationalisation, specialisation and growth which the enlarged market presents. Improvements in the allocation of resources and reorganisa- tion of the industry at the Community level are expected to raise economic welfare by raising the rate of growth of production, employment and income.

Under free-market principles and competition-oriented industrial policy there is no case for intervention in industry by a common industrial policy. Nevertheless, the Community has to create the legal and competitive environment in which competing industries will operate. Consequently, the Treaty of Rome entrusted the Commission with powers, independently of the Council of Ministers (but under the supervision of the

Court of Justice), to dismantle restrictive practices by companies or governments which inhibit free trade between the member states and act against the interest of the consumers. But during the 1970s, when the plans for developing a competition and industrial policy were formulated, the economic climate changed by two dramatic increases in the price of oil and the subsequent rise in the prices of raw materials and the rate of inflation. Simultaneously, the combined pressure of rapidly increasing competition from newly industrialising countries (NIC) and rapid technological change had effects on both domestic production and international trade. Most of the developed and the less developed economies found themselves unprepared for these events, and unable to adapt fast enough to the changing economic conditions. Rigidities in the allocation of resources and the falling volume of demand and production led to rising unemployment. As in some countries the old and uneconomic industry became increasingly uncompetitive, a strong tendency developed towards contraction of the manufacturing sector and decrease in industrial employment (that is, de-industrialisation).

Against a background of halting economic growth, increasing international competition and rapid changes forced by technological progress, many countries altered their approach towards industrial policy by becoming more interventionist and by resorting to increased protectionism by non-tariff barriers to international trade. Change in favour of interventionist industrial policy was also observed among members of the Community.

In the following sections we examine the attempts by the Community, first, to enlarge, liberalise and integrate the internal market and, second, to create a common industrial base and to formulate a coherent common industrial policy.

11.2 COMPETITION RULES

The economic conditions of the 1950s and 1960s favoured the non-interventionist approach to industrial policy. Therefore it is not surprising that in the Treaty of Rome there is no specific reference to a need for comprehensive industrial policy. The Community's aims of integration could be served by opening up the market of the member states to competition and by facilitating the establishment of 'a single industrial base for the Community as a whole' (Paris Summit, 1972). Hence the Treaty deals only with certain aspects of implicit industrial policy, such as the rules of competition, the freedom of capital and labour movements, the right of establishment and the creation of a single market. Under the ideology of the neofunctionalist school of thought, it was expected that within the competitive environment of the Community's integrated market, industry would spontaneously transform itself to take advantage of the opportunities and facilities provided.

For the creation of the single market two elements are necessary: (1) Elimination of barriers to trade of commodities, services and factors of production; and (2) A common rules system of competition. – The liberalisation of commodity trade is pursued by removal of tariff and non-tariff barriers. In spite of the progress made, particularly as regards the elimination of tariffs on trade between the members and the adoption of a common tariff on external trade, many of the original non-tariff barriers to the internal market still remain and some new ones have sprung up. They comprise varying national technical qualifications, health and safety standards, environmental regulations, quality controls, differences in indirect taxation, and so on.

Despite provisions in the Treaty requiring the abolition, within a transitional period of twelve years, of restrictions preventing Community nationals from establishing and providing services in other member states (Article 59–66), the free flow of services is still incomplete. This is due partly to resistance by some members in removing national barriers, and partly to the economic recession of the 1970s which tended to reinforce member states' preoccupation with the protection of their national markets.

The basic legislation for free movement of labour and the professions is almost entirely complete. However, in practice certain obstacles (such as administrative procedures for the granting of residence permits, comparability of qualifications, right of establishment of the self-employed, etc.) are still present and restrict the free movement and residence of labour.

Substantial progress has been made in the liberalisation of capital movements, but, owing to problems with their balance of payments, some member states have maintained or re-introduced temporary restrictions on the grounds of macroeconomic policy objectives (as provided by Articles 73 and 108 of the Treaty). Free movement of capital is expected to raise the possibility of developing a single market for banking and insurance (in accordance with Article 61 of the Rome Treaty) and an integrated European stock market.

Domestic competition policy is the prerogative of national governments. An objective of the common competition policy is to harmonise the competition rules among the members so as to ensure the unification of the European market for the benefit of all—producers, traders, consumers and the economy in general. The common competition rules seek to prevent enterprises from distorting trade by abusing their market power, and provide for action to be taken in cases of anti-competitive practices by governments or enterprises.

The Community competition law has precedence over national anti-trust legislation but does not replace it automatically. Where the Commission finds that a discrepancy between the legislative or administrative provisions of a member state hinders competition in the Community by producing distortions which need to be eliminated, it consults the member state concerned. If an agreement is not reached, then the Council issues the necessary directives and takes any other appropriate measures provided for in the Treaty for elimination of the distortion (Article 101). In general, the Treaty of Rome (Article 177) provided that the implementation and enforcement of Community law would be left to the national courts of the member states, while the Community Court would play a residual yet guiding role (Article 177). Competition rules in the form of regulations are directly enforced by the Commission.

The EEC Treaty contains the basic competition rules in Articles 85–94 which deal with infringement of the principles of competition by agreements among enterprises (85–91) and by state aid (92–94). The provisions of these Articles have been interpreted, clarified and extended by subsequent legislation and by rulings of the European Court of Justice. The EEC competition rules do not apply to the coal and steel industry nor to the nuclear energy field, which are subject to the rules prescribed in the ECSC and Euratom Treaties respectively.

National anti-trust laws exist at varying degrees in every country. The Community anti-trust law is concerned with the preservation of competition in trade between the members of the common market. The approach followed in the Treaty is to define first the prohibited agreements and then to provide for exemptions in certain specific circumstances. Article 85 relates to agreements and practices between enterprises that by their restrictive nature are liable 'to affect trade between member states and have as their object or effect the prevention, restriction or distortion of competition within the Common Market'. Restrictive practices is a general term which refers to collusive arrangements between firms which ultimately aim at price fixing for the purpose of exploiting the market. These agreements may be horizontal, between firms at the same level of production, or vertical, between producers and dealers. Market exploitation does not necessarily mean that the firms involved aim exclusively at monopoly profit maximisation. It may well be that among their intentions are included some degree of market stability, defence of their market share and competition against other, domestic or foreign, firms.

Article 87 has three parts: 87(1) contains the basic prohibition; 87(2) declares the prohibited agreements null and void; and 87(3) describes the specific exemptions. The following agreements are specifically prohibited: (1) price fixing, (2) market sharing, (3) production quotas, (4) discrimination, (5) collective boycotts (market prevention), (6) tie-in clauses (i.e., in order to purchase one good or service, you are obliged to buy another unrelated good or service). The list of restrictions referred to in the Article is illustrative only. Under certain conditions a number of other forms of collusive agreements for buying or selling, goods or services, may be deemed incompatible with perfect competition, for example, joint purchasing, joint selling, exclusive distribution or purchasing, and so on. These prohibitions apply to vertical agreements between manufacturers and the retail sellers of their goods, as well as to horizontal agreements between producers of the same goods, and in principle cover all firms operating in the common market irrespective of whether they are established within it or outside it. The conditions for exemptions from these competition rules are specifically enumerated in Article 85(3). They are that (a) the agreement must contribute 'to improving the production or distribution of goods or to promoting technical or economic progress', and (b) allow 'consumers a fair share of the resulting benefit'. In addition to these specific conditions, Council Regulation 17 (1962) gave the Commission sole power to authorise exemptions from the ban on restrictive practices for agreements with economic benefit. If an agreement satisfies the conditions of Article 85(3), the Commission grants exemption either by an individual decision or by *block exemption*, that is by a regulation covering a whole category of similar agreements. Block exemption has been granted to the following type of agreements: (i) specialisation; (ii) exclusive distribution; (iii) exclusive purchasing; (iv) patent licensing; (v) research and development; (vi) motor vehicle distribution.

Article 86 outlaws 'any abuse by one or more undertakings of a dominant position within the common market' in so far as they affect trade between member states. Dominant position here means concentration or monopoly power which enables the firm or firms (undertakings) to influence by independent action (as a buyer or seller) the outcome of the market. However, following the precedence of national legislation, the Article does not define what degree of concentration, that is what size of market share, is dominant since this may vary from product to product. The emphasis is rather on the *abuse* of power. Dominant enterprises are prohibited from practising price or personal discrimination in the goods they purchase or sell.

This is also the article on which the Commission, following a European Court decision, has based its powers of control over mergers and acquisitions occasioning dominant positions. Certain forms of cooperation agreements between enterprises, which are considered beneficial for the consumers by improving production, distribution, or technical progress, are deemed not to restrict competition and therefore they are exempted. Cross-border concentrations of Community interest, regardless of whether they are brought about by agreement or by take-overs, are also exempted. One major drawback of Article 86 as an instrument of merger control is that is can only be activated after a merger has taken place; pre-emptive action by the Commission is not possible.

National aids are controlled by the Commission under Articles 92 and 93. As a rule, all government aid to business is forbidden under Article 92 of the Treaty: 'Save as otherwise provided in this Treaty, any aid granted by a Member State or through State resources in any form whatsoever which distorts or threatens to distort competition by favouring certain undertakings or the production of certain goods shall, in so far as it affects trade between Member States, be incompatible with the common market'. However, some types of aids, such as transparent development subsidies which are regionally specific, are exempted. Governments are obliged to notify the Commission of any plans to introduce new aid schemes or alter existing ones, and the Commission then decides whether or not these are acceptable under the Treaty. If the aid is found to be incompatible with the Treaty, the Commission has the power to ask the member state to amend it or to abolish it. For example, credit facilities which aid exporters have been terminated at Community instigation. The Commission may authorise certain forms of aid, if it considers that any distortions of competition are offset by advantages to the Community. For example, the Commission has relaxed its application of the competition rules to state aid for companies which are engaged in research and high technology.

Little progress has been made in the field of public procurement mostly because of resistance to changes in the *status quo* by some member states, which consider this function of the government to be an essential element of national 'sovereignty'. Purchases by national or local authorities cover a sizeable part of the GDP, and are still marked by specifications which tend to direct them exclusively to domestic sources of supply. Despite general anti-discrimination provisions of the Treaty (Article 7, 30, 34) and the publication of a number of Directives which specifically seek to terminate discriminatory practices in this field, at the moment less than one per cent of members' public contracts are placed outside the national frontiers.

Articles 87–91 deal with procedures for implementation of the rules of competition. The competition rules of the EEC Treaty can be applied by national courts. However, running parallel to this possibility, the Commission is entrusted with powers, exercised independently of the Council of Ministers, to investigate, to declare restrictive arrangements by companies or government null and void, to order the parties to terminate them, and to impose fines and penalties payable to the Community Budget for infringement of the competition rules. However, the Commission can act only if the relevant agreement has a perceptible restrictive effect, actual or potential, on trade between member states. Restrictive agreements whose effects are purely domestic are a matter for the laws of the member states concerned. Anti-competitive behaviour can be investigated by the Commission on its own initiative. Alternatively, it can be brought to the attention of the Commission by interested parties by way of a complaint. Commission Decisions may be challenged at the European Court of Justice which has the power to confirm, cancel, reduce or increase fines and penalty payments, or to annul Commission Decisions (Article 173). In practice, the competition law has developed through experience and Court rulings, which in general have tended to support the Commission's reasoning, with the implication that the Commission has lost very few competition cases. However, the Commission has been criticised for its preoccupation with excessively bureaucratic procedures which delay decisions for many years.

11.3 EARLY ATTEMPTS FOR A COMMON INDUSTRIAL POLICY

Competition-oriented industrial policy is based on the principle of non-intervention. The role of the central authority is limited to supervision of the process of market integration and the unimpeded functioning of the common market. Hence, in the highly optimistic times of the 1950s, the Treaty of Rome entrusted the Commission to implement the rules of competition and to act only in case of excessive intervention by the governments of the member states. This was not the case with the other two Communities, the European Coal and Steel Community (ECSC) and the Euratom (EAEA) which were empowered to make use of interventionist policies. The ECSC aimed at a common stategy for modernisation of the coal and steel industry- which suffered from overmanning, low productivity, excess supply and uncompetitiveness in the world market. Euratom's objectives were to promote atomic energy and to facilitate nuclear research in the member states.

Implicitly, industrial policy within the Community-wide market includes more than implementation and supervision of the rules of competition. The existing national industrial policies, which were based on different ideologies and power structures between the government, trade unions and employers in each member state, have to be harmonised in such a way as eventually to converge to form the common industrial policy. Direct and indirect subsidies to industry have to be coordinated for those sectors of industry which show signs of growth, and eliminated for sectors in decline and obsolescence. National industrial policies for regional development also have to be harmonised in order to remain compatible with the rules of competition within the common market. Similarly, at the level of the Community it has to be ensured that the existing structure of the industry is amenable to change and adaptation so that it can take advantage of the opportunities presented by the enlarged market to achieve maximum economies of scale. Research and development at the scale of the common market also have to be centrally facilitated, in order to provide the momentum of industrial development and adaptation.

However, the Community policy of a *laissez faire*, free-for-all industrial market did not seem to work towards desired directions. Convergence of industrial policies did not occur, with Germany continuing her policies of neo-liberalism while France and Italy were intensifying their traditional policies of intervention. The industry of the member states did not seem to be able to adapt in the enlarged market or to attempt to gain from scale economies; in the period 1961-9 over half the foreign subsidiaries established within the Community were owned by non-members (primarily USA firms); over half of mergers and take-overs were within the same member country, and two thirds of the rest were accounted for by third countries; and only one fifth of cooperative ventures were between firms of EC member countries. The events showed that the ideology of non-intervention and competition, expatiated in the Rome Treaty, had to be reconsidered in the light of increasing competition by USA multinationals and Japanese firms. The first steps in this direction were taken after the merger of the three Communities in 1967, and the establishment of a separate Directorate-General for Industrial Affairs to coordinate the work of the Commission in the areas of Internal Market, Regional Policy, Industrial Affairs, Competition, Transport and Energy.

The first major task of the Commission was to draw up a profile of the Community's industrial structure, and to put forward priorities for common action. The *Memorandum on Industrial Policy* (the Colonna Report), which was published in March 1970, proposed the setting up of a common industrial policy of the Community aiming at economic expansion and technological development within a European industrial framework. The proposals put forward by the Memorandum dealt with five broad issues: (1) The creation of a single market based on the elimination of intra-Community barriers to trade; (2) Legal, fiscal and financial harmonisation to facilitate the right of establishment, and adoption of a European Company Statute to enable companies to be formed under Community rather than national law; (3) Active promotion of trans-EC mergers in order to enable European firms to withstand increasing competition from outside firms; (4) Improvement in management techniques to ensure smooth adaptation to the changing industrial and employment conditions; and (5) Common front and Community solidarity against competition from abroad, supplemented by the undertaking of research and development through Community financing on a trans-European basis.

However, with regard to practical application of these principles, the Memorandum made rather general statements and recommendations which amounted to a formula for cooperation between the governments of the member states and the Commission rather than a supra-national centrally administered industrial policy. At the same time it proclaimed a policy of intervention which according to some observers had no legal base on the Treaty of Rome, and whose implementation therefore depended on the political will of the member states. The French reacted by submitting their own counter-proposals which stressed the need for coordination of members' national industrial policies but without an independent supranational role for the Commission. The Germans opposed on principle any form of intervention in the industry at the national and the Community level. The other members sided with one or the other of these ideologies. Hence, with different members advocating different economic approaches and pursuing within their own frontiers different national industrial policies, there was no substantive consensus about what the objectives of a Community interventionist industrial policy should be. Therefore, the necessary political will for adopting and implementing the proposals of the Memorandum did not materialise.

The next major breakthrough in the attempt to lay the foundations for a common industrial policy was the communiqué of the 1972 Paris Summit which declared a commitment by the enlarged Community (of nine members) to adopt by January 1974 a programme of action for the establishment of 'a single industrial base for the Community as a whole'. Following this, the Commission submitted in May 1973 a *Memorandum on the Technological and Industrial Policy Programme* (the Spinelli Report) in which it was emphasised that the industrial policy of the Community 'is, and will continue to be, based largely on free enterprise, on agreements freely concluded between workers' and employers' organisations, and on programmes carried out by regional public authorities' (EC, 1973, p. 3). In essence, the substance of this Memorandum was the introduction of a competition-oriented common industrial policy based on: (1) An accelerated but flexible approach towards elimination of technical obstacles to trade and harmonisation of national regulations; (2) Opening-up of national markets for purchasing by public sectors; (3) Encouragement of trans-EC enterprises; (4) Harmonisation of company law and liberalisation of capital markets; and (5) Diffusion of information for the encouragement of cooperation and mergers between Community firms within the context of the competitive market. Although with support from the European Parliament and the Social Committee the programme outlined in the Memorandum was adopted by the Council in December 1973, the practical implications were minimal. What was missing again was consensus on the necessity of a common industrial policy, and also what such a policy should look like and how it would be implemented.

11.4 NEW DIRECTIONS

The two Memoranda and the ensuing discussions highlighted the need for a strategy to improve the business environment by unification of the internal market and by implementing legal and institutional changes to alter the structure of the manufacturing sector. The Community's attempt to create large European firms which would benefit from scale economies and be able to compete effectively in the world markets against the firms of the USA and Japan did not succeed. Despite numerous proposals put forward by the Commission since the early 1970s and the lengthy discussions about them, the European Company Statute has yet to be adopted. Some members of the Community resisted the introduction of the European Company Statute on the grounds that it would interefere with national legal systems. Doubts were also expressed about whether in large firms the benefits of scale economies would exceed the cost of reduced ability to adapt to a rapidly changing economic climate.

Community multinational companies and industrial collaboration schemes exist, some at the company level and a few at the government level. The latter include collaborative schemes which are European but not Community projects, such as the Airbus (which involves companies backed by government financial support), the Joint European Torus (JET, which is a joint undertaking under the Euratom Treaty), and Ariane (which includes some non-EEC participants). But although these collaborations are examples of remarkable initiatives, they are relatively few and at the moment play only a minor role in the strategy for a common industrial policy.

While the Community remained undecided about the necessity for changes in the industrial sector, the economic recession which began in the second half of 1974 had led to rising unemployment and falling output. At the same time, with increasing low-cost export supplies from Japan and Newly Industrialised Countries (NIC), the Community was experiencing loss of competitiveness in both the internal and the world markets. The member states, perhaps under pressure from their electorates, reacted individually to these events by resorting to inward-looking defensive economic policies which gave priority to the short-term protection of industries, jobs and standards of living. These short-sighted policies intensified the fragmentation of the Community market, where the economies of the member states started competing against each other; thus economic convergence suffered a setback and integration reached a stalemate. This situation compelled a reappraisal of both the objectives and policies which would be required for a new drive towards European unity. The ensuing discussions showed clearly that for a solution to these problems three interdependent objectives must be pursued simultaneously: unification of the internal market, common industrial policy and improved competitiveness in international markets.

As a first step for renewing the impetus towards market unification and integration, the EMS was launched on the 13th March 1979, after nearly two years of discussions and planning. More proposals for the elimination of barriers to internal trade were put forward, which aimed at unification of the market as a means of invigorating European industry. They included proposals for opening up public purchasing, setting up a wider system of common standards, increasing cooperation in research and promoting joint projects. Differences among the members emerged again when discussions started about the necessity for a common inteventionist industrial policy. A solution advocated by some members and outside experts (Hager 1982, Richonnier 1984) was to combine liberalisation of the internal market with a certain degree of selective protectionism from external competition. This was justified on the grounds that domestic industry had fallen so far behind the USA, Japanese and NICs' industry that only protection of the domestic market could revive it.

These arguments became more explicit during the Copenhagen Summit of December 1982, when it was proposed that industrial sectors whose existence was threatened by foreign competition must be protected by trade restrictions. Temporary protection on infant industry considerations was also envisaged, for development of advanced technology industries which could not otherwise get a head start in a market already dominated by USA and Japanese firms. The Summit ended with agreement from all sides that the internal market should be strengthened, research related to industry should be speeded up, and more funds should be channelled to investment in industry, high technology and energy.

The Copenhagen discussions were followed by submission of memoranda to the European Council by interested members. The most comprehensive of these was the French memorandum (Richonnier, 1984) which emphasised the need for developing a European industry able to compete effectively against the duopoly of Japan and USA. The memorandum argued that the investment required to achieve this objective is beyond the capabilities of any single European country and requires a market well in excess of the domestic markets of any single member state. A common industrial base would be achieved by industrial cooperation at the level of the Community, and by the adoption of a common industrial policy which would combine reduction of trade barriers within the Community with managed protection from external competition. Detailed proposals were also included regarding harmonisation of company law, opening up of public procurement to intra-Community competition, pooling of research efforts and funds, introduction of common standards and granting of subsidies and other means of assistance to newly emerging industries or sectors in difficulty. Investments by foreign firms would be allowed, but only if they created jobs and directed to sectors which are not already in excess capacity.

The country memoranda present the views of particular

countries but they do not constitute Community policy. The ideas aired in the French memorandum are opposed by Germany, Denmark and the Netherlands which advocate free trade and liberal economic policies. The UK, Belgium and Luxembourg are rather closer to the liberal cause, although they would welcome many of the French proposals. Italy and the three new members of the Community will rather support the French proposals. At the level of the private sector, some big companies, particularly in France and Italy, want the abolition of internal frontiers to be matched by stronger barriers against imports from the world outside. The proposals for more protection by countries and companies, and the possibility that they may become Community policy have increased the lobbying activities of EFTA countries who seek to ensure that closer EC integration will not mean more obstacles for their goods and services. At the same time, some multinationals from the USA and Japan are concentrating more investment and production inside the Community, thus insuring against the possible introduction of restrictive trade policies.

In parallel with the country memoranda, programmes for a common industrial policy were also put forward in 1983 and 1987 by the Round Table of European Industrialists, a pressure group of chief executives, presidents and managing directors of big European companies. Their proposals aim at faster progress towards market integration, virtually free from government intervention. According to the group, this sort of strategy will enable European industry to compete effectively against the industries of the USA and Japan. On the practical side, the group set up a European venture-capital fund in the Netherlands, and continues to lobby European governments and the Commission for swifter action on a list of 300 decisions which must be implemented before 1992 to make the internal market integrated. The group considers that completion of the single market is a step in the right direction for developing a European industry.

Therefore, in conclusion, although each individual member of the community will agree that European industry as a whole is facing severe problems, there is no consensus on what should be done about it. Of the three interdependent objectives which have been considered as necessary for the establishment of a common industrial base and for the revival of European industry only one is currently pursued. This is the objective of creating a single market. The 1985 European Council at Brussels set the date for completion of the single market as the end of 1992. The single market entails the elimination of internal frontiers by concerted action among the members of the Community. However, the drive towards completion of the single market revived the interest on the possibility of introducing the European Company Statute. The European summit in Brussels on the 29–30th June 1987 declared that the Community's 'common economic area' necessitated 'swift progress with regard to the company law adjustments required for the creation of a European company'. In the meanwhile, the Council adopted in 1985 a Regulation for the European Economic Interest Grouping (EEIG), which is an instrument designed to encourage links between independent companies on matters of common interest, such as joint research or joint sales.

11.5   PROBLEM INDUSTRIES

In addition to across-the-board measures relating to industry in general, the members of the Community have been taking specific measures to cope with particular problem industries. Further to action taken at the national level and approved by the Commission, the Community assists by providing financing in the form of grants and loans. For the modernisation and restructure of industry with specific regional or social objectives, financing is provided by the ERDF and the Social Fund. The ECSC provides loans, financed by ECSC borrowing, exclusively to coal and steel industries. For other projects, in particular those relating to small and medium industry, loans can be obtained from the European Investment Bank (EIB) which supplies financial assistance under the powers conferred on it by the EEC Treaty or under the New Community Instrument (NCI). The latter provides loans specifically for investment projects which, through the dissemination of new technology and innovation, tend to reinforce the competitiveness of the Community economy.

For certain key industries, the 'crisis sectors', which are under threat from international competition or are facing problems over a long period of time, coordinated policies have been followed by the member states at the level of the Community. The more important of these industries are:

Steel (1)   This industry was once one of the most important for the Community. But since 1974 it has been contracting in both output and employment. It currently employs only 0.6 per cent of the working population, or 1.5 per cent of all the Community's industrial workforce. Since the steel industry is traditionally concentrated in a few areas, the effects of its decline have created devastating regional problems.

The problems of the steel industry are not new: they were one of the two reasons for the establishment of the European Coal and Steel Community (ECSC) in 1951. But, while in the 1950s and 1960s the problem of the steel industry was how to respond fast to the rapidly expanding demand, in the 1970s and 1980s it is how to contract under the pressure of declining demand and rising foreign competition.

The present difficulties of the industry stem from the sudden change in demand from a long period of growth (6.6 per cent per annum during 1960–74) to a rapid collapse. The reasons for this change are, first, the generalised economic slow-down; second, the technological change in both production and ultilisation techniques; and, third, the emergence of competition from non-traditional producers, Japan and the Newly Industrialising Countries (NICs).

The steady expansion of demand in the 1960s induced major capacity-increasing investment programmes, which continued after the first economic crisis of 1974, under the assumption that the difficulties of the industry were cyclical and temporary. But, when the crisis started to bite, it led the European steel industry to massive underutilisation of capacity (62 per cent utilisation in 1980), substantial staff reductions (by 50 per cent between 1974 and 1986) and a slump in prices. Accumulating financial losses had adverse effects on new investment for modernisation. Thus the industry became old with low productivity, unable to compete effectively with technologically advanced foreign producers, such as Japan. Consequently, between 1974 and 1976 imports in the Community rose by 133 per cent, while exports fell by 32 per cent. Meanwhile, the extra production capacity which was laid down before the crisis came on line, and caused intensification of the competition for orders among the EC producers, with further pressure on prices which on average fell by 50 per cent within two years.

These conditions led in 1977 to a Community programme for steel (the Simonet Plan) which was based on reduction of domestic production by the introduction of voluntary sales quotas. But, with demand falling rapidly and import competition rising, the slump continued and new measures were urgently taken in an attempt to contain the crisis. The new package of proposals, the Davignon Plan, was agreed in May 1977 with the following provisions: (1) Voluntary restrictions of production; (2) Minimum and recommended prices at the Community level; (3) Import surveillance and the conclusion of voluntary export restrain (VER) agreements with exporting countries; (4) Monitoring of investment programmes and national aids.

Although early results showed that these measures had a degree of success, the second massive rise of oil prices in 1979 intensified the crisis to the extent that in 1980 the Community was forced to declare the industry in 'manifest crisis' under Article 58 of the Treaty or Paris (ECSC). Under the 'Merger Treaty' the European Commission has executive authority for the ECSC and is invested by the ECSC treaty with powers to control production and prices of steel. Accordingly, in July 1981 the Commission introduced mandatory quotas on firms and imposed further restrictions on imports. Simultaneously, the efforts for restructuring the industry continued with the objective of reducing excess capacity and increasing efficiency and productivity. State aid was allowed only if it was directed towards implementation of a restructuring programme. The Community would also contribute aid directly to programmes for the alleviation of the consequences of restructuring the industry, as for example for redeployment of redundant workers, the financing of new jobs or early pensions, and for regional regeneration. It is expected that these measures will continue until the industry is restructured on an efficient basis, and some form of long-run equality is established between demand and supply.

Textile and Clothing (2) Foreign competition and slow growth in demand have meant that this industry is in long-run decline, which has recently accelerated with the slowdown in economic activity. Between 1974 and 1980 production dropped by 6 per cent, consumption rose by 7 per cent and imports doubled. But the textile industry is still very important for the Community as an employer of labour, a significant contributor to value added and a supplier of exports.

The textile and clothing industry is characterised by a wide diversity of production with different problems from branch to branch. What all branches of the industry have in common are the stagnant or slightly rising demand, and the intense competition from low-cost producers, which mainly are low-wage NICs of the third world. Between 1973 and 1982 the share of imports in EC consumption rose from 18 per cent to 45 per cent.

With expectations of a moderate rise in the domestic demand and fast rise in foreign competition, the future of the industry does not look promising. Therefore, for survival the industry requires substantial structural changes with reorientation towards branches in which the Community has comparative advantage relative to its competitors, that is capital intensive production using advanced technology and highly skilled labour. However, these structural changes require the financing of vast new investment, and have the undesirable effect that a substantial part of the present workforce will become redundant. The need for financing, and the social and regional implications of policies for the renewal of the industry, are the grounds on which public intervention is justified.

The policy at the Community level includes the reduction of overcapacity and the prevention of forms of government aid which tend to shift the textile industry's problems from one member state to another. Assistance granted by a member state to its industry must be linked to restructuring plans. In addition to measures taken at the national level, the Community is financing research and development programmes and provides limited aid through the ERDF to regions dependent on the textile industry which are affected by the crisis. Financial assistance is also provided by the Social Fund for the retraining of workers still employed by the industry, and of redundant workers, to help them find alternative employment.

The problems of international competition have been temporarily alleviated by the Multi-Fibre Arrangement (MFA) which, under the auspices of the GATT, was first signed in 1974 and extended since twice. The MFA's initial intention was to help the third world exporters in the short-run, without diverting much from the longer-run GATT objective of trade liberalisation, including trade in textile products. However, a clause in the Arrangement, which permitted the negotiation of bilateral trade agreements, has been used by the contracting parties as the basis for negotiating Voluntary Export Restraints (VERs) between exporting and importing countries. In an attempt to help the domestic industry to recover its international competitiveness, the Community has also resorted extensively to signing VERs with most of the textile exporting countries.

Shipbuilding (3) Since shipowners are not in any way constrained to buy from domestic sources of production, shipbuilding is pre-eminently a world industry. The problems of this industry started well before the economic recession. International competition, which has always been intense in shipbuilding, changed in the 1950s and 1960s by the expansion of shipyards in Japan and in countries new to shipbuilding (mostly built with Japanese capital). Characteristic of these shipyards was the substantial production subsidies they were receiving from state funds. In an attempt to offset the comparative disadvantage, other shipbuilding states supplied their industries with subsidies. Although at the time the high rate of growth of world trade sustained a rising demand for more shipbuilding, the subsidies to the industry on a world-wide scale led to excess capacity. When the increase in the price of oil caused recession and a slump in international trade, the market for shipping collapsed, and falling freight rates led to a world shipping surplus and hence to a fall in orders for new ships. The shipbuilding industry thus ended up with a vast structural imbalance between world capacity and world demand.

In countries with traditions of shipbuilding, this situation, which is likely to continue for several years to come, resulted in more intervention in the form of state aid to shipyards, which were facing particular difficulties because many were old and therefore insufficiently competitive. These problems were particularly severe in the EC countries where most shipyards could neither operate on a large scale nor compete with the modern shipyards of the Asian countries. In the Community, despite the cut in production by 50 per cent and in workforce by 40 per cent between 1976 and 1980, the industry is still in need of structural change and modernisation.

In an attempt to correct distortions in competition, the Community issued a series of directives for the harmonisation of members' state aid, by fixing a ceiling and limiting the eligibility for financial assistance to investments that improve productivity and competitiveness. Initially, the intention of the Community was to phase out state aid to the industry and liberalise the market between 1969 and 1975. But, following the oil crisis of 1974, it was decided that 'the continuation of the crisis has serious consequences for the Community shipbuilding industry, which makes the immediate abolition of such aid impossible' (EC, 1981). Hence, the phasing out of state aid was indefinitely postponed and the aid ceiling was pushed up, reaching 28 per cent in December 1986. The state aid is now termed temporary or 'crisis aid' and is associated with an attempt to encourage undertakings to modernise and rationalise shipyards. The long-run objective of the common policy is to restructure the industry by adjusting its capacity and activities to the Community's market, volume of maritime traffic and social and strategic interests. However, in the short run the outlook remains bleak, the recession continues, and so does state aid to the industry. The shipbuilding industry's output (million tonnes gross of ships launched) in 1985 was 2.5 in the twelve member states of the EC, 9.4 in Japan and 5.6 in the rest of the world.

The motor industry (4)   The main car producers within the EC are France, Germany, Italy, Spain and the UK. The producers are state-owned or private firms, some mainly

European and others multinational (mainly non-European). Collectively, the motor industry of the Community produces more vehicles than that of the United States or Japan, which is now the world's most highly automated manufacturer and the foremost exporter of vehicles. In 1984, the motor industry of the twelve Community countries produced 11.8 million vehicles (10.5 million cars and 1.3 million commercial vehicles), against 10.9 million in the United States, 11.5 million in Japan and 8.4 million in the rest of the world. In the Community the industry uses 20 per cent of Community steel production and employs two million workers directly and four million indirectly. However, with the exception of the German motor industry, all other car industries in the Community have been in trouble in recent years.

The production side of the Community market is characterised by fragmentation. Since the motor industry in general offers opportunities of sizeable economies of scale, there is scope for profitable cooperation among the European producers which so far remains unexploited. Changes in production methods by the application of new technology and automation are expected to bring further economies of scale. For example, automation in the manufacture of engines will call for production runs of 0.5 million units a year, and this indicates that the industry will benefit from closer production cooperation, and from relatively greater concentration. With increasing competition from foreign producers, most notably Japan, whose share in the European market is around 10 per cent, the European motor industry is on the defensive, with probably only the German industry able to withstand the effects of market liberalisation and free trade.

The fragmentation of production reflects the fragmentation of the European market for motor vehicles. Motor taxes, technical regulations and approval procedures differ between the member states, and make the same price for the same final product very uncommon among the partners of the common market (see Table 11.1). Hence, motor manufacturers adjust the bulk of their production programme to the conditions prevailing on the markets where they sell most of their output. This in turn leads to resistance to market integration, since manufacturers will object to any sudden changes which will affect their market shares and require them to undertake vast investments in adjustment of their plants. In their turn, manufacturers contribute to the fragmentation of the market by restrictive practices, such as exclusive dealerships, market sharing and price discrimination. Agreements on distribution and after-sales service in the automobile industry have been granted by the Commission *block exemption* from the competition rules prescribed in Article 83 of the Treaty.

Table 11.1: Motor Industry: Tax Spread and Pre-tax price of Final Product*

Country	Pre-tax price for a new car	Tax take on a pre-tax price of 100
B	100	25
DN	92	173
D	109	14
F	108	33
GR	112	156
I	122	18
L	100	12
NL	92	50
P	107	39
E	116	31
UK	147	25

Note: *1.3 I Ford Escort at June 1985 prices, based on an index of 100 for the price in Belgium.

Source: Twelfth EEC Report on Competition Policy.

The present situation is clearly an obstacle to the development of a genuine EC motor industry which, with access to a large internal market—almost 30 per cent of total world new registrations for private cars in 1980—should be able to modernise and compete with its main rivals. At the moment, the member countries do not have common policies regarding the motor industry, nor do they follow policy against competition from abroad. Trade is restricted on a country-to-country basis, mostly by bilateral agreements and Voluntary Export Restraints.

The Community's efforts for the establishment of the basis for a common policy are concentrated in the opening of the internal market by the harmonisation of technical standards, the development of a procedure for issuing Community certificates of conformity, approximation of motor taxation in different countries both on vehicle purchase and on fuel, and standardisation in safety specifications and pollution controls. Unresolved problems are those of common research and development, the monitoring of state aid, and the question of opening the internal market in conjunction with a more aggressive common external trade policy which currently consists of an 11 per cent common external tariff. The fact that most members of the Community have taken the protection of their national market into their own hands means that the Community protection policy is inadequate and in practice not very much used. However, higher protection has the adverse effect that consumers will pay more for their purchases and that restructure of the industry, which is a prerequisite for modernisation, cost reduction and increase in competitiveness, will be delayed.

Advanced Technology Industries (5)   These are key industries which are expected to play an important part in the functioning and development of the economy now and in the future. Electronics, biology and genetic engineering, aerospace, nuclear energy, and advanced engineering are sectors belonging to the category of industries which are marked by further developments obtained from intense research. Therefore, collaboration in research should be a constitutent part of the common policy for development of these industries at the level of the Community. To this effect the Commission has made a number of proposals and has taken initiatives for the formulation of policy, as for example in the sector of information technology.

The market for information technology (computers, electronic components, databanks, modern telecommunications, etc.) is expanding rapidly worldwide. In the Community, the domestic industry is lagging behind its principal American and Japanese competitors, both in development and in market share: in 1982 USA firms won more than 60 per cent of the world market for information technology, against 22 per cent for the Japanese and only 11 per cent for Community firms. To remedy this state of affairs the Community has taken a number of measures: (1) Policies towards market integration by harmonisation of standards and technical procedures, progressive opening up of public procurement markets to all Community firms, coordination of the research efforts of the member states and supplementary funding of technological development by means of Community funds. (2) Setting up of Euronet, the first major European network for long-distance transmission of computerised information. (3) Launching of the European Strategic Programme for Research and Development in Information Technology (ESPRIT). This is a joint Community and private sector programme to promote cooperation in research with potential industrial applications. Under this programme, projects undertaken by private companies which have joined the scheme receive half of the incurred cost from Community funds. The programme involves activity in advanced microelectronics, advanced information processing, office systems, computer-aided manufacture, and infrastructure activity for the promotion of cooperation research and development (R & D) at the level of the Community.

At the private sector level, the industry is pressing governments to get the frontier-free programme moving faster. National markets, even in the larger member countries of the Community, are too small to enable firms to recover investment costs in new products, particularly for innovative high-technology firms.

The Community has also initiated programmes for the development of a Community-wide market for telecommunications and for industrial applications of biotechnology, e.g. in pharmaceuticals, agrifoodstuffs, energy, etc. Like ESPRIT, the research programmes for both sectors will receive half their funds from the Community.

11.6   CONCLUSION

Manufacturing industry is still the most important economic sector of the Community for production, trade and employment. In recent years the industry has operated against a background of economic recession, with slow growth of demand, rising unemployment, increasing international competition and rapid changes forced by technological progress. Although these are problems which to some extent are shared by all members of the Community, industrial policy still remains largely a national responsibility. The reasons for this are that, first, there is no consensus among the members of the community that an industrial policy is necessary; and, second, the partners disagree about whether the common approach should be that of interventionist industrial policy. At the moment, the dominant opinion among the members of the Community is that industrial policy should not have a separate entity, but it should instead be developed as a part of the general strategy for integration which includes internal market unification and common policies for research and development, trade, monetary affairs and competition.

The Community's industrial strategy consists of policies aiming at improvement of the business environment, both by working towards integration of the European market and promoting the necessary changes in the structure of manufacturing industry. The efforts towards completion of the single market continue and, if other problems do not dominate Community activity in the next few years, the barrier-free European market will be realised according to schedule, in 1992. A few broad integrated programmes of research have been launched, but more are required at a scale comparable with that being undertaken in Japan and USA to enable the Community to catch up with its rivals in modern technology, production and trade. Finally, given that Europe's competitive position in international trade is relatively weak, it seems probable that the Community will neither become a free-trader overnight nor resort to protection as the means to industrial growth.

The attempts over the past few years for formulation of a consistent industrial policy have highlighted certain problem areas for which action must be taken at the level of the Community. Such problem areas are: (1) The lack of coordination and inconsistency of national measures, whether undertaken by private companies or by the government. (2) The reluctance of industries to take advantage of the large and integrating market of the Community to raise capital, invest and achieve efficiency via economies of scale and innovation, which will enable it to compete effectively within and without Europe. (3) The need for restructure and industrial renewal in the face of ongoing recession, increasing competition from foreign firms and rapid technological progress.

These are problems which must be solved if industry is to serve the Community of European peoples, and contribute to the effort for reduction of unemployment and increase in growth and welfare.

REFERENCES

EC (1962), 'Council Regulation No. 17', *Official Journal of the European Communities*, 13, 21 February.

EC Commission (1967), *Tenth General Report on the Activities of the Community*, Brussels.

EC Commission (1970), *Industrial Policy in the Community: Memorandum from the Commission to the Council* (the Colonna Report), Brussels.

EC Commission (1973), *Memorandum on the Technological and Industrial Policy Programme*, (the Spinelli Memorandum), Brussels.

EC Commission (1975), 'Statute for European Companies', *Bull. EC.*, Supplement 4.

EC Commission (1981), *General Report on Activities of the European Communities*, Luxembourg.

EC (1982), *The European Community's Industrial Strategy*, European Documentation, Periodical 5/1982, Luxembourg.

EC (1983), *EEC Competition Rules*, European Documentation, Periodical 1983/1984, Luxembourg.

EC (1987), *Europe Without Frontiers–Completing the Internal Market*, European Documentation, Periodical 4/1987, Luxembourg.

Hager, W. (1982), 'Protectionism and Autonomy: How to Preserve Free Trade in Europe', *International Affairs*, 58, pp. 413–28.

Pearce, J. and Sutton, J. (1985), *Protection and Industrial Policy in Europe*, The Royal Institute of International Affairs, Routledge & Kegan Paul, London.

Richonnier, M. (1984), 'Europe: Decline is not Irreversible', *Journal of Common Market Studies*, 22, pp. 227–43.

Swann, D. (1983), *Competition and Industrial Policy in the European Community*, Methuen, London.

12 Epilogue

The European Community will be 34 years old before it becomes a complete common market but still a partial economic union. During the years its membership has doubled from six to twelve and hence disparity between the members on economic and social matters has increased. Nevertheless, the Community continues to pursue two principal objectives: in the medium term, to improve the living and working conditions of the member states; and, in the long term, to unite Europe. Both of these objectives require the members to reconcile their national policies and targets, by abandoning the advocacy of purely nationalistic interests and objectives in such a way that they can be able to work together on the building of economic union.

The procedure and the time-table for completion of the first phase of integration, that of customs union, had been defined in the Treaty. Actually, all customs duties of the six founder members were abolished a year and a half ahead of schedule. But the next steps of the process of integration were only lightly sketched in the Treaty. Insufficient Treaty provisions regarding both aims and time-tables, and the volatile international economic environment of the 1970s and 1980s meant that common policies for the creation of the common market were introduced piecemeal, after protracted negotiations and with long intervals of inactivity. The requirement for unanimity in decisions of major importance for the participating states and the Community has been another factor retarding progress towards integration.

The Commission plays an active part in the policy-making

process by both formulating and promoting the proposals on which decisions are based. But the final arbiter of what must be done is the Council, which has the sole power of decision in all important matters. The Council of Ministers represents the governments of the member states, and therefore the member states themselves (through their governments) are responsible for the degree of integration achieved in the Community at any point in time. We can criticise the Community for using suboptimal policies and indirect ways to reach its objectives or for being slow and ineffective, achieving too little in a very long time. But it would be unrealistic to subject the process of decision making in the Community to optimality criteria. Decisions are reached by bargaining and compromise between (six, nine and now twelve) independent states who, having regard for their national interests, relinquish one aspect of national sovereignty after another every time a decision for more integration is taken. Given that political ideologies and the commitment to integration differ between governments, and that in democratic countries governments change rather frequently, it should not be surprising that Commission proposals take one form after another before they are finally approved by the Council and are transformed into policies. Therefore any attempt to devise welfare maximising economic policies, or to interpret actual economic policies by optimisation criteria is a rather futile exercise.

Integration is a dynamic process which involves the transfer of both economic and political power from the member states to the Community. Economic decisions at the level of the Community have political implications. Indeed, for some observers economic integration is only the means for achieving the ultimate objective, that of political integration. Conversely, politics both domestic of the member states and intra-state, impinge on economic policy-making at the level of the Community. Membership in the Community widens the horizons of politics and reduces the degrees of freedom available to a government to design and execute domestic economic policies. Community policies may be opposed by member countries under pressure from interested parties, by Community-wide pressure groups, or even by the Community institutions such as the Commission or the European

Parliament. For the Community, a policy that conforms with its objectives, increases the cohesion between the members and contributes to the process of economic and political integration is a good policy. For each member state's government, Community policies are acceptable if they do not harm their standing in domestic politics and can be presented to their electorates as advantageous for the country of for specific influential groups of the population of the country (e.g. farmers, consumers, and so on). In general, there are limits to the extent governments can depart from the *status quo* by changing a given situation of domestic politics and economics in search of common policies in the Community. Given these constraints, we should consider the progress the Community has made during three decades as a qualified success.

Integration causes problems which affect the members in different degrees. When the need for solutions can no longer be delayed, coalitions of interests press the members to form alliances in order to force the adoption of common policies. Therefore, as integration causes increasing interdependence of the European economies, governments will be forced progressively to come to terms on their divergent and frequently purely national interests, and to cooperate on the building of the union of peoples.

Index